Japan and East Asian Monetary Regionalism

There is a wide divergence of opinion on the nature of Japanese foreign policy concerning East Asia. Some argue this is decided in accordance with US objectives while others hold that it has a definite position within foreign policy. Consequently Japan's position has been labelled both as reactive and opportunistic, and strategic and effective. *East Asian Monetary Regionalism* investigates this inconsistent interpretation by looking at two main arguments. Firstly that Japan has shown more interest in taking greater political initiative independent of US policy, and secondly that Japanese foreign policy has been characterised by an incremental style which has proved far more effective than often realised.

This book advances the discussion on Japan's new regional activism by offering a fresh observation into regional cooperation in East Asia and the subsequent shift in its regional policy. The investigation is supported through a careful analysis of three case studies that offer key insights into Japanese foreign policy. Combining original fieldwork and interviews with Japanese officials, Hayashi examines Japan and Washington's diverging ideological approaches, Japan's policies towards the East Asian financial crisis and towards East Asian regionalism.

East Asian Monetary Regionalism will appeal to those scholars and intellectuals with an interest in Japanese foreign policy, Japan's international relations and the political economy of East Asia.

Shigeko Hayashi gained her Ph.D. in Politics and International Studies from the University of Warwick in 2002.

Sheffield Centre for Japanese Studies/Routledge Series
Series Editor: Glenn D. Hook
Professor of Japanese Studies, University of Sheffield

This series, published by Routledge in association with the Centre for Japanese Studies at the University of Sheffield, both makes available original research on a wide range of subjects dealing with Japan and provides introductory overviews of key topics in Japanese Studies.

Japan and East Asian Monetary Regionalism

Towards a proactive leadership role?

Shigeko Hayashi

Routledge
Taylor & Francis Group

LONDON AND NEW YORK

First published 2006
by Routledge
2 Park Square, Milton Park, Abingdon, Oxon OX14 4RN

Simultaneously published in the USA and Canada
by Routledge
270 Madison Ave, New York, NY 10016

Routledge is an imprint of the Taylor & Francis Group

Typeset in Times New Roman by
Keystroke, Jacaranda Lodge, Wolverhampton
Printed and bound in Great Britain by
Biddles Ltd, King's Lynn

British Library Cataloguing in Publication Data
A catalogue record for this book is available from the British Library

Library of Congress Cataloging in Publication Data
Hayashi, Shigeko, 1965–
  Japan and East Asian monetary regionalism : towards a proactive
leadership role? / by Shigeko Hayashi.
    p. cm. — (Sheffield Centre for Japanese Studies/Routledge series)
  Includes bibliographical references and index.
  1. Japan—Foreign economic relations—East Asia. 2. East Asia—Foreign
economic relations—Japan. 3. Japan—Foreign relations—East Asia.
4. East Asia—Foreign relations—Japan. 5. Regionalism—Japan.
6. Regionalism—East Asia. I. Title. II. Series.
HF1602.15.E2H39 2005
337.5205—dc22   2005011514

ISBN10: 0–415–36558–9
ISBN13: 9–78–0–415–36558–1

For my husband, Yuji

Contents

Illustrations

Tables

Figures

Acknowledgements

This book was written on the basis of my Ph.D. dissertation at the University of Warwick, where I studied for four years from October 1998 to August 2002. I was very fortunate to have had two fabulous teachers, Professor Richard Higgott and Dr Christopher W. Hughes. I will always be indebted to them for their patient guidance, invaluable comments and advice with considerable insight, which not only guided me onto a broad picture, but also directed my attention to detail. It is not possible to quantify how much I learnt from them.

I would also like to thank the people I interviewed for this research. Despite their extremely tight daily schedules, most of them offered their time generously to answer my questions frankly and seriously. I truly appreciate their warm welcome to a Ph.D. student.

I am very grateful for the precious comments regarding this research from Professor Glenn D. Hook, the series editor. He encouraged me to write a book, particularly when I tended to be lazy after completing my Ph.D. work.

I would like to thank my wonderful family, which is always the backbone of my life, not to mention this research. My parents and brother, Tomoaki, in Japan always understand what their daughter/sister does, even if it is beyond 'traditional Japanese culture'. I am thankful for the gorgeous smiles of my two sons, Kai and Ray, who were born while I was working on this research. They give me energy to work, even when I need to juggle a number of things. This book is dedicated to my husband Yuji. Without his unlimited support and constant encouragement, nothing would have been possible, neither this book nor my Ph.D. research. His intelligence has always inspired me, not forgetting him volunteering to babysit every weekend.

Abbreviations

ABF	Asian Bond Fund
ACCSF	Asian Currency Crisis Support Facility
ADB	Asian Development Bank
AFTA	ASEAN Free Trade Area
AMF	Asian Monetary Fund
AMM	ASEAN Ministerial Meeting
APEC	Asia Pacific Economic Cooperation
ARF	ASEAN Regional Forum
ASEAN	Association of Southeast Asian Nations
ASEAN ISIS	ASEAN Institute of Strategic and International Studies
ASEAN + 3	ASEAN plus China, Japan and South Korea
ASEAN PMC	ASEAN Post Ministerial Conference
ASEM	Asia–Europe Meeting
ASPAC	Asia Pacific Council
BOJ	Bank of Japan
CSCE	Conference on Security and Cooperation in Europe
EAEC	East Asian Economic Caucus
EAEG	East Asian Economic Grouping
EC	European Community
EMEAP	Executive Meeting of East Asia–Pacific Central Banks
EPA	Economic Planning Agency
EU	European Union
FDI	Foreign Direct Investment
FTA	Free Trade Agreement
GATT	General Agreement on Tariffs and Trade
GNP	Gross National Product
G7	Group of Seven Industrialised Countries
IMF	International Monetary Fund
IPE	International Political Economy
IR	International Relations
JICA	Japan International Cooperation Agency
LDP	Liberal Democratic Party
MEDSEA	Ministerial Conference for Economic Development in Southeast Asia

METI	Ministry of Economy, Trade and Industry
MITI	Ministry of International Trade and Industry
MOF	Ministry of Finance
MOFA	Ministry of Foreign Affairs
NAFTA	North American Free Trade Agreement
New AID Plan	New Asian Industrial Development Plan
NGO	Non-Governmental Organisation
NICs	Newly Industrialising Countries
ODA	Overseas Development Assistance
OECD	Organisation for Economic Cooperation and Development
OECF	Overseas Economic Cooperation Fund
OPTAD	Organisation for Pacific Trade and Development
PAFTA	Pacific Free Trade Area
PAFTAD	Pacific Trade and Development Conferences
PBEC	Pacific Basin Economic Council
PECC	Pacific Economic Cooperation Conference
PKO	Peacekeeping Operation
SDF	Self-Defence Forces
UN	United Nations
UNCTAD	United Nations Conference on Trade and Development
WDR	World Development Report
WTO	World Trade Organisation

Glossary of Japanese terms

gaiatsu	Foreign pressure
Gaitame Shingikai	Committee on Foreign Exchange and Other Transactions
keizai kyoryoku	Economic cooperation
seikei bunri	Separation of politics from economics
yosei shugi	Allocation of aid on the basis of requests from recipient governments
zoku giin	Politicians in tribes

1 Introduction

The nature of Japan's relationship with East Asian[1] countries has prompted a large volume of studies in the area of International Relations (IR) and International Political Economy (IPE). These studies argue that Japan has been reluctant to take the lead in the region for various reasons such as its colonial history and the special presence of the US in this region. Within this context, many studies have focused on Japan's economic as opposed to political leadership in the region, leading to a great deal of books and articles on economic relations between Japan and its neighbouring countries. The more critical literature argues that Japan selfishly pursues its economic (and political) interests in a neo-mercantilistic way. A more benign view is that the increased inflow of Japanese private and public capital, specifically in the form of trade, investment and aid, has had a beneficial effect on the region's economy, consequently raising Japan's profile in East Asia.

Despite their significance, these studies on Japanese and East Asian relations have become increasingly inadequate and provide only a partial view, when considering what Japan has been doing in East Asia and what has been happening in the region especially since the 1990s. For one thing, East Asian relations, which tended to be characterised by informal regionalism or regionalisation, can no longer be considered merely as an economic process, and the region has gradually been experiencing a new phase of region building. We have observed since the late 1980s a significant increase in regional institutions that include East Asian countries, such as Asia Pacific Economic Cooperation (APEC), the ASEAN Regional Forum (ARF) and the Asia–Europe Meeting (ASEM). Also, since the late 1990s even an 'East Asian only' group, specifically referred to as ASEAN + 3 (China, Japan and South Korea), has been emerging. At the same time, Japan's relations with the region have been changing. It has become increasingly apparent that Japan is politically more assertive and is willing to accept a greater regional role commensurate with its economic power. This change in Japanese policy has been occurring slowly throughout the last few decades, but is particularly noteworthy from the 1990s onwards.

What this book endeavours to do is to provide important new insights into Japanese and East Asian relations particularly through the close examination of the changes in Japan's regional policy. To be sure, Japan's new approach to regional matters has produced an increasing number of studies for the last decade. For instance, quite a few studies have pointed out the significance of Japan's positive roles in Asia Pacific regionalism as well as brokering the Cambodian peace, as touched on in the next chapter. What this book tries to do is to advance further such discussions on Japan's new regional activism: it approaches Japan's recent regional policy by adding more new empirical evidence particularly on Japan's East Asian, as opposed to Asia Pacific, policy and by more extensively exploring what has caused the shift in Japan's regional policy.

This book puts this investigation into the larger context of the changes in Japanese foreign policy particularly after the end of the Cold War, bringing us to the discussions on the nature of Japanese foreign policy as a whole. In other words, Japan's contemporary regional policy needs to be discussed from the broader perspective of the shift in Japanese foreign policy in general.

The nature of Japanese foreign policy has been the subject of academic controversy over the last few decades. Some claim that Japan does not have any strategy in its foreign relations and has failed to play a role commensurate with its economic power. They argue that Japan is just reacting to outside pressures, specifically from the US (Calder 1998: 517–41), or simply coping with international situations (Blaker 1993: 1–42). Worse, it is argued that Japan is not a sovereign state, i.e. 'a state with central organs of government which can both recognise what is good for the country and bear ultimate responsibility for national decision-making' (van Wolferen 1986/1987: 289). Additionally, Japanese leaders are thought to view the world through the prism of US–Japan relations, and thus the relationship with the US is seen as decisive for Japan's other foreign relations, including its East Asian policy.

Others, however, hold quite opposite views, thinking Japanese foreign policy to be strategic, effective in achieving goals, and even aggressive, particularly in the area of foreign economic policy. While a large part of the negative thesis attributes, to a great extent, the ineffectiveness of the Japanese state in its foreign relations to its domestic political structures, the positive thesis considers that the strong bureaucracy and its network of political leadership and the private sector are the sources of its successful foreign policy. They argue that this system of 'Japan Inc.', which Chalmers Johnson depicted, in a more sophisticated formulation, as the capitalist 'developmental' state (Johnson 1982), has enabled Japan to achieve a number of objectives, including remarkable economic development and higher international status. This leads to the view that Japanese policymaking agents pursue their own agenda in accordance with the national interests, and East Asian policy is not necessarily the extension of US relations, although most scholars accept the strong influence of the US on Japanese foreign policy.

The wide divergence of views on Japanese foreign policy is indeed puzzling, and raises the question of how Japanese foreign policy can be best understood. The argument of this book is at odds with the negative thesis, as discussed throughout. However, the positive thesis also appears to be increasingly insufficient in explaining more recent Japanese foreign policy in that Japan has gradually become more interested in independent initiatives beyond the area of foreign economic policy, and, as touched on above, has shown more positive attitudes towards political (and even security) initiatives particularly in East Asia. It must also be noted that Japan has been increasingly trying to develop deeper relations with its neighbouring countries independent of the US, although this does not mean that Japan has been defying the US. It can be argued that, while its economic resources are still the main policy tool for Japan, it seems that Japan has shown its willingness to get out of the traditional pattern of 'chequebook diplomacy'.

One reason for the negative concept of Japanese foreign policy is that most existing literature on this topic has neglected or underestimated an important characteristic of Japanese foreign policy, namely Japan's quiet and gradual style of pursuing its policy agendas. This book argues that Japan has carried out its policies in a different style from what the dominant international relations litera- ture usually expects: Japan has preferred to keep a low profile while quietly and incrementally carrying out its policies. Indeed, this style of Japanese foreign policy has been quite effective in realising policy goals, given the domestic, regional and international constraints. However, only a small number of studies have noted this important characteristic of Japanese foreign policy.[2] The book considers that neglecting, or underestimating, this has greatly contributed to misunderstandings over Japanese foreign policy.

Reflecting the above background, this book has two main objectives. First, it addresses the above inconsistent interpretations of Japanese foreign policy by presenting two arguments:

1 There has been an important shift in Japanese policy in the postwar period, from political minimalism to more initiative-taking politically, and even in the security area, independent of the US.
2 The quiet and incremental policy style is an important element to consider in the interpretation of Japanese foreign policy.

Second, along with this shift in Japan's foreign policy in the postwar period, particularly in the last decade, the book provides significant insights into the development of Japanese and East Asian relations: it closely examines what Japan has been doing in the region and what has caused the shift in its regional policy.

The analyses of this book will be of great significance not only in the study of Japanese policy and politics but also in the areas of IR and IPE in general. Scholars in these fields tend not to take Japan's weight as an actor in world politics seriously enough; however, neglecting the importance of Japan can lead to failures to analyse correctly important events in the international arena, particularly in East Asia. For instance, Japan's role in the development of East Asian regionalism exemplifies the strong impact of Japanese policies, as detailed in the following chapters. One of the important reasons why East Asia has been behind in establishing a formal regional framework is that the region lacked political leadership: while Japan's initiative was not welcome by regional countries, it was cautious of advancing such a mechanism, as seen in the case of the East Asian Economic Grouping (EAEG, later East Asian Economic Caucus or EAEC) proposal in the early 1990s, in which Japan's ambiguous attitude was largely blamed for its failure. Of course, we cannot attribute the current development in East Asia only to Japan's policy. Indeed, the East Asian financial crisis in 1997 and 1998 has greatly facilitated the process. However, the book would argue that the simultaneous emergence of East Asian regionalism and Japan's growing political presence is more than coincidence. Behind such a development there is a long-term strategy of Japanese policymakers from the early 1990s. In a broader sense, Japan's interests in regional cooperation go back to the 1960s, a history probably at the foundation of the recent development. In short, without a proper analysis of Japanese policy, it is not possible for us to understand what has been going on in the international arena, particularly in East Asia.

In addition to the main objectives above, three case studies – Japan and Washington's diverging ideological approaches, Japan's policies towards the East Asian financial crisis and towards East Asian regionalism – add significance to the book. They provide detailed narratives and analyses of Japan's policies towards the important events in the 1990s, which deserve more scholarly scrutiny considering their great potential for offering insight into Japanese foreign policy.

The analysis of these case studies has been done on the basis of the author's interviews with Japanese policymakers and intellectuals,[3] together with documentary research. In particular, the author asked key individuals in the Japanese foreign policymaking circle what motivated them and what was intended in deciding particular policies. As we will see, these interviews greatly contributed not only to the analysis of the cases, but also to an understanding of the recent change in Japanese foreign policy as a whole. In addition, interviews were used to get behind the inconsistent information in newspapers, journals and other articles and to obtain accurate information about events. It was also helpful to ask for the subjective and objective views of those Japanese intellectuals concerned with Japan's contemporary foreign policy in response to the events of the period.

The existing debates on the nature of Japanese foreign policy

In order to clarify the book's arguments, namely an important shift in Japanese foreign policy during the postwar period and the style of Japanese foreign policy, it is useful to look at the existing debates on the nature of Japanese foreign policy in more detail. We critically examine the current debates from the two angles: whether Japanese foreign policy has been reactive or strategic; and whether Japan's US relations are decisive for the rest of Japan's foreign relations, including East Asian relations, or that East Asia has occupied a definite position in Japanese foreign policy. Subsequently, the arguments of the book are explained in a more specific way.

Japanese foreign policy as reactive or strategic?

Viewing Japanese foreign policy as minimal or even non-existent is still quite common not only among Japan specialists but also general readers. It is true that, for a couple of decades after the end of the Second World War, Japan put its diplomatic fate into the hands of the US so that it could focus on economic development. Its *seikei bunri* (the separation of politics from economics) policy was most conspicuous during that time, and Japan intentionally avoided becoming involved in complicated international diplomatic issues. However, a number of scholars see Japanese foreign policy as passive even after the 1970s, when Japan had risen as a great economic power.

Kent Calder presents Japan as a reactive state, arguing that this concept 'merely maintains that the impetus to policy change is typically supplied by outside pressure, and that reaction prevails over strategy in the relatively narrow range of cases where the two come into conflict'(Calder 1988: 518). He associates this reactive nature with the domestic political structure in Japan, including the fragmented character of its domestic policymaking process and strong interest-group pressures. Calder concludes that external factors determine Japanese foreign policy under such domestic circumstances of policy immobilism, regardless of the interests of Japanese policymakers.

One of the problems with his discussion is that it is quite easy to find cases which contradict his claim. He stresses passivity in Japan's foreign economic policy, whereas much literature notes the more positive and strategic nature of its policy compared with the political and security areas. In addition, some stress that even his evidence of Japan as a reactive state is not very convincing; namely, *gaiatsu* (foreign pressure), which Calder argues is the determinant of Japanese foreign economic policy, has not always worked effectively. Leonard Schoppa, in his analysis of US–Japan trade talks, shows that US pressure on Japan to bring about policy change produced widely varying results in terms of the Japanese government's willingness to go along with US demands. He observes that *gaiatsu* is effective when it works through domestic politics: namely when it has domestic support inside Japan; when it can be arguably characterised as being in Japan's national interest; when there is a domestic problem in search of a solution; and when it is legitimate and ratifiable (Schoppa 1997). In short, the point of Schoppa's discussion is that international factors, specifically *gaiatsu*, could influence Japanese policy through domestic politics, but it could not automatically determine it, which contradicts Calder's contention. In the same context, various articles in the edited volume by Akitoshi Miyashita and Yoichiro Sato stress the strategic nature of Japan's foreign policy despite its numerous concessions to US requests, denying the proposition that Japan is just reacting (Miyashita and Sato 2001).

Like Calder, Michael Blaker denies the importance of strategic considerations in Japanese foreign policy when he describes this policy as minimalist or coping (he actually argues that Japan is trying to cope but unsuccessfully) (Blaker 1993: 1–42). By 'coping' he means that Japan is carefully assessing the international situation, methodically weighing and sorting out each alternative, waiting for the dust to settle on contentious issues, achieving domestic consensus and adapting to the existing situation with the fewest risks. In short, he sees Japanese foreign policy as being highly opportunistic. He is right in that Japan's diplomacy was minimalist until recently, particularly in the security area. It seems also true that Japan's diplomacy was not (perhaps still is not) very sophisticated tactically, which can be attributed to its deferring to the US in many political and security issues, thus sometimes failing to achieve sufficient objectives or missing opportunities to enhance national interests in some individual cases, as illustrated by his two case studies on Japan's policies towards the third United Nations Law of the Sea Conference in the 1970s and the Gulf War in the early 1990s. However, many would disagree that this tactical inability of Japan's diplomacy suggests a lack of strategy in Japanese foreign policy as a whole.

Donald Hellmann points out the contrast in policy across issue areas, arguing that Japan's record on political-strategic decisions is as bad as its record on international economic policy is good, and 'decision-making institutions have produced reactive, not active policies, regarding major *political* issues in foreign affairs' (Hellmann 1988: 369). To him Japan is 'more a trading company than a nation-state, a nation without a foreign policy in the usual sense of the word' (Hellmann 1988: 358), and he attributes this limitation largely to Japan's party politics, characterised by factional struggles, which gives Japanese prime ministers only limited power, together with relatively weak domestic institutions, like the National Defence Council (now the National Security Council) and the Japanese Defence Agency. Although Hellmann accepts the successful record of Japanese policy in the economic area, he does not entirely agree with analyses that credit that record exclusively to Japan's domestic political economy, stressing the importance of the US-made international 'greenhouse' that allowed Japan to pursue its 'neo-mercantilist' policy. By arguing this, he, to a degree, downplays the strategic orientation of Japanese foreign policy even in the economic area.

On the other hand, there is some literature that emphasises the strategic character of Japanese foreign policy, particularly in the economic area. T.J. Pempel holds that for several decades following the Second World War Japanese foreign economic policy followed clearly defined and quite consistently executed objectives (Pempel 1977: 723–74). He argues that 'the definition and implementation of foreign economic policy in Japan rests essentially on the domestic political structures of the country, particularly the strength of the state and its network of conservative support' (Pempel 1977: 726). He does not neglect international forces, but considers that they are less important than domestic political factors in the shaping of Japanese foreign economic policy, and in some cases domestic forces 'proved capable of explicitly resisting unwanted international pressures or of at least creatively manipulating such pressures' (Pempel 1977: 759).

Likewise, Alan Rix, focusing on Japan's trade policy, maintains the significance of its policy objectives in trade policymaking, arguing that Japan's accommodating foreign pressures is not the automatic acceptance of them (Rix 1988: 297–324). He states that 'international pressures are one (albeit highly significant) input to the domestic Japanese policy process', and the 'more important parameters of decision making are domestic: the long-term indicative objectives of government; the diversity of internal processes and the influence of the bureaucratic process itself on policy; and definitions of the national interest' (Rix 1988: 314).

William Nester recognises the more aggressive nature of Japanese foreign economic policy. He is convinced that Japan is skilfully, successfully and single-mindedly securing its economic and political interests, and notes four Japanese foreign policy goals, namely economic and military security, rapid modernisation, acquiring great power status and world recognition of its accomplishments. These were pursued through state-led industrialisation and imperialism before the war and neo-mercantilism after the war (Nester 1990: 71–99). To him, Japanese foreign policy, particularly foreign economic policy, has been purposeful and shrewd, not passive.

Dennis Yasutomo also opposes the idea that the Japanese government is paralysed by policy immobilism and only reacts to external pressures purposelessly, neglecting its national interest (Yasutomo 1995). He accepts that Japanese policy is in a sense as reactive as other governments are, and 'so much of Japan's foreign policy is tailored to responding, either in anticipation or after-the-fact, to the expectations, hopes, and fears of foreign actors, both nation-state and non-nation-state' (Yasutomo 1995: 188). However, he argues that his case studies about Japan's multilateral bank policies and aid policies do not show that Japan is like a billiard ball, bouncing off the movement of others, and that Japan's behaviour reveals a Japanese agenda, often pursued against the wishes of others. In short, what he stresses is that external stimuli provide the initial push, but 'Japan then incorporates the stimuli into its own policy objectives and fashions a policy that may or may not respond directly to the intent or wishes of that stimuli' (Yasutomo 1995: 188).

Furthermore, some scholars note that Japan has successfully advanced its agendas for its national interests but in a low-profile way. Ming Wan points out that what he calls Japan's spending strategies has greatly benefited its national interests, arguing that the fact that Japan has not asserted itself in spending as much as expected does not mean that it does not make strategic choices (Wan 1995: 85–105). Also, as touched on earlier, some discuss that Japan's economic power has successfully created its long-term influence in East Asia; a combination of private and public Japanese capital (trade, investment and aid) has gradually moulded a regional economic order favourable to Japan (Hatch and Yamamura 1996, Rix 1993a: 62–82 and Arase 1995). As discussed in the next chapter, the economic ties of Japan with East Asian countries have considerably strengthened since the 1980s. Such a development has been basically driven by the private sector, particularly through FDI, but government policy has also played a crucial role through aid or other measures to encourage private activity. Arase argues that the institutional structure of Japan's overseas development assistance (ODA) policy reflects the role of the postwar Japanese state in guiding the private sector towards national developmental goals, and, while the private sector is not passive and has greatly benefited from the government's ODA policy, 'it is the state bureaucracy that holds the balance of power' (Arase 1995: 247). Thus, according to them, Japanese foreign policy, specifically foreign economic policy, is very purposeful and skilful. The increased inflow of Japanese private and public capital has had a great effect on the region's economy, which naturally has raised Japan's profile in East Asia and has created the conditions that have led to a gradual, albeit still limited, acceptance of Japan's larger role in the region. Hatch and Yamamura put it as follows: '[the rapid rise in Japan's standing in East Asia] is the product of a deliberate, largely successful strategy to embrace the region in a complex web of personal, governmental, and cooperate ties – all united under the ubiquitous banner of *keizai kyoryoku*, or economic cooperation' (Hatch and Yamamura 1996: 115).

In short, there is quite a large amount of literature that sees Japan's foreign policy as strategic and successful, and presents various arguments that counter the view of Japanese foreign policy as reactive or minimalist. Admittedly, these arguments are mostly limited to the economic sphere, but some scholars, like Michael Green, even argue that Japan is set to be a larger actor in international relations, noting the increasingly independent and political nature of Japanese foreign policy (Green 2001). Also, Reinhard Drifte outlines Japan's pursuit of political objectives in addition to economic ones, arguing Japan has been translating economic power into political influence, which he calls 'leadership by stealth' (Drifte 1998).

Although it is debatable to what extent Japanese foreign policy has been reactive or strategic, as discussed so far, few would probably disagree that Japan has formulated and implemented its foreign policy within given international orders centring on the US. Yoichi Funabashi writes:

> Japan has seldom tried to present itself as a rule-maker in the world community. The rules were already there. Japan simply tried to adapt to them and, if possible, excel at playing the game. When faced with difficulty, however, it tended simply to ignore or reject those rules altogether.
>
> (Funabashi 1991/1992: 60)

Takakazu Kuriyama, a former Vice Minister for Foreign Affairs, accepts this, and argues that Japan did not have to act positively because Japan could reap considerable benefits from the existing international orders (Kuriyama 1991: 113).

Japanese foreign policy – dependent on the US or independent?

Because of this dependence of Japan on the US-centred international order, as well as on the bilateral relations with the US, it is unquestionable that Japan's foreign policy has been greatly constrained, if not determined, by its US relations, and that this unbalanced relationship has made it quite difficult for Japan to adopt independent policies. Makoto Iokibe claims that this policy towards the US has been the basis of Japan's postwar diplomacy, from which no governments have deviated, and within that framework Japan has cultivated other foreign relations (Iokibe 1989: 19–52). In fact, he notes, policies that were contradictory with the US's wishes did not go well, like Prime Minister Tanaka's attempt to deal independently with the oil crises against US policy lines in the 1970s (Iokibe

1989: 38–40). Hellmann holds that '[o]ne international relationship, the U.S. alliance, has totally overshadowed all others since World War II' (Hellmann 1988: 356).

Robert Orr demonstrates the crucial role of the US with respect to Japan's aid policymaking (Orr 1990). He argues that the US has been able to exercise its influence on Japan's aid policy process principally through the Ministry of Foreign Affairs (MOFA), whose officials acknowledge that the US–Japan relationship is the bedrock of Japan's foreign policy (although he notes the US has not always been successful in pressuring Japan). His study is significant in that he actually shows how US pressures have penetrated Japan's domestic policy-making processes by taking advantage of bureaucratic conflicts so that they may affect foreign policy outcomes. However, his analysis gives too much weight to the role of US pressures. As some scholars observe, Japan's aid policy has greatly reflected its own motivations, which Orr refers to only briefly (Yasutomo 1986, Rix 1993b).

In fact, few scholars deny the strong influence of the US on Japanese foreign policy, which is also taken by many as the appropriate context for analysing Japan's regional relations. They argue that most Japanese postwar policies towards East Asia were taken with a view to their effects on the US–Japan relationship. Kazuo Ogura, former director-general responsible for economic negotiations in the MOFA, commented that 'Japan's strategy for Asia is to cooperate with America's Asia strategy . . . This means that Japan's policy towards Asia has really been its policy with respect to the United States.'[4] Although East Asian relations have been considerably important to Japan throughout the prewar and postwar periods, it is probably true that US relations sometimes have taken precedence over East Asian issues. What matters for Japan has been how to pursue regional policy under the constraints of US relations, and this was particularly true for a couple of decades after the Second World War, when Japan was thoroughly embedded in Cold War bipolarity and Japanese policymakers' minds were occupied by the country's economic development while the economic importance of East Asia was not very high. Keiko Hirata argues that even recently Japan has yielded to US *gaiatsu* when the constraints its US relations imposes on its Asian relations are more dominant, and has sacrificed its regional aspirations to take independent policy initiatives in Asia (Hirata 2001: 90–117).

On the other hand, some emphasise the more strategic nature of Japan's regional policy, opposing the idea that Japan's East Asian policy is merely the extension of its US policy. It was argued above that the combination of Japanese public and private capitals has created a regional economic order. Chalmers Johnson holds:

> when it comes to Japan's movement towards a new Greater East Asia Co-Prosperity Sphere, I believe that Japan may know exactly what it is doing, that its bureaucrats are quite capable of guiding the nation in this direction, and that its seeming indecision merely reflects a delicate sense of timing and excellent camouflage for its long-range intentions.
>
> (Johnson 1993: 55)

In an analysis on Japanese policy towards Southeast Asia, Yasuhiro Takeda argues that since the Fukuda doctrine Japan has repeatedly shown careful consideration towards ASEAN, and has given the positions of ASEAN its serious concern (Takeda 1995: 63–88). In fact, the discussion in the next chapter also shows that Japan's East Asian policy has not been an automatic reaction to US policy, and Japanese policymakers have given serious consideration to Japan's regional relations.

In short, we are confronted with two questions, which are closely related to each other, namely (1) whether Japanese foreign policy can be characterised as reactive and opportunistic, or strategic and effective in achieving goals, and (2) whether its US priority in foreign policy has meant that its East Asia policy is decided according to US relations, or that East Asia has occupied a definite position in Japanese foreign policy.

Arguments

The book grapples with these questions about the nature of Japanese foreign policy by presenting two arguments, namely (1) important changes in Japanese foreign policy in the postwar period and (2) Japan's quiet and incremental policy style. This, in turn, provides significant clues to explore the reality of current Japanese and East Asian relations.

The book considers the nature of Japanese foreign policy in the context of gradual but highly significant shifts throughout the postwar period, namely from minimalist to more initiative taking, and from US-centred to more independent East Asian policy. In other words, Japan has become increasingly more interested in taking initiative; while in the past this occurred mainly in the economic sphere, recently Japan has developed more and more initiatives in political matters. These initiatives are most conspicuous in its East Asian relations because of historical, geographical and economic reasons. Accordingly, East Asia has an ever greater diplomatic importance to Japan. This does not mean that the importance of the US to Japanese foreign policy has come to be altered. However, it should be stressed that Japan is beginning to consider ways to offset the importance of the US in the changing international system after the Cold War.

As mentioned above, until the early 1970s, Japan, economically devastated by the war and thoroughly embedded in the Cold War bipolarity, tried to avoid taking diplomatic initiative as much as it could so that it could focus on its own economic development. Its foreign policy interests were quite limited to narrowly defined economic benefits, and relied on US hegemony economically, politically and in security matters for their realisation. This gave the US huge leverage, which quite often made Japan determine its policy in deference to US wishes. Additionally, East Asia was too undeveloped economically to be a serious economic partner for Japan, and there was a very uneasy atmosphere in the region, where East Asian countries disliked Japan's initiatives. As a result, relatively little attention was paid to regional matters. Although East Asia was not completely neglected, its aid policy was easily Japan's most important regional policy at that time.

However, since the 1970s, Japan has gradually become more active diplomatically due to several factors, including the impact of some critical international incidents, such as the oil crises and the collapse of the Bretton Woods system. One could also cite some significant distributional changes, like Japan's economic rise, the relative decline of US power and the increasing interdependence of the East Asian economy. While Japan was no longer allowed to continue its minimalist policy, for economic as well as political reasons East Asia has become increasingly more important to Japanese policy. Japan began to consider utilising its economic resources for political purposes, showing its willingness to take some political initiatives in the region, as shown in the Fukuda doctrine, although on the whole its policy was quite closely related to US policy.

From the 1980s onwards, further shifts in Japanese foreign policy took place. As discussed in Chapter 2, the end of the Cold War, in particular, has completely altered Japan's diplomatic situation, and therefore changed Japanese policymakers' mind-sets. Japan has been more concerned with political and even security initiatives beyond the economic area, for instance, direct involvement in Cambodian peace from the late 1980s. Also, Japan has tried to take more initiatives independently of the US, as seen in the positive policies addressing the East Asian financial crisis and those advancing East Asian regionalism. Despite this the importance of the US has not decreased, nor has Japan begun to defy US wishes. In fact, there has been overall compatibility of Japanese policy with US stances. This is not to say, either, that Japan's policy emphasis has been shifted from the US to East Asia. What should be noted however is that Japanese policymakers are beginning to think about the new ways Japan is pursuing national interests in the post Cold War era: they come to believe that Japanese foreign policy should have more diversity to offset the importance of the US. This is particularly because US policy towards Japan as well as East Asia is highly unpredictable in the long-term in both security and economic issues, given the considerable changes in the international system after the Cold War. This naturally raises the position of East Asia in Japanese foreign policy. Furthermore, it is noticeable that Japan has been participating more positively in debates about how international regimes should be, which contrasts with the previous acceptance of existing international systems.

In short, the picture of contemporary Japanese foreign policy is quite different from that of half a century ago. To be sure, Japan's foreign policy goals themselves have not changed throughout the postwar period. They are: (1) short-term and long-term economic prosperity; (2) the political and security stability of its territory; and (3) higher political status in the world. However, the ways of pursuing these three goals have been changing considerably. This book considers that it is crucial to analyse carefully these changes in Japanese policy in order to characterise effectively the nature of Japanese foreign policy, and in turn to understand what Japan has been doing regionally.

The important point to note here is that, although the book accepts that the minimalist and perhaps reactive nature of Japanese policy sometimes overshadowed the independent aspects in Japanese foreign policy, particularly in the early postwar period, it does not follow that Japan has merely been passive in international affairs and was bereft of its own strategies or policy goals. It is true that Japan had to compromise with US requests quite often, and even now feels the same compulsion. However, it is not correct to interpret this attitude of Japan as merely knee-jerk policies, automatically responding to US requests without any consideration of its own national interests. As discussed later, national interests matter to the same extent that they do in any other country, and Japan has strategies for enhancing its national interests. This book actually considers that such seeming reactivity has been a sort of a strategy for Japan to achieve its long-term policy goals mentioned above and to create situations favourable for its national interests. To put it differently, Japan's frequent reactivity can be regarded as the result of its deliberate manipulation of domestic affairs and international circumstances in order to defend its national interests, as discussed in more detail in Chapters 2 and 6.

This consideration leads to another argument of the book concerning the style of Japanese foreign policy. The view that Japan's economic power has gradually created a sphere of influence in the region has been presented above. The book considers that this idea can be extended to the style of Japanese foreign policy in general. As touched on earlier, this is apparent in Japan's low-profile and incremental approach to advancing its agendas without taking an overt, or dominant, leadership role particularly in East Asia. Domestic factors, such as a consensus-based society, probably have contributed to this policy style, but it is also important to note that Japanese policymakers have recognised Japan's international and more particularly regional constraints, which has made them adopt this way to realise policy goals. The following chapters will show that on the whole this policy has been successful, and Japan has quite effectively advanced the country's national interests throughout the postwar period.

Theoretical position

In addition to empirically examining the above discussions on the shift in the nature of Japanese foreign policy, along with the changes in Japan's regional relations as well as the style of Japanese foreign policy, the book also offers accounts of what has caused these changes and why Japan has preferred such a low-profile approach. This brings us to a broader theoretical debate in IR and IPE about what determines a country's policy in general. It is thus useful to make clear the theoretical position of the book here.

Rather than following a single tradition, the book adopts an eclectic approach and combines the international and domestic levels of analysis. While noting the influence of the international structure and its changes on foreign policy outcomes, it argues that it is crucial to open the 'black box' of the policymaking process of the state. Understanding the views and intentions of individual key policymakers is a fundamental part in analysing a country's foreign policy. Non-governmental actors, such as private firms, interest groups or business organisations, sometimes exert a significant influence on policymaking processes. However, they, like international forces, influence foreign policy only to the extent that they have access to policymaking processes. Accordingly, while the book draws on the insights and strengths of several IR and IPE approaches, the analysis of domestic policymaking processes is given significant weight.

Because postwar Japan has been highly vulnerable to international forces due to its heavy dependence on the US, it is particularly essential to incorporate these factors into the analysis of Japanese foreign policy. It is true that neither realists nor neo-realists, who basically analyse the world outside the state and tend to neglect internal politics, can fully explain the foreign policy of a single country, and it is fundamental to analyse domestic politics. Even neo-realist scholars, such as Stephen Krasner, recognise that it is necessary to examine policymaking processes within a country when dealing with foreign policy (Krasner 1978: 13).[5] Kenneth Waltz also admits that structural causes are not determining, but are influences, and that both unit-level and structural-level analyses are needed to understand international relations.[6] However, this does not discount the importance of international approaches for foreign policy analyses. International structures without doubt constrain, if not determine, state policy, and various works of realist and neo-realist scholars provide some important insights into the understanding of Japanese foreign policy.

First, it can be argued that one of the realist and neo-realist core assumptions, that states pursue their national interests through rational strategies, has some important implications for foreign policy analyses. This does not mean that the book accepts the picture of the state as a unified and autonomous actor, interacting with others pursuing similar goals in the anarchic international system. What should be stressed instead is that the considerations of the policymakers about national interests matter a great deal. Policymakers may not always adopt the right policy, but policy outcomes more or less reflect their assessments of national interests, or their considerations of what is best for a state.

Second, foreign policymaking certainly involves some element of the realist power-politics model, namely the view that international politics is a struggle for power between states in the anarchical system, although this is only one dimension of international politics. Power is a controversial subject, and there is great disagreement among scholars about what it means. Traditional realists define it in terms of military strength, but it is obvious that this narrow definition has been increasingly inadequate in the present international situation. Here power is understood as 'influence', namely a state's ability to influence other states in order to achieve its own policy objectives. One could argue that influence is closely related to the capacity of a state,[7] which is based on various factors: material, such as geography, resource endowment and economic as well as military capability, and non-material, such as status in the world political economy. In turn, the non-material capacity could be derived from various factors, for instance its position in international or regional organisations, and it is probably related to what Susan Strange calls structural power.[8] It can be argued that it is an important aspect of international politics that states are eager to improve these capacities in order to acquire greater influence in international society, so that they can create circumstances favourable to the pursuit of their own national interests. In fact, as touched on above, some

Japanese foreign policies are in part motivated by the desire to secure a voice internationally and to maintain and improve its status regionally and internationally.

Third, and related to the second point, geopolitical circumstances and their changes have constrained and affected the foreign policy of most countries, specifically Japan. In particular, the bipolar structure during the Cold War greatly narrowed the policy options of many countries, and in turn the end of the Cold War has significantly altered the conditions under which they decide on and implement foreign policy. As discussed in Chapter 2, the impact of the end of the Cold War on Japanese foreign policy is immense, and in fact it has greatly contributed to the changes in Japanese foreign policy identified above. Furthermore, the neo-realists' claim that the distribution of power across the international system and the place of a state in that distribution constrain the country's foreign policy has a great deal of explanatory power. It is hard to measure the actual amount of power or capability of states. However, probably few would dispute the fact that the US exerts the prominent influence in the world political economy, which is derived from its overwhelming economic and military strength as well as structural power. Accordingly, the US stance on various issues has significantly affected the foreign policy of other states. Furthermore, Japan's rise as an economic power itself has obviously changed its position in the world, and this was reflected in some of the changes in its foreign policy, as referred to above.

In addition to the realist paradigm, liberalism also has great significance for foreign policy analysis in general and the analysis of Japanese foreign policy in particular. There are considerable divergences within the liberal tradition. Among them, neo-liberal institutionalism is particularly relevant as an international explanation of foreign policy. Specifically, scholars in this tradition stress that deepening economic interdependence has affected the foreign policy of countries, leading states to engage in increasing levels of international cooperation and to construct regional and international institutions. They argue that such regimes mitigate the anarchic condition of the international system. This argument has particular relevance for analysing Japan's stance on regionalism as well as its changing relations with East Asian countries. It can be argued that ever-increasing economic interdependence, or regionalisation, has significantly affected East Asian relations, and in turn, Japan's regional policy. In fact, closer regional economic relations since the 1980s have been one of the important driving forces for heightening interest in regional cooperation in Asia Pacific as well as East Asia, as shown in more detail in Chapters 2 and 6. This is not seen as a functional process of spillover from economic integration to more political issues. Nor does the book necessarily see this as a state's rational response, as many scholars in this tradition do. Instead, it is recognised here that deepening economic interdependence has greatly influenced the minds of East Asian and Japanese policymakers, which has significantly altered regional relations, and in turn Japanese foreign policy.

To sum up, international approaches constitute a significant part in the analysis of foreign policy, and Japanese foreign policy in particular. External factors influence foreign policy by constraining policy options, while providing some opportunities. However, the book does not take the view that there is some universal international force that drives countries in any particular direction. Instead it is argued that international factors only indirectly affect foreign policy through domestic policymaking processes. For this reason, it is essential to analyse domestic policymaking processes, to understand what policymakers actually think, and to combine international and domestic approaches particularly when analysing the foreign policy of a single country.

Although few scholars engaging in foreign policy analysis disagree about the need to open the 'black box' of the state, there is no comprehensive theory or explanation of domestic politics. However, it is probably reasonable to broadly divide arguments into society-centred and state-centred approaches.[9]

Society-centred approaches refute the state centric view of international politics and stress the centrality of other actors, such as interest groups, transnational corporations and non-governmental organisations. These social forces are seen to have a significant influence on foreign policy. For instance, the interest group approach, which is one variant of society-centred explanations, views state policy as the outcome of a competition among organised interest groups for influence over particular policy decisions (Ikenberry *et al.* 1988: 7). Krasner notes that the state is not regarded as an independent entity, but seen as a referee among competing social groups, at worst as a cipher (Krasner 1978: 1).

The applicability of these approaches to analyse foreign policy depends on which issue area is at stake. It can be considered that foreign economic policy, where policy benefits are unevenly distributed across sectors, is generally more affected by social pressures than diplomatic and security issues. It seems not to be difficult to find evidence of social influence when analysing trade and investment policies. As far as Japan's foreign policy is concerned, it is widely known, for instance, that the pressure applied by Japanese agricultural producers, through their cooperatives, has greatly affected Japan's policy towards the agricultural trade. The role of business in Japanese ODA policy is probably more debatable, but many agree that there has been some degree of influence from the private sector on ODA policy-making (Arase 1995, Soderberg 1996: 72–88).[10] Also, Inoguchi and Iwai observe that interest groups are involved in Japanese policymaking process, side by side with bureaucrats and politicians known as *zoku giin* (meaning politicians in tribes) (Inoguchi and Iwai 1987).

This book considers that society-centred approaches explain an important part of foreign policymaking, to the same extent that international approaches do, but that states matter much more than the proponents of these approaches generally assume. It can be argued that society-centred approaches, together with international approaches, supplement state-centred approaches in the way they take into account the fact that private interests affect the considerations of policymakers, as argued below. However, the book opposes the idea that social forces can overwhelm state power and that state institutions merely provide an arena where these interests can compete with each other.

Finally, turning to state-centric approaches, here again, there is no single universal theory, but it is probably useful to start from Graham Allison's classic work, as it still provides a number of important insights into foreign policy analysis

(Allison 1971). Indeed, Margot Light states that 'many of Allison's original insights have become the truisms of FPA [foreign policy analysis], terms which he coined have entered the IR vocabulary, and his work continues to provoke discussion' (Light 1994: 95). Allison formulated three models, namely the rational actor, organisational process and governmental politics models, labelled Model I, II and III, for explaining the Cuban Missile Crisis. He argues that most analysts explain the behaviour of national governments based on the rational actor model, where foreign affairs are understood as 'the more or less purposive acts of unified national governments' (Allison 1971: 4–5). However, this simplification, according to him, obscured the fact that 'the "maker" of government policy is not one calculating decision-maker but is rather a conglomerate of large organizations and political actors' (Allison 1971: 3). Allison's second model is one of the alternative approaches to this rational actor model, and sees government behaviour as the output of large organisations functioning in accordance with pre-established routines or standard operating procedures. Then, his third model takes particular notice of individuals within the government. According to this model, government behaviour is understood as the result of bargaining, or pulling and hauling, among individual policymakers, who act in terms of no consistent set of strategic objectives but rather according to various conceptions of national, organisational, domestic and personal goals.

It could be argued that each of these three models has its own significance, and in a way all of them are correct in their own right, but actual behaviour can be best explained through a combination of the three. Model III suggests that foreign policy is not always decided by monolithic groups. It is probably rare that policymakers concerned with an issue completely agree with each other down to the last detail. Model III appreciates that it is essential to grasp what actors are involved in a decision-making process and how decisions are made through bargaining among those actors. However, assuming that decision-making is a process of bargaining does not necessarily lead to the idea that policies are subject to the parochial considerations of policymakers. Rational considerations discussed in Model I are also involved in decision-making, although it does not mean that policymakers can always make correct judgements or that there is one universal truth about the national interest. Meanwhile, Model II is probably more helpful for understanding the process of implementing a decision, rather than decision-making itself (Hollis and Smith 1990: 148).

From this viewpoint, it could be argued that foreign policy is the product of a mixture of the various interests of several policymakers. As Allison notes, people involved in a policymaking process have a range of interests, which are to do with their background, position, personality and so on, and policy reflects this plurality of interests of the numerous policymakers. This means that explaining why a particular policy has been adopted is a complex exercise, as there could be a number of reasons for a policy, rather than a single one. Building on Allison's analysis, this book divides these interests into four categories, namely national, organisational, domestic and personal interests. It considers that national interests are the policymakers' considerations about what is best for their country. Policymakers, particularly bureaucrats, can also be considered to be interested in 'the health of their organisation'. More specifically they are eager to maintain and increase the influence of the organisation they belong to, as 'where you stand depends on where you sit' (Allison 1971: 176). With respect to domestic interests in particular, politicians tend to be very concerned about the domestic consequences of their decisions on foreign affairs. In the terms of the theory of Public Choice, the greatest interest of politicians is to win the next election. Finally, personal interests could involve anything. For instance, they can be concerned with ideology. They also greatly overlap with organisational interests and domestic interests, and, in a broader sense, with national interests, and perhaps sometimes it is difficult to distinguish private interests from others. It can be argued that several policymakers, each of whom has a different configuration of interests, are involved in a policymaking process, and that what is needed in the analysis of a policy is to distinguish who are involved and what views and interests they have. This procedure is certainly applicable to the analysis of Japanese foreign policy, and for these reasons, the book puts particular importance on the considerations of key decision makers: what motivated them and what was intended in deciding particular policies.

This argument does not deny the significance of international and society-centred approaches, as stressed before. International as well as social factors influence the interests and calculations of policymakers to a great extent. It may be argued that international factors affect policymakers' thinking about national interests in particular, while organisational, domestic and personal interests are closely related to social pressures. In short, international and social factors can be integrated into state-centred approaches by taking into account the ways in which these factors affect the policymakers' thinking, and this book adopts this combined approach.

The plan of the book

Following this introductory chapter, which has set out the arguments of the book, the next chapter (Chapter 2: Historical review of Japan's East Asian policy in the postwar period) provides the empirical background for the arguments of the book, looking thematically and chronologically at Japan's postwar regional policy. By examining Japan's policies in the region, it considers how and why Japan has increasingly become more willing to take the initiative in the region and how it has pursued its policy objectives in the face of the domestic, regional and international constraints imposed on it.

Chapter 3 (The Washington Consensus versus the Japanese approach and implications for the East Asian financial crisis), the book's first case study, looks at the ideological disparity between Japan and the Washington Consensus institutions. It demonstrates that Japanese policymakers, specifically Ministry of Finance (MOF) officials, and academics engaged in the country's aid policy have advocated approaches for economic development and systemic transition that are considerably different from the neoclassical orthodoxy, which has dominated policy debates since the late 1980s. The disagreement between Japan and Washington is not simply a battle for establishing the order of importance between the state and the market as a means of achieving economic goals such as increased productivity, efficiency and growth. The differences emerge in relation to the path that is taken towards a market economy. This chapter demonstrates that, based on Japan's own development experience, Japanese officials have put much greater emphasis on the role of the state than neoclassical economics while favouring a gradualist, or longer-term, approach. The chapter then discusses why Japan has become increasingly vocal with its policies since the late 1980s and how arguments between Japan, specifically MOF officials, and the Washington Consensus institutions, particularly the World Bank, were developed throughout the 1990s. Considering the popular view on Japan's stance of trying not to disturb US relations and of compromising with US policy, MOF officials' assertive attitude towards Washington deserves special attention. The last section of this chapter will discuss how this divergence of views is reflected in their different positions on the causes of the East Asian financial crisis in 1997 and 1998. It suggests that there is a deep-rooted background against which Japan and Washington have taken a different policy stance on the crisis. Thus, this chapter not only offers evidence of Japan's increasing assertiveness in its foreign policy, but it also provides some important background for the understanding of Japan's positive policies towards the East Asian financial crisis as well as its growing interest in regional frameworks discussed in Chapters 4 and 5. Furthermore, the discussion in this chapter suggests that the changes in Japanese foreign policy identified before are based on ideological factors to a certain extent.

Chapter 4 (Japanese policy towards the East Asian financial crisis) is the second case study and offers detailed narratives and analyses of Japan's policies towards the crisis as well as the background against which these policies were conceived and implemented. It looks at how and why Japan became positively involved in this affair, from the Thai crisis and the Asian Monetary Fund (AMF) proposal to the New Miyazawa Initiative. The AMF proposal, despite the fact that the fund was not actually realised then, deserves special attention in analysing recent Japanese foreign policy. The proposal was atypical of traditional Japanese foreign policy in the sense that Japan assertively articulated a policy and tried to take an independent initiative to realise the idea. This raises the question, why did Japan propose the AMF? This, in turn, leads to a more general question of how and why Japan has become interested in regional financial cooperation. The chapter argues that, while Japan's interest in regional financial cooperation is partly due to the lessons learnt from the Mexican crisis in 1994 and partly to discussions among Japanese officials in the 1990s, there are also various underlying factors at play. These factors include the deepening economic interdependence in East Asia, Japan's willingness to assume a greater political role in the region, and its political as well as ideological dissatisfaction with the existing international economic system, centring on the Washington Consensus. In addition, the chapter notes that there is some awareness among the MOF officials of the risk of relying solely on the international organisations, and of the need to establish some self-help mechanism in East Asia.

Chapter 5 (Japanese policy towards East Asian regionalism) expands the previous chapter's discussion on Japan's interest in financial regionalism to East

Asian regionalism in general. The last case study of the book analyses the development of East Asian regionalism, which has been apparent since the late 1990s. It particularly stresses Japan's role in this regionalism, while examining the background factors behind this new trend, including the impact of the East Asian financial crisis. The chapter argues that it is of great significance to consider why Japanese policymakers have been increasingly thinking that East Asia should have some frameworks for cooperation independent of the US. This is not an attempt to exclude the US from East Asia or to discard the frameworks of Asia Pacific cooperation. Rather, the chapter argues, it reflects the belief that, under the increasingly uncertain situation in the post Cold War period, East Asian countries should have other diplomatic avenues in addition to the existing international, regional and bilateral frameworks. This chapter, together with Chapter 4, contributes to the argument about Japan's increasing willingness to take the initiative in the region, and introduce the arguments about Japan's style of foreign policy in Chapter 6.

Chapter 6 (The style of Japanese foreign policy: a low-profile and incremental approach) focuses on the discussion of the style of Japanese foreign policy. Reviewing the postwar Japanese foreign policy from the viewpoint of a policy style, it shows how Japan has pursued its policy goals effectively without taking an obvious and dominant leadership role. The discussions include the evaluation of the Yoshida Doctrine as well as Japan's behind the scenes initiative for Asia Pacific regionalism. Subsequently, the arguments of the previous two chapters, namely Japan's policies towards the East Asian financial crisis and East Asian regionalism, are re-examined in the context of the style of Japanese policy. It is argued that despite the failure of the AMF proposal in 1997, Japan has continued to advance the agenda of regional financial cooperation, and a series of its policies after the crisis have contributed to gradually moving the region towards deeper, though still limited, financial cooperation. These Japanese policies do not demonstrate leadership from the front, nor has Japan overtly articulated what it wants to do. Still, Japan's policies during and after the crisis consistently and effectively advance its agendas slowly but surely in a low-profile way. The chapter also asks how unique the style of Japanese foreign policy is compared with that of other major countries.

Finally, the concluding chapter recapitulates the analyses of the book. It first sums up and assesses the discussions concerning the nature of Japanese foreign policy and its current changes. It re-examines the puzzling question of disagreement on Japanese foreign policy introduced earlier, namely Japanese foreign policy as reactive or strategic, and Japanese foreign policy as dependent on the US or independent. Subsequently, the chapter re-evaluates Japan's regional policy in relation to its overall policy goals identified in this chapter. The chapter argues that the changes in Japan's policy discussed throughout the book, namely the interest in establishing closer relations with regional countries as well as forming some regional frameworks, accompanied by more political and security initiatives particularly for regional matters, are closely related to such policy goals. In other words, replacing the Yoshida Doctrine, these are the effective ways of pursuing

Japan's policy goals under the changing international order particularly since the late 1980s. Finally, the chapter discusses what has caused the overall shift in Japan's interest in regionalism from Asia Pacific to East Asia.

2 Historical review of Japan's East Asian policy in the postwar period

This chapter looks at Japan's East Asian policy in the postwar period historically and thematically. It is, of course, not a comprehensive account of Japanese foreign policy, as such a task would require more than a whole book. The aim of the chapter is to set the background for the arguments of the book introduced in the previous chapter. By looking at what Japan has actually done in its relations with East Asian countries, it considers how and why Japan has increasingly become more willing to take the initiative in the region and how it has pursued its policy objectives under the domestic, regional and international constraints imposed on it. Equally, this chapter shows that Japan has expanded the range of its initiatives, from the economic to the political area. This examination, in turn, will lead to an evaluation of how independent Japan's East Asian policy has been, particularly in connection with its US relations, the considerations Japanese policymaking agents have taken into account in deciding the country's foreign policy, how much the importance of East Asian countries in Japanese foreign policymaking has risen during the postwar period and what are the regional consequences of those changes in Japanese policy.

The chapter is divided into three sections corresponding to three periods: (1) 1945 to the 1960s, (2) the 1970s, and (3) from the 1980s up to the present. Although, of course, some of the issues run throughout two or more of these periods, this division is necessary particularly because the 1970s can be regarded as a turning point in Japanese foreign policy due to some sea changes in international affairs. The 1990s also saw significant changes in Japanese policy, but are discussed together with the 1980s, as some changes in the 1990s originated in the 1980s.

1945 to the 1960s

Japanese foreign policy during this period was basically characterised by the pursuit of economic development whilst maintaining a political low profile and staying within the limits set by the dependence on US hegemony. This Japanese diplomatic principle was first advocated by the Prime Minister Shigeru Yoshida and was then entrenched by his two disciples, Hayato Ikeda and Eisaku Sato. As discussed in the following, this policy was a skilfully conceived strategy to pursue the national interest given the situation Japan faced at the time, namely a totally devastated economy due to the war and the strengthened bipolarity of the Cold War. However, while this policy enabled Japan to devote itself to its economic development, the heavy dependence of Japan on the US gave the US great leverage over Japanese foreign policy. Accordingly, Japan's East Asian policy, which was conducted mainly through economic means, tended to be closely linked with US Cold War strategies.

The Yoshida Doctrine

Yoshida assumed the second term of office of Prime Minister in 1948 (until 1954), and the policy lines that he worked out during this time greatly influenced postwar Japanese foreign policy. His main tenets, which later became known as the Yoshida Doctrine, were concentration on economic development with very limited spending on defence. Japan was under the US security umbrella and had generous access to US markets, both of which Japan was able to obtain in exchange for its support for US foreign policy in the Cold War. This strong dependence on the US has long constrained Japanese foreign policy and it still does, although some of the tenets have been greatly modified and diluted since the 1970s.

It should be noted that Yoshida's tenets were not what the US imposed. On the contrary, they can be regarded as Yoshida's skilful and clever strategy based on his ideas about Japan's national interest under the constraints at work on Japan. In fact, the US urged Japan's rearmament during the Korean War, and John Foster Dulles, special emissary of the Secretary of State, firmly demanded Japan to establish a large military force. However, Yoshida, who saw the Cold War reality as Japan's opportunity and tried to take advantage of it, adamantly resisted Japan's rearmament for the following reasons: the possibility that a militarist could seize power, limited economic capability to spend on rearmament, the fear that the resulting economic plight might lead to social unrest (as the Communists wished), and expected opposition from the neighbouring countries (Igarashi 1999: 96–7). Kenneth Pyle points out that Japan's political passivity in the postwar era was 'the product of a carefully constructed and brilliantly implemented foreign policy [that Yoshida set forth]' (Pyle 1988: 452).

In the end, the US–Japan Security Treaty, which allowed Japan to stick to a minimalist defence policy, was concluded on the same day as the San Francisco Peace Treaty in September 1951. The treaty grants to the US the right to use Japanese bases and provides for a US military presence in Japan. The original treaty, in effect, merely stated that US forces *may be* utilised to defend Japan, and thus it was not a clear US commitment to guarantee Japan's security. However, regardless of this provision the treaty enabled Japan to depend on the US for its security, because it was almost certain that the US would defend Japan in case of emergency given the US strategic interests in the Cold War, and also the existence of US bases in Japan itself could act as a deterrent (Sakamoto 1999: 72). Although Yoshida had to compromise to some extent, for instance by allowing some rearmament in the form of the Self-Defence Forces (SDF), 'Yoshida's firmness spared Japan military involvement in the war and allowed it instead to profit enormously from procurement orders [during the Korean War]' (Pyle 1988: 454).

At the same time, the Security Treaty, which was revised in 1960 by the Kishi cabinet,[1] has framed and constrained postwar Japanese foreign policy. By signing the treaty, Japan was thoroughly embedded into the Cold War framework on the side of the West. Furthermore, the treaty has made Japan highly vulnerable to US pressures, and it has shaped not only security relations between the two countries, but also their overall relations in the postwar period. That is to say, the 1960 Security Treaty is a highly unequal one in the sense that it sets out only the US contribution to Japan's defence, and not the other way round. It recognises as the area for common defence only the territories under the administration of Japan (Article five), and does not include the US territories in the Asia Pacific region, let alone the US mainland. Of course, there are some reasons why the US has accepted this unequal relationship. Japan has provided bases for the US and since 1978 has paid the substantial financial cost[2] for the stationing of US troops in Japan. Importantly, the bases Japan has provided are of considerable significance to the US strategically. Based on the security treaty (Article six)[3] and its interpretations, the US can actually use these bases with great flexibility; their use is not confined to the defence of Japan but can be extended to wider global strategic operations, which is a significant benefit that the US reaps from the treaty (Watanabe 2001: 30–1). Another benefit of the security treaty for the US is that it can expect Japan to take collaborative actions in case of emergency. This was taken further when the two governments signed the Guidelines for US–Japan Defence Cooperation in 1978, which provided for researching concrete military cooperation between the two countries. Nevertheless, despite these benefits to the US flowing from the security treaty, under this system Japan is, after all, a junior partner. It is the US that controls the security fate of Japan. Japan puts the matter of its own security in the hands of the US and cannot affect decision-making even about critical defence issues. Such an unbalanced relationship inevitably has made Japan support US policy and has made it vulnerable to US requests.

Japan's Asian policy in the 1950s

Meanwhile, Asian policies gradually began to come into Japan's diplomatic agenda in the mid-1950s, although they were not very substantial during the 1950s. It is noteworthy that the first edition of the MOFA's Blue Book, published in 1957, stated the association with Asia as one of the three basic principles of Japanese international relations, together with United Nations (UN) centrism and the association with the West.[4] Watanabe points out that the two principles of the association with Asia and the association with the West came out as a result of serious discussions about Asia's position in Japan's diplomatic policy, namely about how the relationships with the West, particularly the US, and those with Asia could be balanced (Watanabe 1992: 84–5). Since then this has been the key issue of Japanese foreign policy. Pempel puts it as follows: 'Japan's relationship with Asia has of course been complicated, but Japan's simultaneous relationship with the West has added further to the complexity. This duality has been an essential feature of Japanese foreign policy for the last century and more' (Pempel 1997: 50).

Japan's Asian relations have been, to a significant extent, dominated by its economic interests throughout the postwar period, as will be shown in this chapter, and this applies particularly to Japan in the 1950s, when the focus was on economic rehabilitation. The resumption of economic relations with Asian countries became a rather urgent and important issue for Japan, as they had provided the majority of natural resources and important markets before the war, even though their economies were very small and less attractive than the rich Western markets. Japan's interest in restoring Asian relations is evidenced in the first diplomatic Blue Book mentioned above, which acknowledged that there was a close complementary relationship between the Japanese and the Asian economies, and without Asia's prosperity and peace Japan would not be prosperous.[5]

In addition, the US, which was concerned about Japan's isolation in the region, was supportive of Japan's closer links with non-Communist Asian countries. For the US, who wished to keep Japan in the Western camp, to increase the importance of Japan's role as an ally, and to make Japan 'the workshop of Asia', Japan's economic rehabilitation was an urgent issue. In this context, the Truman administration took seriously the consolidation of Japan's economic relations with Asian countries, which would ensure Japan's economic recovery and would prevent Japan from moving towards Communism (Igarashi 1999: 116–21).

Against this background, Japan resumed its Asian policies. Prime Minister Yoshida, who was more interested in relations with the West (Shiraishi 1997: 177), but recognised that developing the Asian economies would contribute to the Japanese economy (Sudo 1997: 150–1), proposed some Asian policies concerning economic assistance for Southeast Asia. Most importantly, Japan started the negotiations for reparations payments with Southeast Asian countries as part of its economic assistance programme in 1954. Also, it provided technical assistance through participating in the British Colombo Plan implemented in 1954. The restoration of Japan's ties with the region was not easy however. The negotiations for reparations payments with the Southeast Asian countries were not smooth, and took until the end of the 1950s to complete.[6]

Although Japan did not try to re-establish a significant relationship with China, which had been a vital trading partner before the war as a provider of natural resources and markets, the two countries did maintain some trading relations. Japan was not able to have diplomatic relations with China and instead had to acknowledge the Taiwan government, following the US policy. However, it resumed trading ties with China in 1950 through private channels, based on the principle of *seikei bunri* that Yoshida pursued then. Nester stresses that this policy of Yoshida was greatly motivated by Japan's economic interests, citing Yoshida's remark: 'I don't care whether China is red or green. China is a national market and it has become necessary for Japan to think about markets' (Nester 1990: 78). However, this relationship was disrupted in 1958, mainly because the then Prime Minister Nobusuke Kishi's pro-Taiwan policies angered China.[7]

Prime Minister Kishi (1957–60) adopted a more positive approach to Asia than Yoshida and his other predecessors. Kishi chose Southeast Asia, rather than the US, as the destination of his first official overseas visit in 1957; this was the first visit to that region by a Japanese Prime Minister after the Second World War, and he made another trip to Southeast Asia in the same year. Also, he proposed a Southeast Asia Development Fund in 1957, which was an attempt to develop the Southeast Asian economy by relying on US financial resources. This proposal was not realised, however, because the US did not support the fund.

This relatively assertive Asian policy of Kishi was motivated by Japan's economic interests and its interests in relation to the US. He understood both the short-term and the long-term importance of the region to the Japanese economy (Shiraishi 1997: 177). In fact, during his visit the reparations negotiations with Indonesia were concluded and the Japanese businesses began to turn their eyes to that country. In addition, his positive stance on Southeast Asia fits his style of simultaneously being an 'Asianist' and a 'pro-Americanist'. In other words, he found a positive Southeast Asian policy to be the area where those two norms could coexist (Shiraishi 1997: 176–7). On the one hand, Japan could play a certain leadership role, particularly in South East Asia, which satisfied his Asianist position, though within the international framework set by the US. On the other hand, Japan's contribution to the development of non-Communist Southeast Asian countries was not inconsistent with US global strategies.

On the whole, Japan's Asian policy during this period was a limited success at most. Japan began to re-establish relations with Asian countries through reparations payments and economic assistance, but they were modest in size and political aspects were muted. Although the economic importance of Asia was widely recognised among Japanese policymaking agents, relations with rich Western countries were given priority over relations with the undeveloped Asian countries. Also, Japan's Asian policies at that time were to a large extent associated with US interests, and even the policies of Kishi, who is remembered as an Asianist, were quite consistent with US strategies.

It must be also noted here that, although Japan normalised its relations with the Southeast Asian countries through the agreements about reparations payments, the memories of Japan's occupation of the region were not easily erased. Indeed this has been a continuing constraint on Japanese foreign policy throughout the postwar period. Anti-Japanese feelings were, and still are, most conspicuous in China and the Korean Peninsula. In Southeast Asia, the degree of hostility against Japan seems to have varied among countries: it was largest in the Philippines and Singapore, where there was a great deal of suffering during Japanese colonial rule, while in Thailand and Malaysia, where Japan's aggressions were targeted not on the whole society, but just a part of it, specifically the Chinese, the tension was relatively low compared with others (Sudo 1996: 187–8). However, in general there was a very hostile atmosphere against Japan in Southeast Asia.

The 1960s – solidifying the Yoshida Doctrine

During the 1960s, the Yoshida Doctrine, which recommended a low political profile with the highest priority given to economic development, became institutionalised in the ruling Liberal Democratic Party (LDP) by two prime ministers, Ikeda and

Sato, both protégés of Yoshida. A broad national consensus on economic growth was also formed at the same time. Kishi's administration took up the political issues of Japan's rearmament and constitutional change, and this ended with a political crisis in 1960, when he forced a Diet vote on a revised security treaty. Ikeda, Kishi's successor, returned to Yoshida's lines, but emphasised economic issues more than Yoshida had done. He set forth and implemented the famous Income Doubling Plan, which was aimed at doubling Japan's national income in a decade and resulted in its postwar economic miracle. Subsequently, Sato, who was Prime Minister from 1964 to 1972, further developed the Yoshida Doctrine. Under the concept of the 'peace nation', he formulated two sets of principles: (1) the Three Non-Nuclear Principles, which provided that Japan would not produce, possess, or introduce nuclear weapons onto its territory, and (2) the Three Arms Export Principles, an effective ban on the export of weapons. Michio Muramatsu and Ellis Krauss note that there was no consensus about the Yoshida Doctrine in the 1950s even among the political elite, much less in the public, and that '[it] was not until at least the mid-1960s that the policy line came to be fully developed and institutionalised among the conservative elite and to enjoy widespread public support' (Muramatsu and Krauss 1987: 525). While economic growth was undoubtedly the highest priority, which explains many of the Japanese foreign policies of that time, these 'self-constraints' policies were a part of Japan's carefully calculated actions to legitimise its minimal involvement in US security strategies while reaping economic benefits (Pharr 1993: 246).

Furthermore, there was another important agenda as well, namely enhancing Japan's international status and restoring its self-respect (Yasutomo 1983: 25, Tadokoro 1999: 114). Accordingly, the government put its energy into strengthening economic relations with Western countries and rejoining the international community, by obtaining membership of the International Monetary Fund (IMF) and the General Agreement on Tariffs and Trade (GATT), as equals with Western countries. Whilst marching towards economic success, Japan had achieved many of its diplomatic aims by 1964. It became an Article 8 member of the IMF, joined the Organisation for Economic Cooperation and Development (OECD) and its Development Assistance Committee (DAC), and participated in the Kennedy round of GATT as well as the United Nations Conference on Trade and Development (UNCTAD). In addition to achieving these objectives of economic development and more prominent international status, Prime Minister Sato had another specific agenda, namely realising the return of Okinawa to Japan,[8] and he devoted great energies to this issue.

Considering these goals of Japanese foreign policy, the importance of US support for realising them, and Japan's security dependence on the US, it was not surprising that Japan's policy was influenced by US wishes to a great extent, and its US relations constrained significantly Japanese foreign policy. Accordingly, Japan's approaches towards Asia were closely linked with US strategies, as demonstrated below.

Regional policies in the 1960s

The beginning of economic assistance

While making an effort to expand Western relations, Asia was by no means ignored by Japan.[9] Most prominently, Japan began to expand economic assistance to the region. Subsequent to reparations payments, Japan started to gradually increase both the absolute amount of ODA, through yen loans in the mid-1960s, and also the proportion of it that was given to Asia. Some of the institutions needed to implement these policies, such as the Overseas Economic Cooperation Fund (OECF) and the Overseas Technical cooperation Agency (later the Japan International Cooperation Agency, or JICA), were created during Ikeda's stay in office. Also, in 1965 Japan normalised its relationship with South Korea and began to provide grant aid and yen loans.

Pressures from other developed countries, particularly the US, to make Japan take on a greater economic burden in international society were an important reason for Japanese policymakers' interest in regional matters at that time. The basic Asian strategy of the US was to ensure the political stability of the non-Communist Asian countries as part of its containment policy against Communism. The Johnson Cabinet began to recognise that military assistance alone could not achieve stability and to emphasise the need for economic assistance (Yamakage 1997: 19–20). Accordingly, along with the intensification of the Vietnam War and the deterioration of its balance of payments, the US began to expect Japan to play a larger role in Southeast Asia. Unlike Australia and South Korea, Japan could not dispatch its military forces for Constitutional reasons, while it benefited from the Vietnam War economically. It was no wonder that the US strongly wished Japan to support US policy on the economic side, and pressed Japan to share more in the economic burden so as to keep regional stability (Tadokoro 1999: 132–3, Hosoya 1993: 167). In addition, for the Sato Cabinet, whose priority was the return of Okinawa, proving that Japan was a loyal and reliable ally to the US was crucial to achieving this goal (Shiraishi 1997: 180).

However, Japan was also greatly motivated by the importance of the region in its own national interest. Many studies show that Japanese assistance to the region was linked directly to Japan's economic benefit. The economic cooperation report of the Ministry of International Trade and Industry (MITI) in 1958 stressed the necessity to promote economic assistance to Southeast Asia given the complementary nature of their economies. The report spelt out two objectives of the economic assistance, namely trade promotion and resource acquisition for Japan. In fact, the reparations were paid in the form of products and services provided by Japanese firms instead of cash,[10] which increased the export opportunities of Japanese firms. Also, a large part of the economic assistance (most of it consisted of yen credits) was tied to Japanese business, specifically the purchase of Japanese goods and services, thereby opening Asian markets to Japanese companies and creating ever more important bilateral economic links between Asia and Japan (Pempel 1997: 56). By the early 1970s Japan became the largest trading partner for most Southeast Asian countries, and its role in direct investments and economic assistance increased dramatically, which led to its playing a leading role in the region in the economic sphere together with the US (Hosoya 1993: 172–3). Shiraishi points out that this was 'the beginning of Japan's postwar penetration into Southeast Asia', and that '[the] close cooperation between government and the private financial and commercial sectors was the hallmark of economic cooperation' (Shiraishi 1997: 179).

In addition to these direct economic benefits, there were also political considerations in Japanese aid policy. The Japanese government began to associate Japan's security with political stability and economic prosperity in neighbouring countries. Watanabe points out that Japanese leaders had recognised the poor economic situation and the political instability in Southeast Asia, and they had become increasingly concerned that the plight in the region might lead to a crisis (Watanabe 1992: 91). Furthermore, Japan's positive approach to economic assistance was linked to the objective of enhancing its international status as well. In other words, by contributing to the development of Asia by deploying the economic resources that it had achieved by that time, Japanese leaders wished to obtain some respect and status in international society (Yamakage 1985: 141–2). Southeast Asia in particular was the region where Japan could pursue such a policy, because relations there were easier compared with the hostile relationship with South Korea and the limitation of China policy under the Cold War framework. Therefore, it can be argued that the growth of Japan's economic assistance to Asia in this period was not only a reaction to US requests, but was also closely related to Japan's economic as well as political interests.

Japan's multilateral approach in Asia in the 1960s

In addition to the expansion of economic assistance, Japan took some initiatives in establishing regional frameworks. Japan's motivations for these policies largely overlapped with those for economic assistance, namely Japan's national interests, particularly the belief of the Japanese policymakers that contributing to regional matters could enhance Japan's national status, in addition to accommodating US wishes.

Significantly, Japan attempted to play an important role in the establishment of the Asian Development Bank (ADB). The project to found the bank in the early 1960s appealed to Prime Minister Sato, who wanted to show the US Japan's commitment to Asia, and thus to be seen to be taking a more positive approach in the region.[11] However, Japan's approach to the ADB was not enthusiastic at the outset. This was mainly because of the concern of MOF officials, who were mainly in charge of this matter, that the activities of the World Bank would be reduced and instead Japan would have to assume too many economic responsibilities for the region. Consequently they strongly insisted on the participation of the US and other developed countries. This position of the MOF officials reflected Japan's basic regional approach at that time, namely promoting the collaboration of Pacific developed countries for the development of Asia. It was not until the US decided to participate[12] and the fear that Japan would be the main contributor had lessened that Japan no longer hesitated to become involved. Japan eventually agreed to be the largest contributor together with the US, to have the bank located in Tokyo and to have a Japanese president, and began to participate positively in every process to found the bank.

However, it turned out that this relatively high-profile initiative of Japan was not welcomed by Asian countries. Japanese policymakers' strong hope to have the bank's headquarters in Tokyo was not realised as Asian countries chose Manila, although Japan obtained the presidency.[13] The Asian countries were quite sceptical about Japan's leadership and dominance in the region. This negative response of the Asian countries to Japan's initiative was a reaction against Japan's way of giving aid, which greatly benefited Japanese firms, as discussed above. But, more importantly, it was a reflection of the anti-Japanese sentiment prevalent among the Asian people, a legacy of the war, as well as the Asian governments' rejection of Japanese leadership itself (Yamakage 1985: 147–51). Indeed, as touched on earlier, this sentiment of the Asian countries has long constrained Japanese initiatives in the region throughout the postwar period, and has forced Japan to keep reassuring its Asian neighbours that it is not trying to dominate the region.

In addition to this active role in the creation of the ADB, Japan convened the Ministerial Conference for Economic Development in Southeast Asia (MEDSEA) in 1966. It was the first postwar international conference that Japan organised, and was seen as an institution potentially dedicated to facilitating Japanese economic assistance to the region (Funabashi 1995: 228). Japanese officials, shocked by the defeat in the ADB headquarters contest, intended to utilise the conference, which they thought was less controversial than the ADB, to create a better relationship with Southeast Asian countries (Yamakage 1990: 152–3). Also, by taking the initiative for this conference, Japan tried to display its positive stance on Asia to international society (Tadokoro 1999: 132). However, Japan was again not very successful. The conference met once a year until 1974, but disappeared later on. There were quite frequent disagreements with respect to the projects that Japan tried to advance (Yamakage 1997: 23). Also, the Southeast Asian leaders preferred their own institution, the Association of Southeast Asian Nations (ASEAN) (Yamakage 1990: 152–3).[14]

Moreover, Japan participated positively in the Asia Pacific Council (ASPAC), which was established in the same year as MEDSEA through the initiative of the South Korean President. ASPAC had a strong anti-communist, or anti-China, and pro-South Vietnam bias, given the fact that all the participating countries were American allies except Malaysia, and was in fact to complement and back up US foreign policies, specifically its strategies on the Vietnam War (Yamakage 1997: 21). Whilst it tried to dilute these military characteristics, Japan attempted to use ASPAC as a body of economic cooperation (Yamakage 1997: 21). However, this organisation was also suspended by the mid-1970s mainly due to the rapprochement between the US and China and the US withdrawal from Vietnam.

These early Japanese regional initiatives and their negative consequences are noteworthy, as they had a great impact on Japan's regional policies later on.

Japanese leaders understood that Japan's high-profile initiatives were not welcomed in Asia, and learnt to adopt a low-profile approach (Yamakage 1990: 153). Japan accepted that it had to reassure its Asian neighbours that it was not seeking to dominate the region otherwise it would have to face difficult opposition to its policies. It gave up trying to form a regional framework by its own initiatives until recently, and instead ASEAN, which Japanese policymakers had originally disliked because they feared that it would conflict with Japan's interests,[15] became the main focus of Japan's Southeast Asian policy (Yamakage 1985: 158). Since then, Japan's regional approach has been very cautious and it has not tried to take overt initiatives.

Early development of Asia Pacific cooperation

Japan became interested in another approach to regional issues during this period, namely Asia Pacific cooperation. This approach began to penetrate into Japanese policymaking and intellectual circles and came to be seen as the basis of regional cooperation from around this time, and eventually developed into the Asia Pacific Economic Cooperation (APEC), which will be discussed in a subsequent section in this chapter.

However, the concept of Asia Pacific cooperation was not developed at the official level initially. It was based primarily on a series of academic studies from the early 1960s, where two leading Japanese economists, Saburo Okita and Kiyoshi Kojima, were central contributors. The establishment of the Japan Economic Research Centre in the early 1960s provided an institutional vehicle for these studies (Soesastro 1994: 79). Kojima proposed creating a Pacific Free Trade Area (PAFTA) in 1965, which would have comprised the five developed Pacific countries of the US, Canada, Australia, New Zealand and Japan. This was largely a response to the development of the European Economic Community and it was designed to supplement and strengthen the international trading system.

The concept of Asia Pacific was, for the first time, espoused at the official level by the then Foreign Minister Takeo Miki in the Sato cabinet in May 1967. He recognised the need to address the economic development problems of the Asian developing nations, and considered that these problems should be tackled through the concerted efforts of the Pacific developed countries (Soesastro 1994: 80, Watanabe 1992: 108). Miki hoped that the creation of a free-trade area in the region would lead to increased trade among Asian developing countries, which in turn would help economic development in Asia (Terada 1998: 342). Based on Miki's strong interest in the idea of Asia Pacific cooperation, the MOFA tried to pursue this policy, but, with little enthusiasm from other countries, government level interest in PAFTA became dormant, and instead the idea of Asia Pacific cooperation lived on mainly in academic circles until the end of the 1970s (Korhonen 1998: 27).

The Pacific Trade and Development Conferences (PAFTAD) were started in 1968 under the auspices of the Japan Economic Research Centre with the support of Miki and brought together economists from the five developed Pacific nations and Britain. The participants were top-ranked scholars, who often had important roles as advisors to their governments, and thus the conferences were never ordinary academic gatherings (Korhonen 1998: 2). Likewise, the Pacific Basin Economic Council (PBEC) was established in the same year as a private organisation of Pacific business executives, who were interested in the idea of creating new business opportunities through regional cooperation. Its objectives were to promote the study of regional trade and investment and to advance greater cooperation between public and private interests (Soesastro 1994: 80).

It must be noted that these private organisations became an important vehicle for the later development of the idea of Asia Pacific cooperation (or Pacific cooperation) in the way that they provoked serious discussions about the way towards, and significance of, regional cooperation, which hitherto had been lacking in the region (Kikuchi 1995: 73). Also, they helped to promote regional solidarity and reinforced shared norms, which were the intellectual background of cooperation movements in the area (Higgott 1993: 112–13). In this sense, it could be argued that, although Miki's policy to advance a formal regional cooperation framework was unsuccessful in the short term, in the longer perspective it laid the foundation of the future development of Asia Pacific regionalism. In fact, Terada shows that Miki was aware of the necessity of a long-term policy perspective for that idea, noting Miki's statement: 'we should have a gradual approach to the Asia–Pacific policy by starting with programmes which can be implemented. This would help create a "mood" for producing solidarity among nations in the end' (Terada 1998: 357).

It is important to bear in mind why Japanese policymaking agents, specifically Miki, came to favour the concept of Asia Pacific, and Asia Pacific cooperation. For one thing, as seen in the case of the ADB, Japan was not ready to take regional responsibility alone at that time, although Japan recognised the importance of the development and stability in its Asian neighbours to its national interests. As shown above, the Japanese government initially conceived of Asia Pacific cooperation as a form of collaboration among the Pacific developed countries to assist the developing countries in the region, rather than regional economic cooperation among developed and developing countries on an equal footing. Japan could not afford to assist Asian developing countries alone and had to rely on other developed countries (Terada 1998: 344).

In addition, given the rejection by the other Asian countries of Japan's initiatives in regional matters, Asia Pacific cooperation looked less controversial to Japanese officials, as it could avoid giving the impression that Japan was looking for prominence in the region (Yamakage 1990: 153). In other words, they thought that the US's involvement in Asian frameworks could ease the concern of regional countries about the growing influence of Japan. This would enable Japan, it was thought, to advance regional policies more easily, although, as will be discussed later in this chapter, even the idea of Asian Pacific cooperation was not readily accepted by regional countries.

Furthermore, what must be stressed is that the idea of Asia Pacific cooperation appealed to Japanese policymakers at a deeper level as well. As mentioned before, how to balance the relationship with the US and that with Asia has been a key issue for Japan's international relations throughout the postwar period. The concept of Asia Pacific looks quite attractive to Japan in this context in the sense that, while maintaining and improving its ties with Asian countries, it had a good chance of finding a way to accommodate the US. In other words, it could be argued that Japanese policymakers' interest in Asia Pacific cooperation has reflected the motivation to coordinate these two important relationships. Ohba argues that since Miki the concept of Asia Pacific has been established in Japan as a convenient phrase to combine these two potentially contradictory relationships (Ohba 2001: 267). This is why Japan has stuck to Asia Pacific as the means for regional cooperation, as discussed later.

To sum up, Japanese foreign policy during this early postwar period was characterised by the principles set out in the Yoshida Doctrine, namely concentration on its own economic development, a low political profile, and the priority of and dependence on US relations. Japan's regional policy was pursued under this framework, and it is fair to argue that Western, particularly US, relations were the primary pillar of Japanese policy. Although this situation put its stamp on Japan's regional policy, which tended to be greatly influenced by its US relations, this policy was also motivated by Japan's own political and economic interests, separate from US wishes. Japan's aid to Asia, which started as reparations payments, was extended partly in response to strong US requests, and partly in consideration of Japan's economic and political benefit. Also, it is important to appreciate that Japan's multilateral policies, including Asia Pacific policy, reflected its own political and economic considerations, based on the international and regional conditions at that time. Admittedly, Japan's multilateral initiatives eventually came within the scope of US interests, and Japan's attempt to take on an independent regional leadership role was not successful.

The 1970s

This decade saw an important, albeit limited, shift in the nature of Japanese foreign policy, which can be characterised as a loosening of the framework of the Yoshida Doctrine. Because of the significant transformation of the international political economy, which will be discussed below, Japan was no longer allowed to pursue the same line as in the previous decades. Japan gradually began to promote more independent policies rather than keeping to political and diplomatic minimalism and responding to US requests, even though those policies basically did not deviate from US policy. In other words, the substantial transformation of the international political economy began to force Japan to search for a new diplomatic identity and to expand the scope of its diplomacy within the framework of the US-centred relations. In this respect, Southeast Asia was Japan's renewed focus, and Japan began to show its willingness to take some political initiatives there, though only through economic means. These initiatives were not entirely successful at that time. Nevertheless, it is important to note that Japan began to consider utilising its economic resources for political purposes, and throughout the 1970s the relationship with East Asian countries, particularly Southeast Asian countries, became increasingly more important to Japanese foreign policy.

The impact of the transformation of the international political economy on Japanese policy

One of the dramatic events of the early 1970s was the US recognition of China. President Nixon announced in July 1971 that he would visit China, and in the following year the Shanghai communiqué was agreed between the two countries. The impact of this event on international politics was immense. With respect to Japanese policy, it led to the normalisation of diplomatic relations between China and Japan in 1972, and the conclusion of the Japan and China Treaty of Peace and Friendship in 1978. Since then, economic as well as political relations between the two countries have strengthened markedly. More generally, this gesture on the part of Nixon changed significantly the international structure. It undermined the structure of bipolarity, as it was finally revealed that the Communist bloc was no longer unified.

These altered relationships between the US and China as well as between Japan and China, coupled with the advent of détente between the US and the Soviet Union, and the US withdrawal from the Vietnam War, gave the US sufficient reason for the gradual retreat of its forces from East Asia, which left, to some extent, a power vacuum there. This made Japanese policymakers increasingly concerned about stability in the region. In particular, the 1969 Nixon Doctrine, which stated that the US would not intervene in internal insurgencies in Asia, was seen as a clear call on Japan to contribute to the security and stability of East Asia (Green 1995: 54). It became more or less inevitable for Japan to make up for the declining US presence. Under the circumstances, Japanese policymakers began to recognise the need for the increased political use of Japanese economic resources so as to contribute to the maintenance of stability in the region. At the same time, the Southeast Asian countries, which were probably more concerned about the security situation in the region than Japan, began to view Japan as a potentially greater source of political support (Morrison 1988: 419).

In addition to these geopolitical shifts, there were other factors that influenced the change in Japanese foreign policy. As argued before, the US began to demand that Japan made a larger contribution particularly to East Asian issues in the 1960s, and such pressures were further strengthened in the 1970s, when Japan's economic rise and the US's relative decline (partly due to the cost of the Vietnam War) became evident. Another Nixon shock in 1971, which was the end of gold standard and effectively meant the breakdown of the Bretton Woods system, revealed that the US was no longer an absolute hegemon. In particular, Japan's massive surplus of trade and current balances not only made the US frustrated and led to intensified trade friction between the two countries, but also attracted the criticism of many Western developed nations, who accused Japan of pursuing neo-mercantilistic policies. Japan's more positive policy and the increased use of its economic resources for regional matters can be regarded, in a sense, as a way to placate the US and other Western countries by showing its willingness to shoulder the costs of maintaining the international order.

Furthermore, it is important to note that the Japanese economy began to be more closely connected with the East Asian economy, which not only greatly increased the economic importance of the region in Japanese strategies, but also made Japanese policymakers more concerned with the region's political stability, which by then could affect Japanese businesses directly. Japan had gradually re-established its economic ties to the region during the 1950s and 1960s, but the regional inter-dependence was further increased and deepened in the 1970s. The demise of the Bretton Woods system was a watershed in this process. The resulting appreciation of the yen[16] pressured Japanese firms to go abroad because of the weakening com-petitiveness of their exports. The Japanese government lifted its controls on foreign direct investment (FDI) in the same year, which resulted in a surge of Japanese investment in the region (Table 2.1). This expansion of investment continued steadily throughout the 1970s, with manufacturing companies moving into the four Newly Industrialising Countries (NICs) and raw material extraction companies moving primarily to Indonesia (Stubbs 1994: 371). The increase of Japan's FDI, which involved the rise of trade as well (Table 2.2 and 2.3), ushered in greater regional economic integration, which was furthered in the 1980s, as discussed in more detail in the next section, although at this time it was still based on Japan-centred bilateral linkages rather than regional multilateral integration, as Pempel points out (Pempel 1997: 51).

Based on these changes in the international structure, Japan needed to modify its previous stance of minimalist diplomacy. Accordingly, while Japan consistently and dramatically increased the size of ODA throughout the 1970s (Figure 2.1), and eventually replaced the US as the largest donor in the region in the late 1970s, it began to use its economic resources for diplomatic purposes, particularly in Southeast Asia, as discussed below.[17]

Institutionalising ASEAN relations

Although these changes in the international structure laid the foundation for Japan's more independent foreign policy, particularly in Southeast Asia, they were also a reflection of the regional situation at that time. Throughout the 1970s, high political tension grew in many parts of Southeast Asia, as illustrated by the coup in Thailand in 1971 and the declaration of martial law in the Philippines in 1972. Under such precarious regional conditions, Japan's economic dominance in the region led to incidents in which Prime Minister Kakuei Tanaka was faced with riots in Jakarta and Bangkok in January 1974 during his official trip to Southeast Asia. Although the political tension in the region played a major role in the riots (Morrison 1988: 419), these incidents shocked Japanese policymakers, and made them realise not only the political instability in the region but also Japan's alienation from the region and the necessity to make more efforts to consolidate ties with the region. The incidents also challenged one of Japan's postwar beliefs that the separation of economics from politics was a successful formula for avoiding political conflicts with its neighbours (Morrison 1988: 420), forcing Japanese policymakers, particularly the MOFA, to take a more positive approach towards the region.

Furthermore, it is noteworthy that Japanese policymaking agents were taking a growing interest in East Asia. In the MOFA, the so-called 'Asianists' were gradually

Table 2.1 Japanese outward FDI by regions (1965–2003)

(Million US$)

To:	1965	1970	1975	1980	1985	1986	1987	1988	1989	1990	1995	2000	2003
World	159	904	3,280	4,693	12,217	22,320	33,364	47,022	67,540	56,911	51,932	49,034	36,092
US	33	94	846	1,484	5,395	10,165	14,704	21,701	32,540	26,128	22,650	12,349	10,577
	20.8%	10.4%	25.8%	31.6%	44.2%	45.5%	44.1%	46.2%	48.2%	45.9%	43.6%	25.2%	29.3%
East Asia	32	165	1,078	1,176	1,414	2,310	4,386	5,526	8,120	6,946	11,851	5,788	6,233
	20.1%	18.3%	32.9%	25.1%	11.6%	10.3%	13.1%	11.8%	12.0%	12.2%	22.8%	11.8%	17.3%
China	0	0	0	12	100	226	1,226	296	438	349	4,478	1,008	3,143
	0.0%	0.0%	0.0%	0.3%	0.8%	1.0%	3.7%	0.6%	0.6%	0.6%	8.6%	2.1%	8.7%
NICs	5	60	274	378	718	1,531	2,580	3,264	4,900	3,355	3,236	2,731	1,154
	3.1%	6.6%	8.4%	8.1%	5.9%	6.9%	7.7%	6.9%	7.3%	5.9%	6.2%	5.6%	3.2%
ASEAN 4	27	105	804	786	596	553	1,030	1,966	2,782	3,242	4,137	2,049	1,936
	17.0%	11.6%	24.5%	16.7%	4.9%	2.5%	3.1%	4.2%	4.1%	5.7%	8.0%	4.2%	5.4%

Sources: JETRO homepage, <www.jetro.go.jp/jpn/stats/fdi/data/jfdi111_01.xls> (accessed 20 May 2005)

Notes: East Asia consists of China, NICs and ASEAN 4.
NICs are South Korea, Taiwan, Hong Kong and Singapore.
ASEAN 4 consists of Thailand, Malaysia, the Philippines and Indonesia.

Table 2.2 Japanese exports by regions (1965–2004)

(Million US$)

To:	1965	1970	1975	1980	1985	1990	1995	2000	2004
World	8,452	19,318	55,753	129,807	175,638	286,948	442,937	479,284	565,752
US	2,479	5,940	11,149	31,367	65,278	90,322	120,859	142,475	127,007
	29.3%	30.7%	20.0%	24.2%	37.2%	31.5%	27.3%	29.7%	22.4%
East Asia	1,794	4,595	13,632	33,383	42,275	87,978	186,546	190,356	265,084
	21.2%	23.8%	24.5%	25.7%	24.1%	30.7%	42.1%	39.7%	46.9%
China	245	569	2,259	5,078	12,477	6,130	21,931	30,338	73,913
	2.9%	2.9%	4.1%	3.9%	7.1%	2.1%	5.0%	6.3%	13.1%
NICs	810	2,641	6,972	19,186	22,491	59,667	111,036	114,654	139,654
	9.6%	13.7%	12.5%	14.8%	12.8%	20.8%	25.1%	23.9%	24.7%
ASEAN 4	739	1,385	4,401	9,119	7,307	22,181	53,579	45,364	51,517
	8.7%	7.2%	7.9%	7.0%	4.2%	7.7%	12.1%	9.5%	9.1%

Sources: Compiled Hook *et al.* (2001: 442–9), and METI homepage, <www.meti.go.jp/policy/trade_policy/trade_policy/trade_db/html/f_y2000.html> and <www.meti.go.jp/policy/trade_policy/trade_db/html/f_y2004.html> (accessed 6 June 2005).

Notes: East Asia consists of China, NICs and ASEAN 4.
NICs are South Korea, Taiwan, Hong Kong and Singapore.
ASEAN 4 consists of Thailand, Malaysia, the Philippines and Indonesia.

Table 2.3 Japanese imports by regions (1965–2004)

(Million US$)

From:	1965	1970	1975	1980	1985	1990	1995	2000	2004
World	8,169	18,881	57,863	140,528	129,539	234,799	336,094	379,718	455,254
US	2,366	5,560	11,608	24,408	25,793	52,369	75,408	72,169	62,511
	29.0%	29.4%	20.1%	17.4%	19.9%	22.3%	22.4%	19.0%	13.7%
East Asia	1,288	2,692	10,261	31,396	33,041	62,428	115,519	150,238	196,174
	15.8%	14.3%	17.7%	22.3%	25.5%	26.6%	34.4%	39.6%	43.1%
China	225	254	1,531	4,323	6,483	12,054	35,922	55,116	94,362
	2.8%	1.3%	2.6%	3.1%	5.0%	5.1%	10.7%	14.5%	20.7%
NICs	266	659	2,764	7,365	9,839	25,947	41,218	46,461	46,653
	3.3%	3.5%	4.8%	5.2%	7.6%	11.1%	12.3%	12.2%	10.2%
ASEAN 4	797	1,779	5,966	19,708	16,719	24,427	38,379	48,661	55,159
	9.8%	9.4%	10.3%	14.0%	12.9%	10.4%	11.4%	12.8%	12.1%

Sources: Compiled Hook *et al.* (2001: 442–9), and METI homepage, <www.meti.go.jp/policy/trade_policy/trade_db/html/f_y2000.html> and <www.meti.go.jp/policy/trade_policy/trade_db/html/f_y2004.html> (accessed 6 June 2005)

Notes: East Asia consists of China, NICs and ASEAN 4.
    NICs are South Korea, Taiwan, Hong Kong and Singapore.
    ASEAN 4 consists of Thailand, Malaysia, the Philippines and Indonesia.

(billion US$)

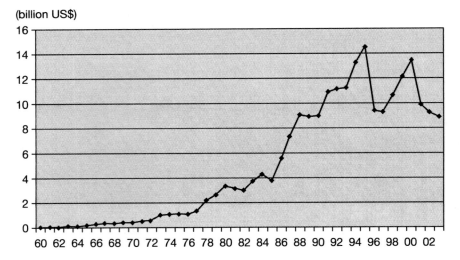

Figure 2.1 The total amounts of Japanese ODA (net disbursements) (1960–2002)

Sources: OECD <www.oecd.org/dataoecd/50/16/5037775.htm> (accessed 1 March 2005)

gaining influence, and they found opportunities for a more active diplomacy in Southeast Asia, at a time when more politicians were also becoming interested in this region (Sudo 1997: 153). This was probably a reflection of the importance of East Asia, particularly due to Japan's closer economic ties there, together with the impact on the Japanese policymakers of the incidents that took place during Tanaka's Southeast Asian visit.

Against this international and regional background, Japan began to establish closer ties with ASEAN. Japanese policymakers came to recognise that the past policy of bilateral economic assistance needed to be reconsidered, but Japan did not have any particular alternative means. Regional organisations that Japan had tried to promote, namely MEDSEA and ASPAC, had not functioned as expected and had disappeared in the mid-1970s. Although, as mentioned earlier, Japanese officials initially did not have a positive stance on ASEAN, under these changed circumstances they began to regard ASEAN as the new cornerstone of Japan's regional policy (Takeda 1995: 65).

The MOFA played a central role in institutionalising ASEAN relations. Prime Minister Takeo Fukuda, during his visit to Southeast Asia in 1977, attended the second ASEAN Summit Meeting by ASEAN's invitation. He made an important speech about Japan's basic philosophy on Southeast Asian policy, known as the Fukuda Doctrine, which became a trigger for the subsequent development of Japan-ASEAN relations. It comprised the following three points.

(1) Japan will not become a military power, and will contribute to the peace and prosperity of the world.

(2) Japan will seek to develop equal partnerships with Southeast Asian countries in the political, economic, social, and cultural spheres based on genuine understanding.

(3) Japan will support the increase in the solidarity and strength of the ASEAN countries; it will contribute to the strengthening of mutual understanding between the ASEAN members and the Indochina nations, and it will help establish peace and prosperity throughout Southeast Asia.

(Takeda 1995: 66, author's translation)

The Fukuda Doctrine expressed the willingness of the Japanese policymaking agents to build up a new relationship with Southeast Asia in collaboration with ASEAN as an equal partner. Most Japanese prime ministers have made an official trip to ASEAN countries since, and each time they have pledged some new commitments for ASEAN's development in accordance with ASEAN's expectations (Sudo 1996: 205–7). Rix argues that there is no doubt that ASEAN has enjoyed a special status in Japanese foreign policy since the Fukuda Doctrine (Rix 1993b: 148).

More importantly, the Fukuda Doctrine displayed Japan's intent to play a larger role in the region by stepping into the political area. Specifically Japan volunteered to be a mediator between the ASEAN and other Indochina countries, for the sake of easing tensions in Southeast Asia. Morrison argues that it is 'regarded as a major turning point in that it provided what Japan regarded as a statement of its political interests in the Southeast Asian region' (Morrison 1988: 422). Japan tried to advance this agenda not through military but economic means, namely the provision of ODA to the Indochina countries. For instance, the MOFA requested Vietnam to use Japanese ODA for importing ASEAN products, which MOFA officials expected would foster a new relationship between ASEAN and the Indochina countries (Sudo 1997: 154). This policy to bridge between ASEAN and the Indochina countries ended in failure at that time, as Japan had to sever aid to Vietnam in 1979 due to Vietnam's invasion of Cambodia in December 1978. However, in spite of this temporary reversal, it is noteworthy that Japan began to show its willingness to utilise economic resources for assuming a political role in the region, and indeed Japan became positively involved in the Cambodian issue later, as discussed in the next section.

This new stance of Japan was not contradictory to US interests. The US was expecting Japan's larger contribution in Southeast Asia, and was positive about its attempt to bridge the gap between ASEAN and Indochina until the Soviet invasion of Afghanistan in December 1979 (Takeda 1995: 67). Watanabe notes that the MOFA planned very carefully the Fukuda Doctrine by creating a domestic and international consensus for it, and its officials had considered that it would not provoke serious external opposition (Watanabe 1992: 113–14).

Since the announcement of the Fukuda Doctrine, the relationship between Japan and ASEAN has become institutionalised. The first Japan-ASEAN Foreign Minister's Meeting was organised in 1978, and they still meet regularly. This first meeting developed into the ASEAN Post Ministerial Conference (PMC) in the following year, which originally included the US, New Zealand, Australia and the European Community (EC) but expanded to others later. Furthermore, an economic ministers meeting between Japan and ASEAN was proposed by the Japanese Foreign Minister; they met for the first time in 1979, and since 1992 they have met on a regular basis.

Since the 1980s

The changes in Japanese foreign policy discussed in the previous section have continued since the 1980s. Japan's minimalist stance on international affairs based on the Yoshida Doctrine has been further diluted. While its foreign economic policy, together with Japanese private capital, have had a significant impact on the regional economic order as well as the economy of individual countries, Japan has become more interested in taking political initiative in regional matters. While policies based on the Fukuda Doctrine represented basically the use of economic resources for political purposes (and in fact economic resources have remained Japan's main foreign policy tool), Japan has become more active diplomatically and has participated in creating new regional frameworks. Furthermore, even security issues have ceased to be a political taboo among Japanese policymaking agents, particularly since the Gulf War, which greatly influenced the thinking of Japanese policymakers and the public, although these issues are still dealt with very cautiously. Few policymakers would dispute that US relations are still most important. In fact Japan is always careful to take into account the US stance, and never wishes to defy US policies. However, it should be noted that Japan's interest in conducting more independent policies that are not merely the extension of, or a derivation of, US policies has begun to be observed. In addition, the position that East Asian countries, not only Southeast Asian countries, but also the NICs and China, occupy in Japanese foreign policy has undoubtedly risen considerably.

The continued changes in the external environment since the 1970s, such as the rise of Japan's economic power and the deepening economic interdependence in the region, have laid the foundation for these further shifts in Japanese foreign policy during this period. However, what has to be particularly noticed is the sea change in the international system triggered by the end of the Cold War. Funabashi argues, '[t]he 1990s and the end of the Cold War have brought Japan's Asia policy to a new stage. Increasingly, politics and a greater spirit of interdependence have been infused in Japan's approach to the region' (Funabashi 1995: 230). Accordingly, this section will first look at the impact of the end of the Cold War on Japanese foreign policy, followed by an examination of Japanese policies in three areas: (1) Japan's economic relations with the region, (2) its policies towards regional cooperation and (3) its political and security initiatives.

The end of the Cold War and its impact on Japanese foreign policy

Despite several years of the renewed heightening of Cold War tensions in the early 1980s, by the end of the decade it became apparent that the Cold War was coming to an end. Although some may argue that the impact of the end of the Cold War in East Asia has not been as great as in Europe, it has greatly changed Japan's diplomatic environment, and has significantly influenced Japanese foreign policy.

One of the significant impacts that the end of the Cold War has had on Japanese foreign policy is that it has made Japan's status in world politics more uncertain. While the Cold War order strictly constrained the scope of its foreign policy, Japan in turn had a secure position in such a framework, which it sought to safeguard by indirectly contributing to the Western camp and supporting US policy mainly through economic means. The end of the Cold War has completely altered these coordinates of Japanese postwar foreign policy, and has forced Japanese policy-makers to think anew what sort of role the country should play in order to maintain and enhance its political status. The following remark of Former Foreign Minister Yohei Kono indicates the shift in Japanese foreign policy: since the end of the Cold War the concept of Japan as a member of the West, which was the basis for deciding Japan's political and security policy, has had no significance, and this has brought a significant change to Japanese foreign policy (Kono 1995: 13).

Furthermore, the changing world order in the post Cold War era no longer guarantees the conditions in which Japan has pursued its national interests, specifically its stability and prosperity. As discussed before, Japan was, to a great extent, a beneficiary of the existing international order during the Cold War and was able to achieve these objectives, but such a favourable environment is not guaranteed any more. As a consequence, the Japanese policymakers have increasingly recognised that Japan has to be more involved politically in the architecture of a new international order to avoid being left out and to secure a voice to defend its national interests.

This orientation of the Japanese policymakers is particularly evident in the security area. During the Cold War, the US was strongly committed to the security of its allies within its broad security framework based on the containment of the Soviet Union. The end of the Cold War has inevitably forced it to change its long-term policy stance. The reduction of the US defence budget and the gradual withdrawal of the US forces from East Asia from a long-term perspective is unavoidable to some extent and so is its limited political presence there, although for the time being the security relationship between Japan and the US has been strengthened particularly since the issuance of the Nye Report in February 1995,[18] and the US has shown its determination to maintain around 100,000 troops in East Asia for at least the next 20 years. In fact, the US has declared that it has ceased to be the world policeman, and it has requested greater burden sharing from its allies (Iwata 1997: 110–1). Japanese and East Asian officials have recognised that East Asia has to prepare for a gradual US withdrawal from the region. Under the circumstances, Japan's political role in the region has definitely become more important than before. It is not that they wish a diminution of the US presence in East Asia, and in fact some regional frameworks, such as the ARF and APEC, are in a sense intended to keep the US involved. However, in the long term the US cannot be expected to maintain the same policy towards East Asia as it did during the Cold War, which Japanese and East Asian officials have to accept.

The Gulf War actually revealed to Japanese policymakers that the old formula did not work well any more, and had a considerable impact on Japanese security thinking. Japan's huge economic contribution did not satisfy the US policymaking circles or the US public, and its failure to participate in the UN coalition force generated international criticism. Iokibe argues that what the Gulf War asked the Japanese was to consider whether their fundamental belief concerning the country's security was wrong, namely the belief that all Japan has to do to be accepted by the international society is not to instigate or to be involved in a war in any way (Iokibe 1999: 228–9).

Thus, the end of the Cold War and subsequent changes in the international environment, and the Gulf War in particular, have significantly influenced Japanese society, and have provoked huge debates in Japan. Although a new consensus on this issue has not emerged yet, many people seem to have come to be aware that some change is necessary. It is noteworthy that there have been increasingly positive views on a more extensive, albeit still limited, role of the SDF. When the government submitted a United Nations Peace Force Cooperation Bill to the Diet in 1990, when a war in the Gulf seemed likely, public opinion was very negative about the overseas dispatch of military personnel and the Bill (Stockwin 1999: 73–4). However, a decade later, a poll showed that 70 per cent of people backed the SDF's logistical and non-combat involvement in the operations of the US and other states that followed the attacks in New York and Washington on 11 September 2001.[19] This has been a highly controversial issue as it could lead to a shift in Japan's fundamental security policy, but an increasing number of voices not only among policymakers but also the Japanese public have asked that Japan should cease to be a junior partner to the US. In fact, there have been discussions about the revision of the constitution, specifically the revision of Article 9,[20] which provides the basis of state pacifism and on which much of the discussion has revolved, and still revolves (Hook and McCormack 2001: 4). Debates are still going on,[21] but one thing to be noted is that the number of people who accept the revision of the constitution has increased in the last decade, although most advocates of the revision do not wish to get rid of Article 9, or to push for independent remilitarisation (Hook and McCormack 2001: 31–4, Green 2001: 25–6 and Stockwin 1999: 168–72).

In short, the end of the Cold War has created various conditions under which Japan has to be more positively involved in international affairs politically, and even in the security area. It is believed, increasingly, that the past minimalist policy is no longer beneficial for Japan.

At the same time, the end of the Cold War has influenced Japan's East Asian relations in the sense that the East Asian countries have come to hold an ever more important position in Japanese foreign policy. For one thing, East Asia is naturally the place where Japan's political initiatives are more likely to be directed for historical, geographical and economic reasons. Japan has to consolidate the basis that allows its more positive roles there. Accordingly, the region has attracted more attention from Japanese policymaking agents.

Furthermore, Japan's interest in East Asia is more or less the reverse side of its increasingly difficult relations with the US. The end of the Cold War has affected

Japan's relations with the US in the sense that the conflict of economic interests between the two countries, which had been mitigated by the presence of a common enemy during the Cold War, became more exposed and straightforward. This was particularly seen in the high tension in the bilateral trade negotiations between the two countries from the late 1980s to the early 1990s. Takayuki Kimura, a high-ranking MOFA official, argues that during the Cold War, even though economic negotiations had their moments of heated discussion, they could reach a last-minute compromise because the US 'considered the overall relationship with Japan more important in the face of communist adversaries than minor economic gains in negotiations' (Kimura 1997: 57–8). However, the end of the Cold War made such considerations unnecessary for the US, and made it pursue direct economic benefits particularly during the term of the Clinton administration. These aggressive US attitudes made not only Japanese policymakers, but also a large part of the Japanese public, the media and academics, grow dissatisfied with the overall relationship with the US, although few dispute the significance of US relations.

While these changes attributed to the end of the Cold War have provided the background for Japan's greater political initiatives in the region, Japan's policy in the economic sphere has also continued to affect the region. In the following, Japan's economic role in this period will be discussed first before moving on to examine Japan's initiatives in the political and security areas.

Japan's economic relations with the region

Japan's economic power has greatly influenced the fate of the regional economy throughout the postwar period, and it has been particularly significant since the mid-1980s, when a combination of Japanese private and public capital began to flow into East Asian countries. This has resulted in a much greater integration of the regional economy and a new regional economic order. While this development has contributed to the rising importance of East Asian countries in Japanese foreign policymaking, it has created in turn a more favourable regional environment that allows a greater role for Japan. This section will discuss this development and show how Japan has successfully pursued regional policies by deploying its economic resources.

It must be noted that, while the economic policies of the Japanese government have played a significant role, as discussed below, Japanese private capital has been an essential driving force in integrating the East Asian economy. Japanese FDI in the region had grown continuously since the 1970s, as discussed before, but this growth was accelerated dramatically in the mid-1980s, particularly after the Plaza Accord in 1985. The value of the yen almost doubled between 1985 and 1988, which forced Japanese firms to go abroad. Japanese FDI in East Asia tripled from 1985 to 1987, and increased five times by 1990 (Table 2.1). Although the US is still by far the largest investment destination, this rise of Japanese FDI to East Asia has had a great impact on the region. In fact, in many East Asian countries Japan has become the largest investor nation, replacing the US.[22] The surge in Japanese FDI in absolute terms was accompanied by the rapid increase of Japanese trade with the region. Both Japanese exports to and imports from East Asia almost doubled from 1985 to 1990 (Table 2.2 and 2.3). Also, Pempel notes that, while about one-half of US investment in East Asia is concerned with natural resource extraction, Japan's investments in manufacturing have become more conspicuous, which has made the East Asian economy highly dependent on Japan (Pempel 1997: 62).

Japanese FDI has not only strengthened the economic relationship between Japan and other East Asian countries, but has also altered the region's trade and investment pattern as a whole. The pattern of East Asian development has been described as the 'flying geese model of development'. According to this explanation, Japanese FDI first went to NICs, contributing to their development, and then began to invest massively in ASEAN and China. The latter were also the destination of significant investment from the multinational companies of NICs. Also, according to the model, these countries were then able to move up the technological ladder through this investment process by following the example of countries that had already been successful. For instance, as Japan moved out of textiles, Korea and others took over. What this discussion suggests is that such an investment process has encouraged further regional development, being accompanied by a great expansion of multilateral intra-regional trade, which has further integrated the East Asian economies in a web of relations not only bilaterally with Japan but also with each other.[23] This process has been deepened by the emergence of the Chinese FDI network, where overseas Chinese investors in Singapore, Hong Kong and Taiwan move into China (Pempel 1997: 64). In fact, the amount of exports within East Asia (including Japan) increased from US$123.2 billion in 1985 to US$628.6 billion in 1995 (JETRO 1997).

While the economic integration between Japan and other East Asian countries, or among regional countries, has been basically market-driven, the role of Japanese government policies in that process cannot be underestimated. In particular, the extension of substantial amounts of Japanese aid to the region has made Japanese investment in the ASEAN and China easier, underpinning the regional investment linkage (Stubbs 1994: 372–3).

Japan has steadily increased the volume of aid, having become the largest aid donor in the world in 1989 for the first time, and East Asian countries have always been in a special position as recipients of Japanese aid. Although the percentage of total Japanese aid to East Asia has declined due to the diversification of Japanese aid, the sum that East Asia received has substantially increased in absolute terms (Table 2.4). In addition, East Asian countries have always dominated the top ten list of aid recipients (Table 2.5). Of particular notice is China's emergence as a major recipient after the two governments signed the 1978 Peace and Friendship Treaty. After the end of the Cold War Vietnam has joined China as a main target of Japan's ODA in accordance with Japanese policy of promoting the development of both socialist and capitalist economies of the region (Hook 1996a: 176).

For many East Asian countries, Japanese aid has been of considerable importance to their economies, although it may be debatable to what extent it has actually affected their economic growth. As mentioned in the preceding section, Japan has been the largest donor in the region since 1977, and in most of the ODA recipient

Table 2.4 Japan's bilateral ODA by regions (1980–2002)

(Million US$)

	1980		1990		1995		2000		2002	
Asia	1,383	70.5%	4,117	59.3%	5,745	54.4%	5,283	54.8%	4,086	60.7%
Northeast Asia	82	4.2%	835	12.0%	1,606	15.2%	700	7.3%	865	12.9%
Southeast Asia	861	43.9%	2,379	34.3%	2,592	24.6%	3,155	32.7%	1,754	26.1%
Middle East	204	10.4%	705	10.2%	721	6.8%	727	7.5%	209	3.1%
Africa	223	11.4%	792	11.4%	1,333	12.6%	969	10.1%	584	8.7%
Others	151	7.7%	1,327	19.1%	2,758	26.1%	2,661	27.6%	1,847	27.5%
Total	1,961		6,941		10,557		9,640		6,726	

Sources: MOFA homepage <www.mofa.go.jp/policy/oda/summary/1999/d_g2_01.html#c_2_2> (accessed 2 April 2002), and <www.mofa.go.jp/policy/oda/white/2003/image/p4c2s3chart14big.gif> (accessed 25 May 2005)

Table 2.5 Japan's bilateral ODA by recipients of largest amounts (1970–2003)

(Million US $)

Rank	1970 Country	Amount	1980 Country	Amount	1988 Country	Amount	1998 Country	Amount	2003 Country	Amount
1	Indonesia	125.84	Indonesia	350.30	Indonesia	984.91	China	1,158.16	Indonesia	1,141.78
2	South Korea	86.76	Bangladesh	215.14	China	673.70	Indonesia	828.47	China	759.72
3	Pakistan	39.55	Thailand	189.55	Philippines	534.72	Thailand	558.42	Philippines	528.72
4	India	32.73	Burma	152.46	Thailand	360.62	India	504.95	Vietnam	484.24
5	Philippines	19.23	Egypt	122.97	Bangladesh	341.96	Pakistan	491.54	India	325.79
6	Thailand	16.91	Pakistan	112.42	Pakistan	302.17	Vietnam	388.61	Pakistan	266.22
7	Iran	11.96	Philippines	94.40	Myanmar	259.55	Philippines	297.55	Sri Lanka	172.26
8	Burma	11.94	South Korea	76.30	Sri Lanka	199.83	Sri Lanka	197.85	Kazakhstan	136.27
9	China	9.53	Malaysia	65.63	India	179.46	Bangladesh	189.05	Afghanistan	134.42
10	Singapore	5.75	Sri Lanka	44.78	Egypt	172.90	Malaysia	179.10	Cambodia	125.88

Sources: Orr (1990: 70–1), MOFA homepage <www.mofa.go.jp/policy/oda/summary/1999/d_g2_02.html#c_2_3> (accessed 2 April 2002), and MOFA homepage <www.mofa.go.jp/mofaj/gaiko/oda/shiryo/oda/shiryo/04_hakusho/ODA2004/html/siryo/index.htm> (accessed 25 May 2005)

countries in East Asia, Japan is the largest donor.[24] Furthermore, Japan is the second largest contributor to most multilateral banks, and the largest to the ADB, together with the US, which also affects the economic fate of many East Asian developing countries. Rix stresses the importance of Japanese aid, arguing the aid has 'been able to affect the economic future of most of the countries of Asia, and come to be the greatest single influence in the economic decision-making of many governments within the region', and aid 'speaks loudly of Japan's importance to the region' (Rix 1993b: 159). Japan's economic assistance has become more important particularly after the end of the Cold War, as the US, under Congressional pressure, has become a less generous donor.

Furthermore, it could be argued that what the Japanese government has done is more than merely giving aid. It has adopted various measures to encourage private capital flow to the region. For instance, it gave Japanese firms financial incentives, such as low-interest loans for foreign investment, foreign investment insurance, as well as information.[25] Also, there is evidence that the government was, through its associated agencies, engaged in various activities, like technical training of engineers, to enhance the quality of human resources in the region. In 1987, the MITI announced the New Asian Industrial Development (AID) Plan, which was the attempt of the MITI to combine state resources such as aid and technical cooperation with private capital and technology. It seems that this plan did not actually achieve significant results and ceased to be part of the ministry's cohesive policy in the early 1990s. Nevertheless, the plan deserves some note. Doner argues that 'many of the mixed institutional arrangements that the AID plan both drew on and encouraged have continued to function', and it reinforced the Japanese private sector's own initiatives toward internationalisation (Doner 1997: 224–5). Hatch and Yamamura regard what has been happening in East Asia as the attempt of the Japanese government to expand the Japanese political economy, namely it is 'regionalizing the developmental policies and practices' (Hatch and Yamamura: 1996: 55). Likewise, Shiraishi argues that the basic point about the current formal policy line in Japan is 'the encouragement and promotion of an Asian economy dynamism with Japanese direct investment, Japanese aid for structural adjustment, infrastructural and human resources development, and Japanese imports from Asian NICs and the ASEAN countries', namely 'extension of its politics of productivity beyond Japanese borders onto Asia' (Shiraishi 1997: 187).

To sum up, these Japanese economic policies, accompanied by the huge inflow of Japanese private capital into the region, have had a considerable impact on the regional economy, which has led to a closer economic integration in East Asia. Accordingly, the East Asian economy has become more incorporated in Japan's overall economic strategy, while the importance of Japan's economic power in the region continues. Despite the current prolonged stagnation of the Japanese economy, Japan is still of great significance for East Asian countries economically and has still a great influence on the regional economy, as the discussions on the East Asian financial crisis in Chapter 4 will show.

What has to be noticed here is that the deepening economic interdependence in the region has greatly influenced Japan's emphasis on East Asia in its foreign policymaking. Closer economic ties with East Asian countries have increased Japan's economic stakes in the region considerably, as the regional development and stability have been directly linked to the interests of Japanese business. This has made policymakers adopt a more positive policy to secure such stakes, as discussed below. Furthermore, the increasing importance of the East Asian economy, together with the more difficult relations with the US after the end of the Cold War, have triggered vigorous debates in Japanese intellectual and policymaking circles concerning the 'new Asianism' or 'Japan's Asianisation'. A number of leaders of opinion have begun to stress that Japan should put more importance on its East Asian policy.[26] At the same time, this development has also contributed to a greater interest in East Asia among the Japanese public. This awareness of the importance of East Asia by the vast range of the Japanese people could affect Japan's growing interest in becoming more involved in regional matters politically.

Another point to note is that these concerted activities of Japanese public and private sectors have not only influenced East Asia economically, but have also contributed to enhancing Japan's political position in the region, particularly Southeast Asia. Arase argues that Japanese ODA creates considerable leverage over recipient governments, while consolidating Japan's political relations with East Asia (Arase 1995: 252–3). In other words, while Japan's low-profile economic diplomacy, involving a combination of private and public capitals, has moulded a regional economic order that is essential for Japan's prosperity, it has affected the overall relationship between Japan and the region. This has created long-term Japanese influence, economic as well as political, in the region, and has expanded the sphere of Japan's political activity. Rix describes this as Japan's 'leadership from behind', namely 'a style of leadership that aims at creating long-term Japanese influence in the region, and has been a successful form of long-standing "entrepreneurial" leadership that has carved out a regional role for Japan as investor, trader, aid donor and political actor' (Rix 1993a).

In fact, it seems that Japan's regional initiatives have become more accepted by neighbouring countries since the early 1990s (although not all the countries, particularly China and South Korea, are positive, and Japan still has to deal with its diplomatic relationships with its East Asian neighbours in a very cautious manner). The Malaysian Prime Minister's 'Look East' policy and the EAEG proposal, which will be discussed shortly, probably suggest such a change. Some countries like Thailand have supported Japan's larger role even in the security area. It is also notable that ASEAN countries generally supported the deployment of the SDF in Cambodia to participate in the UN peacekeeping operation in September 1992. Furthermore, the recent development of the framework of ASEAN + 3 can also be seen as an illustration of the region's growing acceptance of Japan's political role in East Asia. Also, it is worth mentioning that, as discussed in Chapter 4 and Chapter 6, Japan's substantial aid during the East Asian financial crisis has significantly improved its relations with regional countries including South Korea, with which Japan has had a very difficult and sensitive relationship throughout the postwar period.

Of course, it should not be forgotten that there are other reasons for this changing regional position of Japan as well, specifically Japan's consistent efforts to improve its regional relations after the adoption of the Fukuda Doctrine, such as almost regular prime ministerial visits to Southeast Asian countries. Also, Hook points out the importance in this respect of Japan's more forthright apologies in the 1990s for its wartime aggression, as 'without addressing the outstanding issue of wartime responsibility, no Japanese government will be able to play a full political and military role in the region' (Hook 1996a: 198). In addition, with the end of the Cold War, East Asian resistance to a regional security role for Japan became less uniform and salient (Hook *et al.* 2001: 139), while the fear of the revival of Japanese militarism has been abating to some extent, though it has not disappeared. The Chinese government, for instance, often expresses its concern about the possibility that Japan would emerge as a military power in the region in order to check Japan's growing presence in the region (Kojima 1992: 27–8). In any case, this changing regional relationship of Japan has enabled it to make a more independent policy and to exercise more political influence in the region.

Japanese policy towards Asian Pacific cooperation

These low-profile Japanese initiatives through economic resources, or leadership from behind, to use Rix's phrase, have also been a feature of its policy towards regional cooperation. Japan's interest in Asia Pacific cooperation goes back to the 1960s, as discussed before, and since then Japan has consistently and cautiously promoted it. That culminated in the establishment of APEC in 1989, although it has been more eagerly engaged in East Asian cooperation recently. The latter will be detailed in Chapter 5, and this section focuses on how and why Japan has participated in the development of Asia Pacific cooperation.

The concept of Asia Pacific cooperation, or Pacific cooperation, was developed throughout the 1970s, but was discussed mainly in academic circles like PAFTAD. where Japanese and Australian scholars played a significant role. The original idea behind PAFTA was to help build a free trade area, but it was abandoned during the 1970s and PAFTA evolved into a more loosely structured, government-level organisation to deal with trade and development issues, similar to the OECD. The new organisation was called the Organisation for Pacific Trade and Development (OPTAD), and, by the late 1970s, came to be favourably received in PAFTAD. In this, while the issue of development of regional developing countries became more central, the initial project of a free trade area of developed countries was sidelined.

The concept of Pacific economic cooperation generated by academics gradually penetrated into official circles in the region from around the end of the 1970s. The official espousal of the idea of Pacific Basin cooperation by the then Japanese Prime Minister Masayoshi Ohira, who took office after Fukuda in 1979, triggered this move. Ohira formed the Pacific Basin Cooperation Study Group as one of his personal policy-advisory bodies in March 1979. The group was headed initially by Saburo Okita, who had been a leading economist involved in developing the idea of Pacific cooperation in the 1960s and 1970s. In addition to Japan, the US also took the idea seriously at the official level. Congress contracted Hugh Patrick of Yale University and Peter Drysdale of the Australian National University for a study in 1978, and they submitted a detailed report about OPTAD. Furthermore, some politicians in the ASEAN countries became interested in OPTAD, though they had preferred their own institution of ASEAN (Korhonen 1998: 121).

Thus, the development of Pacific economic cooperation entered a new era in the 1980s. The term 'Pacific' as a region, which had not been accepted in the first PAFTAD conference in 1968, came to be used extensively by that time, though confined to the PAFTAD circle (Korhonen 1998: 112). Although, when it was first advocated in the 1960s, the concept of Pacific cooperation referred to the idea of concerted efforts of the Pacific developed countries for the development of the region's developing countries, this time it was proposed as a framework aimed at advancing regional economic interdependence by cooperation among both developed and developing countries in the region.

The background against which Ohira became interested in Pacific Basin Cooperation can be looked at from two perspectives: international as well as domestic. Internationally, facing the fact that the deterioration in US–Soviet relations, triggered by the Soviet invasion of Afghanistan, reversed the trend of détente of the 1970s, Fukuda's regional policy, which had assumed that Japan had a regional role as an arbiter and intermediary between ASEAN and Indochina, did not work effectively any more. Japan needed a new regional policy in order to show its will to play a larger role in the world as well as in the region. Funabashi argues that 'Japan's Asian policy rapidly re-established the primacy of Cold War concerns', and that Ohira's Pacific design 'widened the scope of Japan's regional diplomacy and reflected an acknowledgement of Cold War realities' (Funabashi 1995: 229).

Furthermore, China's changing relations with the West gave Japan an easier environment to advance regional cooperation. China's isolation in the region until the early 1970s had created an obstacle to Japan's regional policy, as its positive policy towards Southeast Asia, either through bilateral aid or advancing institution-alisation, could possibly be taken for an anti-China policy domestically and internationally (Watanabe 1992: 117). However, the new development of China-West relations reduced the risk that Japan's regional policy would be considered in that way. Kikuchi points out that Ohira's visit to China in December 1979, when he confirmed his belief that China preferred economic modernisation and a peaceful international environment to conflict with the Soviet Union, became the turning point in the development of his thinking about the Pacific Basin Cooperation, as it implied the possibility of incorporating China into an Asian framework (Kikuchi 1995: 104–5).

Domestically, Ohira was contesting Fukuda for the premiership and to do this effectively he needed a different foreign policy platform. While Fukuda was identified with an Asian orientation, Ohira fought Fukuda with a package of grandiose visions (Korhonen 1998: 123). Also, Korhonen argues that Ohira had to prevent Japan from being drawn into the reborn Cold War. That is, Ohira, who had inherited an intra-factional tradition from Ikeda and Yoshida, 'had to find a way to identify Japan clearly with the United States, but by using such language that Japan's economic orientation could continue. This is where a Pacific economic cooperation initiative fitted in perfectly' (Korhonen 1998: 125–6). In addition, Lawrence Woods refers to the influence of almost two decades of discussions about Pacific cooperation within Japanese policymaking circles (Woods 1993: 90).

Meanwhile, Malcolm Fraser, the then Australian Prime Minister, responded positively to Ohira's idea, and, at two meetings held between the two Prime Ministers in May 1979 and January 1980, they agreed to cooperate in realising Ohira's idea, which led to the Canberra Seminar in September 1980, later referred to as the Pacific Economic Cooperation Conference (PECC) I. Despite the initial reservations of some countries, particularly ASEAN countries, the second PECC conference was held in 1982 in Bangkok, and since then PECC has become a regular conference.[27] PECC featured a tripartite involvement of academics, business people, and government officials participating in a private capacity from a wide variety of countries, both developed and developing.[28] This is partly because ASEAN countries were reluctant to have an official level conference due to fear that it could compete in importance with its own institution of ASEAN (Yamakage 1997: 284–5, Kikuchi 1995: 127).

It must be noted that the private nature of PECC was in accord with what Japanese policymaking agents considered preferable.[29] The report of Ohira's Pacific Basin Cooperation Study Group stated that it would be difficult to create a governmental level organisation immediately, given the complicated diplomatic relations in the Pacific area. MOFA officials, basically agreeing with the advice of the report, considered that it was essential to take a cautious and gradual approach to advancing Pacific cooperation. They thought that forming an extensive and formal framework would not be practical at that time, and that such an agenda had to be worked on in the middle and long-term perspective. In order to keep the momentum, Japanese officials hoped that the Canberra seminar would reach an agreement to establish an informal body to further the idea of Pacific cooperation.

Another point to be noted is that despite its unofficial status, PECC has strong official links. Woods argues that state officials in an unofficial capacity are 'regarded by many as a polite fiction', and that they are 'state representatives, though the state belief that they are attending as private citizens does allow them to attach a disclaimer to everything they say and ensures that their home governments will not be obliged to uphold any decisions taken' (Woods 1993: 117). Thus, while the private nature of PECC gives flexibility in the way in which participants discuss and interact across countries as well as sectors, their activities in a series of conferences has greatly affected government-level thinking on regional cooperation through deepening the understanding and knowledge of state officials. In fact, Woods notes that PECC activities stimulated some inter-governmental initiatives later, such as the establishment of the ASEAN-PMC as well as the initiation of the Cairns Group and, more importantly, APEC (Woods 1993: 115).

It is important to note that, despite Ohira's strong attachment to the idea of Pacific cooperation, Japan hesitated to come to the fore alone, and chose to advance the idea by supporting Australian leadership on this issue. As soon as the interim report of his Pacific Basin Cooperation Study Group was presented, Ohira visited Fraser to discuss the agenda in January 1980, stressing the significance of Pacific cooperation. According to the agreement reached at this meeting, Foreign Minister Okita asked John Crawford of the Australian National University, who had been one of the prominent scholars in PAFTAD, to organise the first seminar at the Australian National University. This can be interpreted as a choice on the part of Okita against holding the conference in Japan, where he would have been put in a more exposed position. The choice of venue for the conference was in a sense reasonable, as Japanese and Australian scholars had been at the centre of efforts to develop the concept of Pacific cooperation in the 1960s and 1970s. It is reported that Ohira's secretary thought that because of Australia's strong research and interest in Pacific cooperation, Australia would best understand and promote Ohira's Pacific Basin Cooperation Concept ahead of other countries (Terada 1998: 349–50). However, it is reasonable to assume that there must have been some other reasons why Japan had not proposed that idea on its own. For one thing, if Japan had done so, East Asian countries could have criticised it as Japan's attempted control of East Asia or its new effort to create a Greater East Asia Co-prosperity Sphere. By taking the initiative in partnership with Australia or allowing Australia to assume a central role, it could evade such criticisms to some extent (Kikuchi 1995: 123). In addition, the US was also quite sceptical about Japan's positive move on regional projects, as it was worried that Japan was trying to create an East Asian block and to accumulate power over the region. Japanese policymaking agents considered that jointly proposing and advancing the concept could contribute to lessening this concern of the US (Kikuchi 1995: 123).

To sum up, the idea of Pacific cooperation, which had been developed mainly in academic circles in the 1960s and 1970s, gradually came to be entrenched among Japanese policymaking agents, following the then Prime Minister Ohira's strong interest in it. However, Japan was very cautious in the way it promoted this agenda. Japanese policymakers considered that it was not practical to push ahead a governmental organisation, and that this should be a long-term goal, which could be pursued through a series of discussions and interactions within a private-level body. Japan was also cautious not to be regarded as taking an independent regional initiative, and preferred to act with Australia so that it could apparently dilute its influence, in consideration of the concerns of East Asian countries and the US about Japan's dominance in the region. Indeed, this style of promoting regional cooperation incrementally and cautiously can be observed repeatedly in Japan's later policies on this subject.

The formation of APEC in 1989, which is a government-level economic forum as opposed to the unofficial status of PECC, marked a watershed in regional cooperation in Asia–Pacific. The fear that the expanding regional arrangements in North America and Europe might become protectionist as well as the possibility that the multilateral trading system would collapse in light of the difficulty of the Uruguay Round of the GATT made countries in the Asia Pacific region concerned about the future of the international trading system. This was the impetus for the creation of APEC. However, it should be noted that the remarkable economic growth of the East Asian countries and increasing economic interdependence in the region laid the foundation for APEC, which was greatly supported by the continuing processes of unofficial cooperation, namely PAFTAD, PBEC, and PECC.

Against this background, both the Japanese and the Australian governments came to consider some new framework in the region. However, it was Australia that took a direct initiative. The then Australian Prime Minister Robert Hawke called for a formal regional mechanism for cooperation in Asia–Pacific in January 1989, and this led to the establishment of APEC, which originally comprised the six ASEAN nations, Australia, Canada, Japan, New Zealand, South Korea and the US; China, Hong Kong and Taiwan joined in 1991, Mexico and Papua New Guinea in 1993, and Chile in 1994. Australia's original plan excluded the US, but later accepted the MITI's strong insistence on the need for including the US in the original list of members.

Despite the significant initiative of Australia in founding APEC, some stress that Japan assumed more than a supportive role in the initial process (Funabashi 1995 and Krauss 2000: 473–94). Prior to the Hawke initiative, the MITI's study group had started to consider the issue in early 1988, and its interim report, which came out in June 1988, proposed the establishment of a government-level framework for economic cooperation in Asia Pacific. Krauss notes, 'this report envisions APEC in the form it eventually developed: an open, regional forum of economies with government participation cooperating to achieve more integrated and balanced growth with a gradualist and consensual approach respectful of the region's diversity' (Krauss 2000: 477). Hawke responded to the report very positively, and since then the MITI and the Australian government worked together to persuade other countries.

However, Japan let Australia take the initiative, and itself assumed a behind-the-scenes role. Funabashi points out various reasons for this: bureaucratic turf battles between the MITI and the MOFA, domestic pressure from agricultural constituencies to oppose trade liberalisation, especially of rice, the Japanese decision-making processes such as bottom-up consensus building, and the lack of political leadership (Funabashi 1995: 211–20). The MOFA's adamant opposition to the MITI's initiative was based not only on jurisdictional territorial rivalry, but also in its belief that the East Asian nations do not accept Japan's prominent leadership (Krauss 2000: 480). MITI officials also shared the same concerns as the MOFA. It was reported that there was a fear among MITI officials that the idea of a regional grouping could raise for some countries the spectre of the Greater East Asian Co-Prosperity Sphere concept of the 1930s and 1940s, and thus the MITI contented itself with a secondary, low-profile role.[30] A remark of Shigeo Muraoka, the then vice-minister in international affairs and responsible to the MITI for creating APEC, confirmed this point:

[t]he reason I thought Japan should maintain a low-profile and that Australia should take the initiative in organising APEC instead, lay in the belief that memories of the Co-Prosperity Sphere still pervaded the region and people

would not readily support a Japanese idea which might remind them of the old awful days. I thought the problem of the Co-Prosperity Sphere was deeply rooted.[31]

In short, it can be argued that the concern about the possible negative reactions of regional countries to Japanese initiatives again prevented Japan from taking a prominent leadership role, and made it keep a low-profile, as in the case of PECC.

As to the significance of APEC in Japanese foreign policy, it was argued before that the concept of Asia Pacific cooperation fits in well with the fundamental diplomatic goal of Japan, namely balancing its relations with the US and East Asia. APEC is indeed a successful means for pursuing such a policy, and accommodates the diplomatic situation of being caught between the US and East Asia, which Japan has been grappling with for a long time. It was the realisation of what the Japanese government had pursued since the 1960s, namely regionalism incorporating the US and East Asian countries. Japan in fact aimed at dealing with a number of important diplomatic agendas with the US and East Asia simultaneously through the framework of APEC. The inclusion of the US in APEC was seen by Japanese officials to contribute to the containment of US unilateralism and to prevent the US from turning away from multilateral frameworks in their trade policy and becoming inward-looking. Also, in terms of security, Japan, feeling nervous about a possible US withdrawal from the region after the Cold War, expected APEC to play a role in keeping the US engaged in the region. The US commitment to regional security is still important to Japan as well as to the region, as there remain a number of potential conflicts in East Asia, such as the Korean Peninsula. Also, Japanese officials are aware that many of its neighbours accept Japan's growing presence, economically as well as militarily, in the region only because the US–Japan security alliance guarantees that Japan will not disturb regional order and threaten its neighbours. At the same time, APEC is regarded as 'an instrument that Japan is using to strengthen its ties with ASEAN' (Funabashi 1995: 197). This has become particularly important for Japan when it was aspiring to a political role in East Asia in the 1990s, as touched on before.

However, the alternative option that came from the Malaysian Prime Minister Mahathir in 1990 created a problematic issue for Japan. It was the proposal to form EAEG, which was to be an 'Asian only' group that excluded North American and Oceanian countries. Japan's participation was considered crucial. Mahathir intended to anchor Japan to East Asia (Low 1991: 375) and expected it to take the lead. Apparently the US and Australia strongly opposed such an idea.

Japan's response was ambiguous and it did not take a decisive stance on the Malaysian proposal. On one hand, Japan obviously could not risk its US relations by endorsing EAEG in the face of US objections. In fact, the US strongly pressured Japan not to accept the proposal. The fact that there was no consensus on EAEG even among the ASEAN countries made Japan's stance more difficult as Japan was still very wary of the sensitivity of East Asian countries about Japan's regional presence. Furthermore, the negative image that EAEG would give the world, and thereby the possibility of risking important American and European markets, was another concern of Japan, although the Malaysian government explained that it did not intend to establish an exclusive economic block.

On the other hand, Japan was not able to dismiss the EAEG concept, either. The proposal struck a chord with a great number of 'Asianists' in Japan, including prominent politicians, many bureaucrats in elite ministries such as the MOF, the MOFA and the MITI, and business people and organisations like Keidanren and Keizaidoyukai (Higgott and Stubbs 1995: 527, Funabashi 1995: 208). The increasing economic interdependence in the region as well as the heightening tension of economic relations between the US and Japan were partly the reasons for more favourable views on EAEG in Japan. Also, the fact that the US itself had committed to the North American Free Trade Agreement (NAFTA) provided reasons for supporting EAEG. However, what is more noteworthy is that they reflect Japan's growing willingness to play a greater political role in the region beyond merely exercising economic power, independent of the US. It is no wonder that Japanese policymakers saw the idea of EAEG as a great opportunity to take a leadership role in East Asia.

It can be argued that this indecisiveness of Japan with respect to EAEG amounts to saying that Mahathir's proposal re-awoke Japan's long-standing identity question of where Japan belongs, or 'Japan's East versus West dilemma' (Funabashi 1995: 231). Likewise, Yamakage argues that the proposal 'worked as a litmus test of the Japanese public's inclination to either Asia or the United States' (Yamakage 1997: 299). Hook joins these views, stating that

> Japanese response to competing forms of regionalism can be said to have crystallised around the question faced by respective governments since the Meiji era: how relations with Asia, on the one hand, and the West, on the other, should be balanced.
>
> (Hook 1996b: 25–6)

As long as Japan advocates the concept of Asia Pacific, it could escape from meeting the question head-on, and indeed the EAEG proposal forced Japan to consider this identity question anew.

Although Japan could not respond decisively to the EAEG proposal in the early 1990s, the idea has re-emerged since the late 1990s, and this time Japan has not hesitated to give full support to the framework. The change in Japan's stance on East Asian regionalism is indeed radical, given its consistent support for Asia Pacific cooperation and its earlier indecisive attitude towards EAEG. It will be discussed in detail in Chapter 5 how and why Japan has been positively involved in that process.

Japan's increasing interest in taking more political and security initiatives in the region

Japan also began to show greater interest in taking more political initiatives particularly in East Asia. As mentioned before, by the 1980s Japanese policymaking agents began to realise that economic policy, specifically aid policy, alone was not enough to fulfil the international responsibilities that befitted a country of Japan's economic strength. Prime Minister Yasuhiro Nakasone, who assumed office in 1982, tried to pursue more positive political roles and to enhance Japan's presence internationally. He was proactive particularly in the security area, and abolished the 1 per cent (of gross national product – GNP) ceiling on military spending,[32] although this policy caused domestic and regional concerns about Japan's military intentions. Subsequent Prime Minister Noboru Takeshita, given the thaw in Cold War tensions, suggested that Japan had to participate in forming a new international order. He specifically proposed three pillars of this international contribution, namely (1) further economic cooperation through the expansion of ODA, (2) the advancement of cultural exchange and (3) cooperation for peace including more positive diplomatic efforts and the dispatch of people. Tadashi Ikeda, a senior MOFA official, explains that this third pillar of cooperation for peace reflects the thought that Japan has to contribute to settling international conflicts not only through economic means but also by diplomatic efforts and the dispatch of people, which led directly to discussions in the ministry concerning Japan's participation in UN peacekeeping operations (PKO) (Ikeda 1996: 19). In fact, the MOFA began to discuss this issue at that time, although the resignation of Takeshita, due to a political scandal, made the ministry put these plans on hold (Iokibe 1999: 234). In short, Japan's rise as an economic power by the 1980s, along with strong external pressures, made Japanese policymakers aware that Japan had to take a more positive political stance internationally. This consideration has been strengthened since the end of the Cold War, as discussed above.

Japan's direct involvement in the Cambodian peace process from the late 1980s is particularly noteworthy, as it shows Japan's willingness to take an independent initiative in a regional conflict, where Japan had previously avoided being involved. After the outbreak of the Cambodian dispute in 1978, ASEAN took the lead in forming the framework of a dialogue for resolving the conflict, and Japan consistently supported ASEAN's policies, independently of US interests, although Japan did not itself play an important role in the events (Takeda 1995: 70–1). Successive Foreign Ministers and Prime Ministers in the 1980s kept stressing Japan's full support of the ASEAN stance concerning the dispute resolution.[33]

However, Japan went a step further in the late 1980s, when the end of the Cold War completely changed the political situation in Indochina. With the demise of the Soviet block, Vietnam withdrew its forces from Cambodia in 1989, turning to a more economy-oriented policy, while the US interest in the Cambodian issue declined. At the same time, China was isolated diplomatically after the Tienanmen Square incident. This situation gave Japan more room to conduct its own diplomacy there.

Following the above Takeshita proposal for international cooperation, Japan maintained good cooperation with ASEAN but took a more independent line, and became involved more directly in that regional dispute. Japan began to establish contacts between the four warring parties in Cambodia, while strengthening the negotiation channels with the countries concerned. In July and August 1989, Japan participated in a Cambodian peace conference in Paris, and co-chaired with Australia the third committee, which covered the refugees and economic reconstruction issues and produced substantial results. Yukio Imagawa, one of the senior MOFA officials involved in the Cambodian peace process, evaluated Japan's role in the conference as a highly significant event in postwar Japanese diplomatic history (Imagawa 2000: 70). After that, Japan began to move on its own despite the shift of the peace process to the permanent members of the UN Security Council (P5), where Japan was not a permanent member and was thereby completely dismissed from the talks. Japan dispatched a senior diplomat to Phnom Penh to contact the Hun Sen's government in February 1990. It is noteworthy that this visit was made even with the reluctance of the US, who supported the anti-Hun Sen (and anti-Vietnam) coalition government. Then, in June 1990 Japan invited the four Cambodian factions to Tokyo, convening a conference among them. Despite the boycott of the Khmer Rouge, the Tokyo meeting produced some significant results. In particular, Sihanouk and Hun Sen agreed that the tripartite coalition and the Phnom Penh government would share equal representation in the Supreme National Council, which was established in September 1990.[34] This Tokyo meeting was highly significant in the sense that Japan, for the first time in the postwar period, convened a political conference aimed to solve a dispute among third parties (Imagawa 2000: 96). Also, the Tokyo conference and the agreement there was one of the important contributions Japan made with respect to the Cambodian peace process, adding momentum to the peace talks (Ogasawara 2000: 139–40, Green 2001: 175 and Hirata 2001: 108).

After the Tokyo conference, Japan also made an effort to convince all of the Cambodian factions to accept the draft agreement, which had been drawn up by the P5 and other countries concerned excluding all the Cambodian factions, there thus remained a tough task to persuade them to accept the agreement. In February 1991 Japan proposed to the Cambodian factions a modified agreement, and continued to negotiate with them even when other countries were too busy to think about the Cambodian issue due to the outbreak of the Gulf War. This independent effort of Japan was not welcomed by the US, but Japan's initiative eventually persuaded the countries concerned that some modification of the agreement was inevitable to keep the momentum of the peace process (Ikeda 1996: 129). In the end, all the four factions settled on a new plan, and in October 1991 the Paris peace agreement was signed by all the Cambodian factions and countries concerned.

Thereafter, Japan continued to contribute to Cambodian issues. Japan hosted almost all of the major international conferences on Cambodian economic reconstruction, and pledged a substantial amount of economic contributions. In addition, Japan finally dispatched the SDF to take part in the PKO in Cambodia, after the Diet passed the International Cooperation Law in June 1992. Drifte argues that this has become the focal point for Japan's ability and willingness to contribute to the maintenance of the international system beyond cheque book diplomacy (Drifte 1998: 140). Also, Japan committed personnel to monitoring the Cambodian election in 1993.

It can be argued that Japanese policies towards Cambodian peace and economic reconstruction showed that Japan is willing to take more independent initiatives diplomatically. Green claims that the most striking motivation for the above Cambodian diplomacy of Japan was ideational, namely the MOFA's desire to demonstrate that Japan could play a leadership role in Asia as a normal country (Green 2001: 179). Ogasawara analyses that Japan's positive attitude to the Cambodian peace derives from its two motivations: participating in establishing international order rather than accepting it as given, as well as reconstructing its South East Asian policy, especially its Indochina policy, after the Fukuda doctrine (Ogasawara 2000: 132–6). Furthermore, Ikeda adds to this debate, stating that it is getting difficult to justify why Japan would not or could not participate directly in the processes through which the new order that Japan considers to be right becomes established, as just paying a bill has become domestically unacceptable (Ikeda 1996: 18–19).

In addition to the diplomatic effort concerning a series of Cambodian issues, Japan began to engage in the establishment of some regional frameworks in an area of great sensitivity, namely regional security arrangements. After the Second World War, Japan contributed to regional security only indirectly through the US–Japan Security Treaty. The US preferred the hub and spokes system in East Asia rather than multilateral arrangement as in Europe, while Japan showed only the slightest interest in a direct leading role for security issues as that was considered not to be acceptable domestically and regionally. Thus, the change in Japan's stance in this area is particularly notable.

Japan was first unenthusiastic about this issue, when Australia, followed by Canada, proposed an Asian version of the Conference on Security and Cooperation in Europe (CSCE) in 1990. This proposal was dropped when it could not obtain support from ASEAN or any major country in the region including the US and China. Nevertheless, soon after that ASEAN began to consider the idea that ASEAN-PMC could be expanded to multilateral security arrangements in the post Cold War period, while the Japanese government also became interested in the possibility of a new framework for regional stability.

In July 1991, the then Japanese Foreign Minister Taro Nakayama formally proposed to use the ASEAN-PMC for a region-wide security forum. Although the Japanese proposal failed to get support from the countries concerned at that time, it was a significant gesture for Japan: it formally announced a substantial change in its stance on security policy, which used to be very negative about multilateral security arrangements (Kikuchi 1995: 269). Likewise, Midford claims, '[t]he Nakayama proposal represents a bold departure from Japan's reactive policy toward regional security, and marked the first time since the end of the Second World War that Japan made a regional security initiative on its own, let alone in the face of clear American opposition' (Midford 2000: 368).

At the same time, regional countries gradually became more receptive to the idea of a regional security forum. Despite their initial negative reactions, the Nakayama proposal encouraged ASEAN countries to think about this issue more seriously, and eventually the ASEAN leaders declared at the Singapore summit in January

1992 that ASEAN should intensify its external dialogues in political and security matters by using ASEAN-PMC. Akiko Fukushima argues that behind this shift was their perception of the region's changing security situation: they came to realise that a multilateral security framework in Asia Pacific could serve as an insurance policy to prepare them for a possible withdrawal of the US forward deployment in the region, in addition to their concern over China's military buildup (Fukushima 1999: 141–2).

Japan also tried to convince the US of the importance of multilateral approaches with respect to regional security. In fact, there is evidence that the then Prime Minister Kiichi Miyazawa and the MOFA explained quite assertively Japan's stance on various occasions (Drifte 1998: 84, Kikuchi 1995: 271–2), although the US did not fully accept the idea of a security framework in Asia until Bill Clinton took office in 1993 (Kikuchi 1995: 271–2).

At the same time, ASEAN played a significant role in advancing the agenda through examining the issue at the ASEAN Institute of Strategic and International Studies (ISIS). The idea to use ASEAN-PMC as a regional security forum ran into difficulties, as there was strong resistance within ASEAN to including Russia and China in ASEAN-PMC, an idea which was developed in talks between ASEAN and Western developed countries (Ohba 2001: 271). In the end, it was agreed at the ASEAN foreign ministers' meeting in July 1993 to establish a new framework, the ARF, separately from ASEAN-PMC, and the following ASEAN-PMC meeting endorsed the idea. The first meeting of the ARF was held in 1994 in Bangkok, joined by ASEAN (then six countries), its dialogue partners (Australia, Canada, Japan, New Zealand, South Korea, the US and the European Union (EU)), China, Russia, Laos, Papua New Guinea and Vietnam.

In short, the process through which the ARF was created is of great significance when considering recent Japanese foreign policy. It shows that Japan is beginning to consider regional multilateral security arrangements, and actually took quite assertive actions and tried to make the US understand its intentions. While ASEAN assumed a central role in realising the ARF, it is reasonable to say that Japan's positive policy on this matter also contributed to pushing ahead the agenda to a significant extent.

The change in Japan's stance on regional security reflected the various impacts of the end of the Cold War on Japanese foreign policy discussed above. In particular, the inevitable reduction of the US military presence in East Asia and the limitation of Japan's security contribution only being through the US–Japan Security Treaty under post Cold War conditions have made Japanese policymaking agents recognise the need for a larger security role in the region for Japan, taking into account the potential benefits of some new regional security orders that could supplement the existing regional framework based on bilateral relations. Such regional multilateral security frameworks could not only help to fill the possible security vacuum in East Asia, but could also help Japan to define its political status and roles in the region in the post Cold War era. Kikuchi argues that such an initiative could give Japan an opportunity to recover the honour of its diplomacy that was tarnished during the Gulf War (Kikuchi 1995: 267). Furthermore, Midford points out that a unilateral

Japanese contribution to regional security would likely backfire, considering Japan's uneasy relations with regional countries; instead, Japan has an interest in developing stronger multilateral frameworks (Midford 2000: 389–90). He further claims that Japanese policymakers identified the multilateral approach as a primary means for directly reassuring ASEAN states about the implications of its expanding security role (Midford 2000: 389–90). In the same context, Fukushima notes that for Japan multilateral security forums appear to be an effective way to become involved in regional security matters without posing any threat to its neighbouring countries (Fukushima 1999: 150).

It should be stressed, however, that Japan is not replacing the existing security system in East Asia centred on the US–Japan Security Treaty with regional frameworks. Rather, multilateral mechanisms in East Asia (or Asia Pacific) are considered as supplements, not substitutes, to existing bilateral frameworks (Kikuchi 1995: 284), and they are not aimed at creating firm relations, like a security alliance, but a looser entente (Kikuchi 1995: 277). As Fukushima puts it, the ARF is not a multilateral institution in its formal sense, but is a forum for Asia Pacific governments to discuss security questions at various levels so as to understand mutual security concerns and to explore possible areas of cooperation (Fukushima 1999: 149). Furthermore, Yukio Takeuchi, a senior MOFA official, comments that the ARF can offer opportunities for regional security dialogues, but is not enough to maintain regional security, nor is it realistic to consider the establishment of a NATO-like organisation for collective actions in East Asia, hence it is necessary to keep the US engagement through the existing network of bilateral alliances.[35]

Conclusion

This chapter has thematically looked at what Japan has done in East Asia since the end of the Second World War, and has demonstrated some important shifts in Japanese foreign policy. Japan's foreign policy during the early postwar period was quite limited in scope and greatly influenced by US global strategies, although it would be an exaggeration to say that Japan's policy was merely a reaction to US pressures. However, Japan has gradually been more eager to take initiatives not only economically, but also politically. Even in security issues Japan has become more positive, compared to its earlier reticence, particularly since the 1990s. Economic resources are still the main tool of its foreign policy, but Japan has begun to make more diplomatic efforts than before, and has shown its willingness to participate in creating new international and regional orders. Also, Japan has begun to pursue regional policy more independently, rather than conducting it as an extension of US policy, although there is overall consistency with US interests, and the continued US engagement in East Asia is an important priority. The chapter has also discussed the style of Japanese foreign policy, and has shown how Japan has quietly pursued its agendas. In many cases Japan has avoided taking dominant initiatives, and preferred low-profile approaches, but in a long-term perspective, this style has enabled Japan to achieve its interests. The subsequent chapters will look at these discussions in more specific cases, which will not only offer empirical narratives of great significance to the study of Japanese foreign policy, but also consider in more depth what has caused the shifts in Japanese foreign policy identified above and what has made Japan adopt a low-profile style in its foreign policy.

3 The Washington Consensus versus the Japanese approach and implications for the East Asian financial crisis

This first case study is about how Japanese policymakers, specifically MOF officials, have tried to challenge the popular discourse of the neoclassical doctrine among policymaking agents in international organisations and major developed countries as well as Western academics, referred to as the Washington Consensus.[1] One of the main aims of this chapter is to demonstrate the difference between the Japanese approach on economic development and systemic transition and that of the Washington Consensus. It will discuss how different their approaches to development and transition are, why Japan has become increasingly vocal in its policies since the late 1980s, and how arguments between Japan, specifically MOF officials, and the Washington Consensus institutions, particularly the World Bank, had developed throughout the 1990s. Subsequently, the last section of this chapter will highlight how this divergence of views is reflected in their different positions over the causes of the East Asian financial crisis in 1997 and 1998.

These points are of great significance for the arguments of the book. First, the quite critical manner in which Japan has advocated its approach against the Washington Consensus offers additional evidence of Japan's increasing assertiveness in its foreign policy, contradicting the argument that Japan has merely been reacting to outside pressures. Second, this ideological disparity and the resultant difference of views on the crisis, together with the growing discontent of Japanese officials about the fact that Japan does not have a voice in the Western dominated organisations despite its large contribution, will help to understand Japan's policies towards the crisis as well as the new regional frameworks, as discussed in Chapters 4 and 5.

Policy debates on development and transition between Japan and Washington

As mentioned above, Japanese policymakers, specifically MOF officials, and academics engaged in the country's aid policy, backed by various Japanese and Western academic works, have advocated approaches for economic development and systemic transition that are considerably different from the neoclassical orthodoxy, which has dominated policy debates since the late 1980s. The Japanese government convened numerous workshops and conferences within the Japanese development aid circles, which were attended by officials and economists, and which led to a broad consensus on the alternative approach towards development and transition (Ohno 1998: 1).

Strictly speaking, it is highly debatable as to what extent there is 'consensus' among the major players in Washington and among those in Japan. In particular, as discussed below, the World Bank and the IMF do not always speak with the same voice, as the World Bank has been searching for a new approach to development throughout the 1990s. Even within the World Bank and the IMF, there are quite diverse opinions (Inada 1997: 15–16). Furthermore, after the predominance of the neoclassical doctrine in the 1980s and 1990s, the East Asian financial crisis that occurred in 1997 and spread worldwide has generated a 'mood swing' from this consensus to another, which is emerging as the 'post-Washington Consensus'. The essence of this change is a greater emphasis on civil society, institution building, safety nets and governance, which are added to the well-known vocabulary of the neoclassical orthodoxy, namely liberalisation, deregulation and privatisation (Jayasuriya and Rosser 1999). In particular, the recognition of the significance of governance, which 'is underwritten by: (1) a managerialist ideology of effectiveness and efficiency of governmental institutions and (2) an understanding of civil society based on the mobilization and management of social capital rather than one of representation and accountability', is not historically trivial (Higgott 2000b: 140–1), and contrasts with the emphasis of the Washington Consensus on the shrinking role of the state. On the Japanese side, there are, of course, a number of Japanese neoclassical economists, therefore it may be that the Japanese consensus is limited to a specific community responsible for Japan's aid policy.[2]

Nevertheless, it is important to note that there have been fundamental differences of opinion between the development assistance communities of Washington and Japan on what policies developing and transition economies should adopt. The disagreement between them is not simply a battle for establishing the order of importance between the state and the market as a means towards achieving economic goals such as increased productivity, efficiency and growth. Japan has never disregarded market mechanisms. It has in fact put great importance on them, while Washington-based officials and economists admit a certain role for the state. The differences emerge in relation to the path that is taken towards a market economy. In other words, the crucial point is the difference of their views on how developing, or transition, economies can achieve a market economy and can begin to enjoy its benefits. Based on Japan's own development experience, Japanese officials have put much greater emphasis on the role of the state than neoclassical economics. In this sense, the recent swing in international political communities and academics towards a greater appreciation of the role of institutions seems to have made the gap noticeably narrower between the Washington Consensus and Japan, although there still is a divergence of views between them. The following section will discuss the differences between their approaches by considering two issues, which are closely related: (1) the role of the government in development and transition and the efficacy of industrial policy, and (2) the issue of the sequence and time span of liberalisation.

The different views on the role of the government and the efficacy of industrial policy

Neoclassical economists basically assume the existence of markets, or, at the very least, they consider that markets are achievable in a few years, while trying to remove government involvement in the economy as soon as possible. Accordingly, to them the way developing and transition countries should proceed is to merely liberalise their economic systems immediately, through domestic and external deregulation and the privatisation of state-owned enterprises while following strict macroeconomic restraints. On the other hand, in the light of Japan's past economic achievements as well as that of other East Asian countries, Japanese policymakers and academics put more importance on the role of the government. They think that governments should take more active roles than neoclassical economics assumes in introducing and establishing market mechanisms. According to people in the Japanese policymaking circle, effective market mechanisms exist only in economies that have reached a certain level of development and cannot be created merely by liberalisation and deregulation. Throughout the 1990s, the World Bank has partially modified its position on the role of the government. For instance, some of its officials have watched governance issues more closely, as argued below. At the same time, it seems that the IMF has been sticking more strictly to its traditional approach, at least until the East Asian financial crisis.

The above difference of views about the role of government has been particularly contentious over arguments on the efficacy of industrial policy. The rationality of targeted intervention by government to alter an industrial structure has been subjected to intense debate not only between Washington and Japan, but also academics in general, but as yet no clear consensus has emerged.

People working within the neoclassical orthodoxy deny that industrial policy is effective, arguing that it distorts market mechanisms and that such a policy is not only unnecessary, but can also be harmful. They argue that each country's industrial structure must be achieved through efficient allocation of resources by market mechanisms. Krugman and Obstfeld point out the following reasons why most neoclassical economists studying this issue have been sceptical about the importance of industrial policy. First, East Asian economies have followed a wide variety of policies, ranging from extensive government intervention in Singapore to virtual laissez-faire in Hong Kong, or from deliberate intent to form very large industrial firms in South Korea to the dominance of small, family-run companies in Taiwan. Yet all these economies have achieved similarly high growth rates. Second, the actual impact on industrial structure is not certain and is difficult to assess, despite considerable publicity given to industrial policy. Third, there have been some notable failures of industrial policy, for example, South Korea's promotion of heavy and chemical industries from 1973 to 1979 (Krugman and Obstfeld 1997: 269).

On the other hand, Japanese officials argue that there are certain sectors, particularly in developing countries, that require special support from the government at least for a limited period in order to achieve a faster and sustainable economic growth. For instance, Masaki Shiratori[3] argues that a country's 'competitive advantage should be understood in a dynamic context, not a static one as used in the neoclassical approach', and 'to select a currently uncompetitive industry that is judged important for an economy's future and accelerate its development using policy instruments' is justifiable (Shiratori 1998: 81).

The economic basis of the Japanese argument is that government intervention can be rationalised where there is a case of market failure, including the case of infant industry and economies of scale. In particular, most developing countries lack the basic conditions that enable market mechanisms to work properly. Of course, economists and policymakers in Washington understand that there are certain cases in which markets fail to achieve the optimum distribution of resources. However, they are still sceptical about the efficacy of large government involvement in the economy in general, and industrial policy in particular, pointing out the following problems. First, market failures are hard to identify. Second, it is difficult to establish what policies would be appropriate to address market failures, even if they are identified. Under the circumstances, policy should be non-discriminatory. rather than sector-specific. Third, governments can also fail. They can fail to pick possible successful industries. Also, there are risks that policies intended to promote development are subject to capture by special interests, and this sort of thing is more likely to happen in developing countries. Fourth, it is difficult to assess the cost and benefit of government interventions.

In addition to economic grounds for industrial policy, there has been significant academic research to support Japan's assertion about the importance of the state and the role of industrial policy in the light of past economic development in Japan and other East Asian countries. This academic support has come mainly from people labelled as revisionists.[4] They share the view that Japan and some East Asian countries have achieved outstanding economic development in a way traditional economics cannot fully explain, and their economic performance is not merely the result of efficient resource allocation that comes from well-functioning market mechanisms. Much of the literature in this school historically and empirically analyses the policies implemented in these countries and carefully explains how these policies played significant roles in the countries' development.

The most pioneering work of the revisionists is Chalmers Johnson's *MITI and the Japanese Miracle* (1982), which 'spawned a veritable cottage industry of books on the role of the state in the economy, and it framed both popular and scholarly debate' (Woo-Cumings 1999: 27). In this book, Johnson argues that the key to understanding the Japanese economic miracle during the postwar period is through the organisation and mechanism of the capitalist developmental state. According to Johnson, there are two different types of state in the capitalist world, namely the regulatory, or market-rational states, such as the US, and the developmental, or plan-rational states, like Japan. While the former type of state concerns itself with the forms and procedures of economic competition, the latter has as its dominant feature precisely the setting of substantive social and economic goals. He also argues that in the developmental state 'the government will give greater precedence to industrial policy, that is, to a concern with the structure of domestic industry and with promoting the structure that enhances the nation's international competitiveness' (Johnson 1982: 19). Other characteristics of the developmental model, discussed in the book, are the existence of an elite bureaucracy committed to state objectives, a pilot agency like the MITI, a political system that enables the bureaucracy to operate effectively, and state institutional links with the private sector that work in a market-conforming way, such as administrative guidance.

Since this book was published in 1982, and as the remarkable development of East Asian economies received particular attention, several scholars have taken up this issue and have extended it to East Asian countries, advancing Johnson's arguments.[5] Among the extensive literature on the developmental state, of particular importance is *Governing the Market* by Robert Wade (1990), which closely analyses Taiwan's economic development. In this book, Wade proposed the 'governed market theory' to explain East Asian[6] economic success (Wade 1990: 26–9). The theory contains a three-level explanation. First, the high performance of East Asian countries was the outcome of (1) very high levels of productive investment, making for fast transfer of newer technology into actual production; (2) more investment in certain key industries than would have occurred in the absence of government intervention; and (3) exposure of many industries to international competition, in foreign markets if not at home. Second, the government guides, or governs, market processes of resource allocation so as to produce different production and investment outcomes than would have occurred with the policies supported by neoclassical economics. Third, the government could successfully pursue these policies because of a particular set of political organisations, essentially authoritarian, as opposed to democratic, regimes, and the government's corporatist, as opposed to pluralist, relations, with capital and labour.[7]

The issue of the sequence and time span of liberalisation

In addition to the differing views on the role of the government and the efficacy of industrial policy, another critical aspect of the divergence of opinions between Japan and the Washington Consensus is the speed and sequence of economic reforms and liberalisation in developing and transition economies, namely gradualism versus a big bang or a shock therapy approach. This issue arose in the 1990s in particular, when transforming the former centrally planned countries into market economies became a serious international agenda, but the argument also applies to economic development in general. As mentioned above, Japan does not dispute the efficacy of market mechanisms in circumstances where a country has an economic system that can compete in the world economy. What makes Japan's approach different is the fact that it asks whether the same policies that apply to free markets should be implemented immediately in all countries irrespective of their stage of economic development. This leads to a methodological difference between Japan and the Washington Consensus, namely that, in the view of Japanese officials and academics in the aid policy community, there is too much deductive bias in neoclassical economics, in which one universal principal is pursued and applied to all countries in the same way.[8]

The prevailing view in the international financial institutions, supported by a number of neoclassical economists, is that domestic and external liberalisation and the introduction of rational price structures have to be implemented as soon as possible so that market mechanisms can begin to work properly and countries can become better off, although in the short term there could be some confusion in the economies. What is necessary in developing and transition economies is merely to comprehensively and promptly remove the impediments to the free operation of markets. The reforms in Russia and other former Soviet republics and Eastern European countries in the 1990s have been implemented on the basis of this big bang approach. People that follow this approach assume various time spans, but not more than five years (Ohno and Ohno 1993: 166). The big bang approach recommends that the following policies are implemented simultaneously: (1) macroeconomic stabilisation through the reduction of the financial deficit and the control of money supply, which is what the IMF usually demands of recipient countries as conditionality; (2) microeconomic liberalisation including price liberalisation, trade liberalisation, the establishment of currency convertibility, and the creation of new institutions that enable these policies to function properly; (3) the comprehensive privatisation of state industries.

On the other hand, Japan, backed by numerous Japanese scholars as well as some Western scholars, favours the gradualist approach, which stresses that liberalisation and economic reforms must be sequenced properly from a longer-term perspective than neoclassical economists assume, and should not be carried out all at once. In other words, domestic and external liberalisation must be implemented step by step, depending on a country's economic and social situation as well as the ability of its government, and there is not a universal rule on this process. This approach recommends that the government should retain a certain control of the economy until the new institutions that allow market economies to operate are firmly established and take root in the economy. The idea is that if the government loses all control of the state sector at an early stage of transition, the social cost can be too costly, even intolerable. As far as trade and foreign exchange are concerned, the gradualist approach considers that there is a great risk that rapid liberalisation will cause domestic industries to collapse and lead to too much dominance by foreign firms. Therefore, external liberalisation should be carried out very cautiously, and the government should protect some industries by restricting trade and capital transactions for a certain period, until domestic industry obtains a certain degree of competitiveness.

This approach also opposes the immediate privatisation of state industry, arguing that hasty privatisation does not necessarily lead to efficient management, and could cause high unemployment. For instance, Yoshiaki Nishimura, evaluating Russian privatisation in the early 1990s, doubts that rapid privatisation brought about the desired results, pointing out various problems, such as huge transfers of wealth from the poor to the rich, insider control (control by managers and employees of the enterprise), which has preserved socialist inefficient management, a concentration of state assets by the *nomenclatura* (a privileged class) and the conduct of the privatisation process amid accusations of rampant corruption and fraud. He claims that a basic point has not been properly recognised in Russian privatisation, namely the point that '[p]rivatisation is a complicated process because ownership is not just a matter of economic activity but also closely related to people's consciousness which in turn depends on will and ideology' (Nishimura 1998: 259). Ohno comments that Nishimura's negative view about Russian privatisation is now widely shared in Japan and abroad (Ohno 1998: 44).

The gradualist stance of the Japanese government is clearly shown in a research paper of OECF on transition published in 1995 entitled *Transition Strategies and Economic Performance: Gradualism Revised.* It examines the transition process in Russia, Poland, China and Vietnam, and concludes:

> Because institutions conducive to market activities are slow to develop, it is vitally important to put institutional aspects at the center of the analysis. The 'big-bang' approach tends to pay too much attention to the need to shatter the old system, and insufficient attention to the dangers of institutional breakdown and self-reinforcing fiscal and macroeconomic collapse.
>
> Greater attention needs to be paid to an 'optimal' order of reforms, in view of the interrelationship among macroeconomic stability, liberalisation and institution building. Immediate liberalisation and privatisation tend to result in a drastic fall in government revenues and impair price stability, unless an alternative public finance system is put in place; without the institution of a new social security system, privatisation would impose heavy social costs.
>
> It appears [from the transition experience to date] that rapid 'privatisation' is neither necessary or sufficient for successful transition.
>
> (OECF 1995: 9–10)

Finally, it is probably relevant to refer here to Japan's view on the promotion of democratisation and human rights in developing countries in connection with aid policy, because it shows some difference between Japan and Western countries over the time span to deal with this issue. Since the end of the Cold War, Western countries, particularly the US, have become very eager to promote democracy and human rights. This has provoked an angry response from East Asian countries. Some leaders, such as Lee Kwan Yew of Singapore and Mahathir of Malaysia, argue that human rights ideas are inappropriate in East Asia and will undermine East Asian growth and its domestic law and order (Neary 2000: 85). This has put Japan in an awkward dilemma as a member of advanced Western economies and of East Asian nations (Watanabe 2001: 68).

Japan has begun to show its commitment to democracy and human rights. Japan's ODA Charter, approved by the Cabinet in June 1992 and considered the most important basic document concerning the country's ODA policies, reads: 'full attention should be paid to efforts for promoting democratization and introduction of a market-oriented economy, and the situation regarding the securing of basic human rights and freedoms in the recipient country'.[9] Also, the MOFA is beginning to take the lead in signing and ratifying a number of international human rights covenants and intends to play a more positive role in human rights promotion at UN conferences (Neary 2000: 89–90).

Nevertheless, Japan is still criticised for being passive on this issue by Western countries, and, in fact, it does not necessarily side with Western countries in giving and suspending aid according to human rights criteria. Take the example of China. Although having followed Western nations in sanctioning China after Tiananmen Square in 1989, Japan did not express its political position. It avoided straightforward reference to human rights and democracy and simply pointed to the practical difficulties of implementing ODA-related negotiations under the confused conditions following the incident (Watanabe 2001: 81). Also, the Japanese government made every effort to prevent prolonging this situation. In the Group of Seven industrialised countries (G7) summit in July 1990, Japan pressured the other participating countries to soften the sanctions against China, and soon Japan resumed aid. In one way, China's economic significance to Japan (and the Japanese policymakers' assessment that they did not want to risk bilateral relations) explains its activist policies. However, in addition to this economic consideration, there seems to be another factor that did not make Japan necessarily follow the West. A MOFA official commented that the issue of democratisation is important, but the cutting of aid does not necessarily advance democratisation, and therefore it is more important to support Chinese open policies rather than isolate China.[10]

Another example that shows that Japan has not always sided with Western countries on the issue of democratisation and human rights is that of Japanese policy towards Myanmar. Japan first suspended aid to Myanmar in September 1988, when the military regime suppressed a democratisation movement, because of the strong international criticism against the military government. However, in February 1989 it recognised the military authority and resumed aid for continuing projects as well as humanitarian aid. Also, despite that regime's violation of democracy and human rights in the 1990s, Japan tried to soften a resolution by the Commission on Human Rights and the Third Committee of the UN General Assembly (Arase 1993: 946). Furthermore, unlike the US, Japan did not impose a trade embargo and economic sanctions against new investments by Japanese companies in Myanmar, neither it did oppose Myanmar's membership in ASEAN (Peng Er 2001: 126).

In a sense, this disharmony between Japan and Western countries is rooted in its historical relations with its neighbours: Japan cannot be seen to be dominant in the region. It is interesting to note that Japan joined other Asian nations and signed the Bangkok Declaration (at the UN-sponsored Asia Regional Preparatory Meeting for the World Conference on Human Rights in March 1993, attended by 40 Asian countries, including Indonesia, China, Malaysia and Singapore). Arase argues that the key points of the Declaration were that developed countries should not tie aid to human rights, and should respect the sovereign right of states to manage human rights within their borders, and Japan signed it after being criticised by some Asian governments for being too Western with regard to its stance on human rights in ODA policy (Arase 1993: 939–40).[11]

It also cannot be denied that there were considerations related to Japan's direct economic interests at play. With respect to the resumption of aid to Myanmar, Orr points out that there were pressures from some in the Japanese business community through LDP members. He also notes the MOF and the MITI's concerns over issues falling under their bureaucratic purview. More precisely, MOF officials wondered whether stopping aid would result in financial chaos, forcing Rangoon to default on previous yen loans from Japan, while the MITI was worried about the effects on future business in Myanmar. Orr argues that although the MOFA was concerned about Japan's international image if it did not follow other donors, these combined reasons were simply too much for the ministry to ignore (Orr 1990: 84–6).

Furthermore and especially relevant to the discussions in this section, this discord can also be attributed to the difference of views between numerous officials and influential scholars in Japan and their Western counterparts over how to promote democracy and human rights. Inada argues that the thinking of Japanese officials and scholars can be summarised as follows: democracy has universal value, which many countries share; however, the way towards a democratic system varies, according to the situation of each country, and democratisation should not be imposed uniformly and hastily; in some developing countries, particularly in East Asia, economic stability comes first, and then stability leads to democratisation. Inada further argues that Japan's approach is to encourage indirectly the democratisation of developing countries, and it is unlike the American approach, which imposes directly the values of democracy onto those nations (Inada 1995: 169–70). Likewise, Takeda points out that Japanese officials and intellectuals believe that democratic transition in developing countries would be better achieved through changes in economic and social structures, and that democratisation can be promoted indirectly through economic development (Takeda 1997). Watanabe presents a similar line that Japanese officials are apparently of an opinion that verbal fighting is not conductive to substantive improvements in the human rights situation and that instead creating institutions, necessary for the protection of human rights, is, in the long run, more productive (Watanabe 2001: 75). Related to this point, people in the Japanese aid community consider that an authoritarian regime is not necessarily evil, and although not ideal, it can be regarded as a transitional regime for the purpose of rapid industrialisation (Ohno 1998: 32–4).

The development of the arguments between Japan and the Washington Consensus

The previous section has discussed the divergence of views on the role of states as well as on the sequence and time span in policy implementation between Japan and the Washington Consensus. The discussion now turns to the point of how Japan has articulated its policy stance since the late 1980s.

Neoclassical economics has provided the mainstream approach to the study of economic development since the 1970s, when it became the policy basis of the World Bank and the IMF. The hegemony of the neoclassical economics was secured against the background of state-centred development in the 1950s and 1960s which was believed to have revealed problems of government failure and to have resulted in economic difficulties, such as the accumulated debt problem in the 1970s and 1980s in many developing countries, with the exception of some East Asian countries (Ishikawa 1994: 3–6). Neoclassical economics gained further momentum during the Reagan administration in the US and the Thatcher administration in the UK, both of which were ideologically devoted to the neoclassical orthodoxy. In the 1980s, the World Bank and the IMF began to demand of developing countries medium-term microeconomic policy that was more concerned with the countries' economic structures, supplementing traditional policy with macroeconomic stabilisation. This came in the form of the structural adjustment policy, which typically included comprehensive reforms of institutions, liberalisation and privatisation, and was stipulated by the IMF and the World Bank as a conditionality to their loans. Ishikawa argues that structural adjustment policy is an attempt to rapidly replace the dirigisme that characterises the economic regime of most developing countries with a market economy (Ishikawa 1994: 2).

Despite the fact that Japan gradually increased the volume of ODA throughout the 1970s and 1980s, having become the largest aid donor in the world in 1989 for the first time and having substantially increased its financial contributions to international organisations including the World Bank, Japan did not articulate its development philosophy and merely contributed funds during this period. This silence of Japan was due, Yasutomo points out, to the Japanese officials' lack of knowledge about development processes (Yasutomo 1995: 75).

However, some MOF officials began to raise questions about the prevailing orthodoxy in international organisations, particularly the World Bank, and started to openly express their disagreement with the orthodoxy, as the Bank's development approach began to clash with, or contradict, the Japanese aid policies in the late 1980s. Isao Kubota[12] states that the debate between Japan and the World Bank on what is the right development approach was triggered by a divergence of opinions concerning Japan's subsidised policy-directed loans to developing countries (Kubota 1993/4). Specifically, the World Bank criticised Japan's policy of giving developing countries two-step loans, which are aid loans that are extended to a financial institution of a developing country with low interest rates for the purpose of being passed on to specific, or targeted, sectors in the country at lower interest than ongoing commercial interest rates.

This issue surfaced over the ASEAN–Japan Development Fund, which was established in 1987 by the Japanese government, with the aim of extending two-step loans to ASEAN countries to promote the development of the private sector in those countries and to help finance joint ventures in East Asia (Doner 1997: 226, Fishlow and Gwin 1994: 3). The plan was not successful largely because Japan failed to provide subsidised loans in the face of opposition from the World Bank and the IMF. The World Bank insisted that credit should be extended at market or non-subsidised rates, for the following reasons: (1) the system that treats specific sectors favourably will distort market mechanisms in financial markets; (2) in many developing countries, governments lack the institutional capability to distribute funds fairly within the countries; and (3) in the case of subsidised loans, these problems become more serious (Shiraishi 1997: 191). Shiratori writes that these arguments from the World Bank were hardly acceptable to Japanese officials for practical reasons, as two-step loans were one of the main vehicles for Japan's ODA loans, as well as reflecting Japan's postwar experience of economic development (Shiratori 1998: 77). Japan, which basically believes that financial policies should be subordinated to a broader industrial strategy, insisted that: (1) aid unavoidably distorts market mechanisms in developing countries, and it is a contradiction that the World Bank only criticises the distortion of financial markets; and (2) the institutional inability of governments to distribute funds properly supports the necessity for their institutional reforms, but it cannot be a basis for denying subsidised loans (Shiratori 1998: 77).

The MOF, along with numerous Japanese academics, also became very sceptical about the effectiveness of the World Bank's structural adjustment policies and their universal application to developing economies (at the same time that Japan considerably increased the portion of co-financing with the World Bank in its total ODA in the late 1980s). Yasutomo notes that as Japanese officials studied the Bank's approach to structural adjustment loans as well as the Japanese and East Asian development in the past, they found contradictions: Japan and East Asian countries have achieved marked economic development in a different way from what the World Bank instructed developing countries to do, while in Latin American countries, who had followed the neoclassical orthodoxy, the crisis of accumulated debt intensified (Yasutomo 1995: 77). Japan did not completely refute the effectiveness of structural adjustment loans, but it opposed the universal application of the same set of conditionalities to every country and insisted that loan and aid conditionality should take into account each country's development stage and economic condition in a long-term framework. These divergences over two-step loans and structural adjustment loans led to a serious debate between Japan and the World Bank concerning development philosophy in the 1990s.

The Japanese government openly questioned the World Bank's policies for the first time in an OECF report released in October 1991 entitled *Issues Related to the World Bank's Approach to Structural Adjustment* (OECF 1991). The report criticises the Bank's overemphasis on market mechanisms and macroeconomic issues in structural adjustment loans, arguing that: (1) structural adjustments are not enough to generate sustainable growth, and there should be measures aiming directly at promoting investments; (2) trade liberalisation must be implemented cautiously from a long-term viewpoint, and it is too optimistic to expect that industries capable of sustaining the economy of the next generation will come up automatically through the activities of the private sector, and therefore some measures for fostering industry are required; (3) the significance of lending at subsidised interest rates, specifically two-step loans, to financial institutions for developmental projects should not be disregarded; and (4) the World Bank tries to apply the same policies to every country universally, but the various conditions of each country should be taken into account.

Since publishing the report, Japan has become increasingly more assertive about its development philosophy as well as its view on aid policy. At the annual

IMF/World Bank meeting the same month, Yasushi Mieno, the then Governor of the Bank of Japan, made the following statement:

> Experience in Asia has shown that although development strategies require a healthy respect of the market mechanism, the role of government cannot be forgotten. I would like to see the World Bank and the IMF take the lead in a wide-ranging study that would define the theoretical underpinnings of this approach and clarify the areas in which it can be successfully applied to other parts of the globe.
>
> (Cited in Shiratori (1998: 78))

Also, it was observed that there was growing assertiveness in Japan's development approach from Japanese officials at the World Bank, including Japan's executive director and his deputy.[13] It is also reported that, in a symposium sponsored by the OECF in early 1992, the then Vice President of the World Bank was strongly challenged by several Japanese panellists who stressed the important role of governments in the development of Japan and East Asian countries.[14] An OECF official was reported to have commented that what fuelled this assertiveness was the increasing frustration with the World Bank economists' lack of attention to the role of the state.[15]

On the other hand, since the beginning of the 1990s the World Bank has somewhat changed its stance and has begun to pay more attention to the role of the state in development. The 1991 *World Development Report* (WDR) proposed the market-friendly approach, which the World Bank itself later described as a middle ground between the neoclassical economics and the revisionist views. The report stresses that development is associated with the proper role of government, which is larger than merely standing in for markets if they fail to work well, and markets must be complemented by government policies such as investing in people, building better social and regulatory systems, and providing stable macroeconomic conditions. The report considers that the role of the government should be wider than neoclassical economics would allow, but it holds a negative view about government interventions that distort the resource allocation by market mechanisms.

Meanwhile, Japan convinced the World Bank to conduct a major study on the role of the state and industrial policy in the past development of Japan and East Asia (Shiratori 1994: 70).[16] Although Japan appreciated the 1991 WDR in the sense that the World Bank had begun to turn its attention to the importance of the state in development rather than just preaching the value of markets, it was still dissatisfied with the Bank's under-estimation of what the governments had done in Japan and some East Asian countries. The study, which was mainly sponsored by Japan, was conducted for two years by World Bank staff and some outside experts, and the report entitled *The East Asian Miracle: Economic Growth and Public Policy* was published in 1993.

The report basically takes the same middle position, as the 1991 WDR did, between neoclassical orthodoxy and the Japanese approach. The study grappled squarely with the issue of the role of the state in economic development, stating that governments had played an important role in Japan and other East Asian countries. It particularly notes that their policies for getting the fundamentals right had contributed to the rapid growth, while admitting that some government interventions beyond getting the fundamentals right (particularly in Japan, Taiwan and South Korea) were effective. It says that in these countries 'government interventions resulted in higher and more equal growth than otherwise would have occurred' (World Bank 1993: 6). However, the report gave a negative view about the effectiveness of industrial policy in general, which had been the main point of controversy between Japan and the World Bank since the early 1990s. It argues that, despite the achievement in these countries, 'the prerequisites for success were so rigorous that policymakers seeking to follow similar paths in other developing economies have often met with failure' (World Bank 1993: 6). The report also stresses that the use of industrial policy to achieve more rapid productivity growth by altering the industrial structure was generally not successful even in these three countries, and industrial growth 'tended to be market-conforming, and productivity change was not significantly higher in promoted sectors' (World Bank 1993: 354).

Although Japan was not completely satisfied with the arguments of the report, as it never went outside the confines of neoclassical economics, it welcomed the report to a certain extent. In fact, Japanese officials were not surprised at the content of the report, given the dominance of neoclassical economics in the World Bank's management, staff and organisational culture.[17] Kubota argues that the report is not perfect from the Japanese viewpoint, but nevertheless he finds substantial changes from the previous stance of the World Bank (Kubota 1993/4). He also considers that there is not one absolute approach to development, and thus Japan should keep exerting pressure on the World Bank from the outside to make the bank officials consider policies more flexibly (Kubota 1993/4). It can be argued that Japan's aim through sponsoring the East-Asian-Miracle report was not to upset the established orthodoxy completely. It was more modest. Japan wanted its development experiences and philosophy to be more widely acknowledged and tried to restrain the establishment from relentlessly and narrow-mindedly pursuing its emphasis on market mechanisms. In this sense, Japan's attempt was fairly successful as it could at least put its development approach on the agenda.

The 1997 WDR, *The State in a Changing World*, goes further than the 1993 World Bank report, and pays more attention to the role of the state. It particularly focuses on the governance issue. The report stresses that, without an effective state, development, both economic and social, is impossible. It classifies the functions of the state into three categories, minimal, intermediate and activist, and suggests matching the state's role to its capability: countries with low state capability need to focus first on basic functions, the provision of pure public goods, and those with strong capability can take on more activist functions. According to the report, the activist functions involve industrial policy, but it is careful to say that 'high-intensity government support' such as coordinating investment (by the public and private sector) or picking potentially successful industries must be limited to countries with unusually strong institutional capability. Instead, the report suggests more flexibility in 'light-touch initiatives' such as government initiatives to private-to-private networks. The report is significant in that, although it does not recommend implementing active interventionist policies, it hints that they cannot be dismissed completely. The comments of James Wolfenson, President of the World Bank, following the publication of the report, are noteworthy. He states that people learnt that many states were not able to implement what they promised, and thus they began to believe in the minimalist state. However, such a state is not harmful, but neither is it effective.[18]

This change in the attitude of the World Bank can be attributed to various factors. It is widely recognised that the change in attitude, particularly the 1997 WDR, is associated with Joseph Stiglitz's taking on the post of Chief Economist of the World Bank from February 1997 to December 1999. He is a leading academic on the economics of the public sector and has written extensively on the role of the government. He is also a leading critic of the Washington Consensus, and exposed the limitations of neoclassical economics. Also, Kenichi Ohno comments that it is not clear how much Japan's voice has contributed to such a change, but perhaps it has had some impact, in addition to other factors such as Wolfenson's personal initiative, the voice of non-governmental organisations (NGOs), and the difficult economic situation in transition countries after implementing neo-classical reforms.[19]

These changes in the stance of the World Bank indicate that in the 1990s the World Bank increasingly began to adopt a philosophy different from the line of the IMF, which remained confined to neoclassical orthodoxy, although their disagreements and confrontations are not necessarily a new issue (Mohri 2001: 56–61). It could also be argued that in a sense the World Bank's position moved closer to that of the Japanese, and became positioned somewhere between the IMF and Japan. Furthermore, as argued above, given the mood swing from the Washington Consensus to the Post-Washington Consensus after the East Asian financial crisis, the difference between Japan and Washington has somewhat narrowed.

However, there still seems to be a gap between their views, and it is not certain whether the gap will narrow or widen in either the long or short term. It is arguable to what extent Stiglitz's thinking has been accepted within the World Bank, particularly after he left the institution. Izumi Ohno is quite sceptical about this point. In her book, she discusses a World Bank report entitled *East Asia: The Road to Recovery*, published in September 1998, and argues that overall the report shows a change of course away from the Stiglitz line in the World Bank: the policy proposals of the report for the East Asian economy are inspired by the Anglo-American approach (Izumi Ohno 2000: 199–203). She also stresses that, although under Wolfensohn, the World Bank has pursued a new approach, in which non-economic factors are incorporated into its policy considerations in addition to economic factors (the latter having been the only consideration of neoclassical orthodoxy), the approach is still based on Western thought. Therefore, the new line of the World Bank is not in defiance of the Washington Consensus, but it extends the arguments of this Consensus to other aspects like non-economic factors, while keeping its basic philosophy (Izumi Ohno 2000: 212–15). Likewise, Jayasuriya and Rosser argue:

> It would be an error to see policy frameworks emerging from the new consensus as a departure from the earlier emphasis on open markets, deregulation and less government. Rather, the new consensus should be understood as a political counterpart to the earlier economic emphasis on structural reform. Indeed, it may be useful to think of these new policy frameworks as attempts to institutionally 'bed down' the structural reforms championed by multilateral policy in the last two decades.
>
> (Jayasuriya and Rosser 1999)

Furthermore, methodologically the Post-Washington Consensus has not left behind the Washington consensus. Kenichi Ohno points out that Washington's belief that there is one best practice for development to be adopted for every country has not changed throughout the 1990s, and Washington still tries to apply the same policies to every country uniformly by using a checklist or a matrix.[20] Higgott also notes that the Post-Washington Consensus is no less universalising, and attempts to be no less homogenising, than the Washington Consensus, and its prescriptions still demonstrate a 'one-size-fits-all' formula (Higgott 2000b: 146).

Finally, it is worth referring to the silence of other figures such as MITI and MOFA officials. Despite the fact that the MITI was without doubt a central institution in the past Japanese industrial policy (Komiya and Suzumura 1988, Johnson 1982), and the fact that the MITI and the MOFA as well as the Economic Planning Agency (EPA) have been involved in aid policymaking processes (Orr 1990: 31–51), they have not actually participated in the MOF's assertive policies towards the Washington Consensus concerning development and transition. This is partly because the relations with the IMF and the World Bank are within the jurisdiction of the MOF. Other ministries conducted some research about these subjects within their organisations, but they did not have any means to show their views to these international organisations.[21] This is also to do with the general nature of the MITI as an economic ministry, whose prime interest is the direct economic benefit of Japan, and that of the MOFA, whose priority is to maintain cordial relations with the US. As Orr argues, the MITI tends to determine the extent to which aid will help or hinder Japan's overseas market and domestic industry (Orr 1990: 36–9), and it does not get ideologically involved. Also, Green notes that the MITI and the MOFA were not included in the MOF's ideological campaign, as they were worried about the impact of MOF officials' aggressive stance on bilateral trade and security relations (Green 2001: 238). In addition, Ohno comments that few MOFA officials have expertise in international finance and economic development, and thus do not seek to engage with the international financial organisations.[22] As far as the EPA is concerned, it has convened several workshops and conferences, attended by prominent Japanese scholars. However, the agency does not have enough influence to make its views known even within Japan, and its reports, some of which were written in English, did not have any impact, either in Japan or abroad.[23] In addition to these factors, Ohno points out that personal initiatives were also important. In the early 1990s, there were powerful advocates of the Japanese approach, such as Masaki Shiratori and Isao Kubota in the MOF, and Yasutami Shimomura[24] concerning OECF reports, but there were no similar voices in other institutions.[25] These factors explain the silence of other bodies (except the MOF and the OECF), although they have basically shared the same view with the MOF and the OECF and have conducted some internal research on development.

The divergence of opinion on the causes of the East Asian financial crisis

It has been argued so far that, although it shares with the Washington Consensus institutions the goal of promoting economic development, Japan has quite different opinions about how economic development and systemic transition can be achieved, and has consistently articulated its views openly since the early 1990s. It could also be argued that, although MOF officials were the main actors in the debates with Washington, these views are, on the whole, shared among Japanese intellectual and policymaking circles.

This led to a divergence of opinions between Japan and Washington, particularly the IMF and US Treasury,[26] about the causes of the East Asian financial crisis and the necessary measures for easing the crisis, when it spread beyond East Asia in 1997 and 1998. The following discussion relates their respective views on the crisis to their ideological differences presented above by drawing a broad picture of their stances on the crisis.[27]

The IMF and the US basically regarded the crisis as originating in structural problems in the affected countries, stressing the problems of the financial sectors and the inappropriate relationships between the public and private sectors. The IMF explains, in its published document *The IMF's Response to the Asian Crisis* issued in January 1999, its view on the causes of the crisis as follows. The primary reason for the crisis is not macroeconomic imbalances, but weaknesses in financial systems and, to a lesser extent, governance.

> A combination of inadequate financial sector supervision, poor assessment and management of financial risk, and the maintenance of relatively fixed exchange rates led banks and corporations to borrow large amounts of international capital, much of it short-term, denominated in foreign currency, and unhedged. As time went on, this inflow of foreign capital tended to be used to finance poorer-quality investments.
>
> Although private sector expenditure and financing decisions led to the crisis, it was made worse by governance issues, notably government involvement in the private sector and lack of transparency in corporate and fiscal accounting and the provision of financial and economic data.[28]

Therefore, the core of the policies adopted by the IMF was, together with austerity macroeconomic policies, the 'forceful, far-reaching structural reforms', which involve the comprehensive reform of financial systems and measures to address the governance issues, namely 'the measures designed to improve the efficacy of markets, break the close links between business and governments, and ensure that the integration of the national economy with international financial markets is properly segmented'.[29] The US government in essence shared these views (Aramaki 1999: 84–6).

On the other hand, the Japanese officials regarded the crisis as a liquidity problem, or a sort of panic, which could be ascribed to some faults inherent in the global financial markets. They accepted that there were some problems in the affected countries particularly in the financial sectors, and also that their real economies were declining somewhat, partly due to the pegging of their currencies to the dollar, and partly to the rise of China's economic competitiveness. However, they thought that it was totally wrong to only blame the economic systems of the affected countries for causing the crisis, arguing that these countries had achieved remarkable development, praised as the East Asian miracle, under the same systems. Instead, the Japanese officials insisted that what has to be considered is the present state of the governance of international financial markets. A speech by the then Japanese Finance Minister Kiichi Miyazawa in December 1998 reflects these arguments:

> The Asian crisis revealed the weakness of the financial sectors and the lack of proper financial sector supervision in these countries . . . Still the sense of crisis did not seem to be shared evenly throughout the world: I suppose that this was because some observers attributed the Asian crises to specific deficiencies in the economic management of the Asian countries, including seemingly opaque and improper relationships between governments and businesses.
>
> However, when turmoil also took place in Russia and Brazil this year, it became very clear that crises such as those experienced in Asia are more general phenomena. One cannot help but realise that these successive crises stemmed not only from specific problems in particular economies, but also from general problems inherent in today's global economic system.[30]

The Subcommittee on Asian Financial and Capital Markets under *Gaitame Shingikai* (Committee on Foreign Exchange and Other Transactions) established in the MOF also discussed the issue. According to its report, although there were some problems such as macroeconomic imbalances particularly in Thailand, the spread of the Thai crisis to the neighbouring countries was due to the contagion effect, which was generated by a radical shift in market perceptions. In the case of South Korea, various economic problems had surfaced well in advance of the crisis, which led to the situation that foreign creditors who had become increasingly sensitive to their investments due to the crises in South East Asia rapidly withdrew their funds (Subcommittee on Asian Financial and Capital Markets 1998: 3–9). Also, the then Japanese Vice Finance Minister Eisuke Sakakibara argues that the crisis was caused not by the structures peculiar to East Asia, but by 'global capitalism', and that could happen anywhere in the world (Sakakibara 1998).

It must be noticed that with the spread of the crisis to Russia and Latin America, attributing the crisis only to the domestic problems of the affected countries in East Asia lost a degree of credibility, and the systemic defects of global financial markets have become more widely recognised. This has led to a 'mood swing' towards the Post-Washington Consensus. It is important to note that G7 Finance Ministers discussed the issue of the international financial architecture and agreed on the necessity to reform and strengthen it. Haruhiko Kuroda, former Vice Minister of the Japanese MOF, argues that the meeting was significant particularly in the following aspects: (1) the Ministers agreed that capital account liberalisation in developing countries should be carried out in a careful and well-sequenced manner, accompanied by measures to support a sound and well-regulated financial sector and by a consistent macroeconomic policy framework; (2) they recognised the importance of improving transparency by all market participants, including the disclosure of the exposure to hedge funds; (3) they agreed that the international financial community needs to set out a framework for involving the private sector in the resolution of crises, stating that private creditors should not believe that their credits are protected by the IMF, and that in some cases it is likely that net debt payments to the private sector are reduced. Kuroda stresses that it is particularly surprising that the champions of the market economy, the US and the UK, agreed on these points, which are completely different from G7's traditional stance (Kuroda 1999).

Returning to the divergence of opinions between Japan and the Washington Consensus concerning the causes of the crisis, this difference is to a large extent a reflection of their arguments on development and transition that was discussed in the early part of this chapter. It is no wonder that the IMF and the US held the views on the crisis outlined above. As the efficacy of markets mechanisms is their basic assumption, it seems to them that what was wrong could not have had anything to do with the global financial markets, but something that had hindered the markets from working effectively in the affected countries. Therefore, such hindrances to the operation of market mechanisms, specifically statism, 'crony capitalism' and mercantilism, had to be blamed and hence the call to have them removed from the economies immediately. To Washington, the crisis looked as though it was justifying its philosophy, marking the triumph of its philosophy over other capitalist models (after having defeated the Soviet style planned economy), and was a window of opportunity to dismantle what it saw as obstacles to spreading the free market systems to the East Asian economies. Furthermore, some scholars point out that their ideological interest for such a policy was reinforced by economic considerations: namely, the crisis was not only significant ideologically, but was a great opportunity to promote the US national interest by removing the barriers to US businesses expanding in the East Asian markets (Wade and Veneroso 1998, Bhagwati 1998: 7–12).

On the other hand, Washington's views on the causes of the crisis and its subsequent policies, which completely refute what Japanese officials and intellectuals had considered to be important for developing and transition economies, were totally unacceptable to Japan.[31] It is true that the East Asian economies are not a copy of the Japanese economic system or its developmental model. On the contrary, their economic and social systems are quite diverse (Weiss 2000: 21–55). However, Japanese officials and academics consider that these countries have achieved remarkable economic development by following some of the core elements of the Japanese experience in the past. In most of the countries, the governments played an important and leading role in economic development, which was much larger than neoclassical economics recommends as the appropriate role of government, and selectively promoted specific sectors. To Japanese officials and academics, these are the essential parts of the success of East Asian development, and what the IMF was doing was trying to convert their economic systems to the American framework based on market mechanisms. Higgott puts it as follows: 'what has been challenged in the crisis of the East Asian NIES in the late twentieth century is the very model on which they have built their success. It should be seen not only as an economic crisis, but as an "ideas battle" or an ideological battle' (Higgott 1998a).

To Japan the crisis was, in a sense, caused by Washington's over-emphasis on market mechanisms, namely the policies to encourage developing countries to liberalise their financial and capital markets. This argument of Japan may have had the benefit of hindsight. Japanese officials and academics did not articulate their opinions on this issue before the crisis, largely because they failed to give much thought to the issue of financial liberalisation. However, the crisis crystallised their views on this issue, and now they strongly advocate that the liberalisation of financial and capital markets in developing countries must be dealt with very cautiously, as sometimes it could be harmful for their economic stability. For instance, Kenichi Ohno argues that financial liberalisation should not be demanded uniformly from developed and developing countries, and it should be considered according to their level of development (Ohno 1998: 60–1). In fact, Japan apparently supported Malaysia's capital controls in the midst of the crisis. Despite the IMF's reluctance, Japan included Malaysia in the list of countries to be supported under the New Miyazawa Initiative, as will be discussed in the next chapter.

With respect to the IMF's policies, Japanese officials and academics considered that they were an attempt to impose market mechanisms hastily and rigidly with little consideration of each country's situation, and would dismantle what had been vital for the development of East Asian countries. In particular, Japan's discontent grew as the IMF's policies became more far-reaching and comprehensive with the spread of the crisis, and went far beyond a sensible line as far as the Japanese were concerned (Sakakibara 2000: 195–201). Japan's stance on this point is as follows: East Asian countries have to address the problems that they are facing, revealed to them by the occurrence of the crisis, and they have to deal with the liberalisation of their economic systems in the long term, including trade and financial liberalisation. However, this must be done step by step, according to the economic situation and the level of development, and in certain areas, government involvement is still justified in these countries. At the very least, it is not a matter to be addressed in the midst of the crisis.

Conclusion

This chapter has looked at the ideological disparity between Japan and the Washington Consensus institutions, which has led to their different views on the East Asian financial crisis. Although they start from common policy goals that developing and transition countries should pursue, namely introducing market economy and democracy, Japan has a quite different view about the way to achieve these goals, particularly in terms of the role of the government and the policy time span. Considering Japan's past stance of trying not to unsettle its US relations or of compromising with US policy, MOF officials' quite assertive attitude towards Washington itself deserves special attention. In addition, the discussions in this chapter will help to understand Japan's policies towards the crisis and East Asian regionalism in the following chapters. This chapter suggests that there is a deep-rooted background against which Japan and the Washington Consensus institutions have taken a different policy stance on the crisis and Japan has advocated its policies assertively during the crisis. Also, Chapters 4 and 5 will show that MOF officials' interest in financial regionalism has been closely related to these ideological debates throughout the 1990s.

4   Japanese policy towards the East Asian financial crisis

Following the discussion in the previous chapter about the causes of the East Asian financial crisis, this chapter offers a detailed narrative and analysis of Japan's policies towards the crisis as well as the background against which these policies came out and were implemented. It looks at how and why Japan has become interested in regional financial cooperation in general, and the AMF in particular, while considering the significance of the New Miyazawa Initiative in analysing recent Japanese foreign policy. It is also discussed how and why Japan became positively involved in this incident together with the IMF. The chapter argues that the findings presented here advance one of the central arguments of the book about Japan's increasing willingness to take the initiative in the region. Also, the relevance of this evidence about Japan's interest in regional financial cooperation will be explored further in the discussions about East Asian regionalism in the next chapter. Additionally, by noticing some elements of the style in which these policies were pursued, this and the next chapter prepare the ground for a comprehensive analysis of the style of Japanese foreign policy in Chapter 6. The Thai crisis, which eventually triggered the region-wide, then global, crisis, provides the starting point of this chapter.

The Thai crisis

In Thailand, share prices and real estate prices fell significantly in 1996, and eventually the problems of its economy came to be revealed on 13 May 1997, when an unprecedented level of market attack against the Thai baht took place. The Thai government tried to defend the currency by intervening in the market alone or coordinated with Singapore, Malaysia and Hong Kong, and by imposing a ban on taking the baht out of the country. However, it finally announced, following IMF advice, that it would let the baht float on 2 July, judging that it was impossible to keep the baht pegged to the US dollar any more. Nevertheless, in response to the announcement, the speculative attacks of the market increased and the value of the baht against the dollar dropped further,[1] which caused the crisis to expand to neighbouring countries such as Malaysia, the Philippines and Indonesia. In the end, the Thai government called in the IMF on 28 July.

Prior to the decision to resort to IMF assistance, the Thai government asked Japan to provide bilateral assistance to help weather the situation, but the Japanese government did not accept the request. Japan's stance at this stage was to coordinate with the IMF, although, as the crisis spread, it came to take a critical position against IMF policies. It was not that Japan was indifferent to the plight of the Thai economy, and in fact the MOF dispatched its senior officials on a mission to Thailand in order to obtain accurate information about the Thai economy at an early stage in mid-May, and a second mission in mid-July, while the Thai Finance Minister met his Japanese counterpart in Tokyo later in July.[2] However, Eisuke Sakakibara, who was a central figure in dealing with the East Asian financial crisis as the Vice Minister of the MOF, argues that, although it might have been possible for Japan to put up most of the necessary funds to stabilise the currency and to ask other East Asian countries to contribute a small share, it considered this option too risky, as the Thai government did not disclose any essential information about its economy, such as the exact amount of its foreign reserves and the extent of the government intervention in the market (Sakakibara 2000: 177). Another finance official commented that Japan had to coordinate with the IMF, because Japan did not have unlimited funds for intervention, and also because only the international organisations were in a position to advise other countries about their policies.[3] Under the circumstances, Japan suggested that the Thai government request IMF assistance, while Japan itself began to contact the IMF to discuss closely the Thai issues.

Japan's persistence in believing that the IMF should play an important role at this early stage of the crisis should be noted. As argued in the previous chapter, while there has been a great deal of disagreement about economic management between the Washington Consensus institutions and Japan, few Japanese officials and academics failed to dispute before the crisis the tenet of the Washington Consensus with respect to the governance of international finance, namely the tenet that the liberalisation of financial and capital markets will lead to economic benefits even for developing countries. Many East Asian countries followed this position, having rapidly liberalised their financial markets and having positively taken foreign capital into their economies since the early 1990s. Thailand, for instance, established an offshore market called Bangkok International Banking Facilities in 1993, through which it tried to obtain short-term capital for economic development. These policies of the East Asian countries were supported not only by the IMF and the World Bank, but also by the G7 countries, including Japan, at that time, although later they admitted that the eventual reckless inflow of foreign capital was one of the factors that caused the crisis, as discussed in Chapter 3. This support for liberalisation in East Asia on the part of the West and Japan was, to a degree, a response to pressure from their own financial institutions, who had been keen on lending to East Asian firms since the early 1990s, and who lobbied their governments to encourage East Asian governments on the path towards radical financial deregulation. Furthermore, when the idea of floating the baht, which became the trigger of the crisis, was suggested by the IMF, Japan failed to oppose it. In short, despite the apparent difference between Japan's stance and that of the IMF with regard to economic development, Japan failed to contest the Washington Consensus in the field of finance at this time.

In spite of refusing to grant Thailand's request for bilateral assistance, Japan played an important role in organising the Thai rescue package under the IMF scheme. Although an agreement was promptly reached between the IMF and Thailand, it soon became clear that the estimated US$14 billion necessary fund far exceeded the available resources from the IMF and other international organisations.[4] Under the circumstances, Japan, who, after consulting with the IMF, convened a meeting for rescuing Thailand in Tokyo on 11 August, went to great lengths to make the meeting successful. MOF senior officials flew to East Asian countries to try to persuade them to contribute to the package by stressing the importance of cooperation by regional countries and emphasising that Japan would contribute US$4 billion, which was equal to the IMF contribution (Kimura 1998: 15).[5] Eventually, the meeting was a greater success than expected, and a total of US$17 billion was committed to the package. In addition to US$4 billion each from Japan and the IMF and 1.5 billion and 1.2 billion from the World Bank and the ADB respectively, East Asian countries and Australia offered a total of US$6.5 billion, while the US failed to make a contribution,[6] although the US instead pressed for an increase in Thailand's access to the IMF's regular loan facilities from 300 per cent of its quota to 500 per cent. Sakakibara writes that the hall of the conference was filled with unusual enthusiasm that could be described as 'Asian solidarity' (Sakakibara 2000: 180), and Japan's positive attitude continued after the Thai meeting.

The AMF proposal – the origin and initial discussions

Given impetus by the great success of concluding the Thai rescue package, which demonstrated an inclination towards collaboration among East Asian countries with the US refusing to participate in it, the idea of establishing the AMF, which would be a permanent fund contributed to by regional countries to prevent a future crisis from occurring, was put forward and discussed intensively among Japan, other East Asian countries, the US and the IMF during the rest of the year.

There is no consistent view about who, Japan or ASEAN, originally initiated the idea and how it was discussed among the countries concerned. However, by putting all available information together, it is reasonable to suggest that a similar, but not identical, idea was examined among the ASEAN countries and also separately within Japan before it became public in mid-September. On 19 August, the Thai Foreign Minister was reported as saying that he would propose the establishment of an ASEAN monetary fund (as it was tentatively named then) by the ASEAN countries to support their currencies against foreign speculations.[7] Later, the Philippine Foreign Minister revealed that the ASEAN countries had been considering the idea and that it would be discussed in September during the meeting of ASEAN Foreign Ministers.[8] The ASEAN countries agreed in principle to have such a preventive organisation of their own at that time, but wondered about the feasibility of financing an adequate fund by themselves and the discussions were at a standstill.[9] It was under these circumstances that Japan told them that it was thinking about a region-wide financial organisation in East Asia, and was ready to be the largest contributor to the organisation.[10]

The MOF started to work on establishing the AMF immediately after the conference on 11 August. Sakakibara writes in detail about how Japan proceeded with negotiations with the countries concerned. Before drafting Japan's proposal, Sakakibara first sounded out the Governor and the Vice Governor of the Hong Kong Monetary Authority on 24 August as well as the Finance Minister of Singapore on 30 August. Then the MOF worked on the Japanese plan, which was proposed unofficially to Hong Kong, Singapore, Malaysia, Indonesia, and South Korea by Sakakibara himself on 10 September, while other senior officials in the International Finance Bureau of the MOF visited China and Australia to explain the proposal on the same day. On 12 September, the Japanese Finance Minister sent out the Japanese proposal to the nine countries of Australia, China, Hong Kong, Indonesia, Malaysia, the Philippines, Singapore, South Korea and Thailand, which were expected to be members of the AMF according to the Japanese plan. Then Japan requested these countries to hold a session to discuss the proposal during the IMF/ World Bank meeting scheduled on 23 and 24 September in Hong Kong (Sakakibara 2000: 182–5).

The original Japanese plan was to establish a fund of US$100 billion, out of contributions by member countries. It was reported later that Japan intended to contribute US$50 billion.[11] The proposal contained several controversial issues, which provoked the strong opposition of the US and the IMF, as discussed below.

The first contentious point of the proposal was the issue of membership. According to the Japanese plan, membership was limited to the countries that Japan had sent its proposal to, and the US was not included. Japanese officials insist that Japan did not try to exclude the US from East Asia, but that they assumed there was no chance that the US would contribute to such a regional fund, given the US reluctance to participate in the Thai package.[12] Also, Sakakibara states that if the US were included in a regional framework, it would not be really regional, and no different from the IMF, as it would be expected that the US would interfere in what Japan and other East Asian countries would like to do.[13] Apparently, his comment indicates that Japan (or at least Sakakibara) wanted a regional organisation free from US intrusion. The US unsurprisingly became very anxious about Japan's intentions.

Second, the AMF proposal was not clear about what the relationship between the AMF and the IMF would be, and there was a question about what sort of conditionality, if any, the money provided by the AMF would carry with it. Japan's stance on these issues was not necessarily consistent throughout the negotiation process that lasted until mid-November. Hiroshi Mitsuzuka, the then Japanese Finance Minister, was reported on several occasions as insisting that the AMF would be a supplementary organisation to the IMF. However, Anthony Rowley writes that, despite the MOF's insistence that the new regional facility should be contingent upon IMF approval and the money it provides should be additional to IMF resources, sources close to Tokyo's official thinking suggested that the new facility could offer funds in cases where no policy conditionality was required or in cases where the IMF might be slow in coming up with the money (Rowley 1997). A finance officer said that, although there was not necessarily consensus about this matter, some were of the opinion that the AMF should be independent of the IMF. But, he continued, later the MOF came to stress the AMF's consistency with IMF conditionality in response to the fierce criticism of the US and the IMF claiming that the AMF would be a potential cause of moral hazard.[14]

The US and the IMF began to attack the AMF, after Japan sent its AMF proposal to the intended member countries. On 17 September, the then US Treasury Secretary Robert Rubin alerted the Japanese Finance Minister by telephone that the US was definitely against the AMF, while the US government sent letters to the Finance Ministers of the member nations of APEC, which were signed by Rubin and the US Federal Reserve Board Chairman Alan Greenspan. The letter stated that the US was ready to consider regional concerted actions to manage economic crises instead of the AMF and that the IMF had to be at the centre of any such attempt (Sakakibara 2000: 186). Meanwhile, Japan tried to counter this move of the US.

The climax of the battle over the AMF came on 18–21 September 1997, when the finance ministers and senior officials of the countries concerned came together to attend a series of meetings. The Japanese proposal concerning the AMF was discussed among the ASEAN finance ministers on 18 September in Bangkok, preceding the finance ministers' meeting of the ASEM countries scheduled on the next day, and the proposal was supported there. Then, the venue was changed from Bangkok to Hong Kong. The AMF was one of the items on the agenda of the G7 meeting on 20 September, when some European countries expressed reservations about it. On 21 September, prior to the annual IMF/World Bank general assembly on 23 September, the ten proposed member countries plus the US and the IMF held a Deputy-level meeting to discuss the proposal. As expected, ASEAN countries and South Korea were in favour of the proposal, while the US strongly opposed it. China, Hong Kong and Australia did not express their stance clearly, but Australia had given Japan a negative message before the meeting. The meeting finally failed to reach a conclusion.

The politics surrounding the AMF

In order to understand this outcome, it is necessary to make clearer the stance of the countries concerned towards the AMF proposal.

Not all the ASEAN countries were enthusiastic about the Japanese proposal particularly after the US had expressed strong opposition,[15] although none of them objected to it publicly. Malaysia, particularly Prime Minister Mahathir Mohamad, which had long been against the IMF or perhaps 'Western values' and never wanted to rely on the IMF, was unsurprisingly a strong supporter for the AMF. It may be that the Malaysian officials did not want to accept the reforms suggested by the IMF of the country's industries, in which they had vested interests.[16] Thailand and Indonesia were also in favour of the proposal. In Thailand, who was already under the IMF program, there was resistance to the severe structural reforms that the IMF had demanded. The situation was similar in Indonesia, who wanted to avoid IMF reforms that could damage the government, although it was soon to request IMF assistance. On the other hand, Singapore, who was the closest to the US among the ASEAN countries and strongly wished to keep the US engagement in the region, was not in favour of the framework that excluded the US, and neither was the Philippines, which was concerned that the formation of a new economic organisation in the region could cause a decline in the authority of the ADB, whose headquarters were located in the country's capital.

South Korea was supportive of the AMF. Although the country tends to dislike any Japanese initiative in the region because of Japan's colonisation during the war, it can be inferred that it wanted to secure a way to achieve liquidity, without making a humiliating request for IMF assistance, given that its foreign reserves had been critically diminished since the Thai crisis. In fact, the level of South Korea's foreign reserves was only about US$21 billion as of the end of September and foreign capital was still being withdrawn.

Although China did not oppose the Japanese proposal directly, it remained cautious about Japan's leadership in East Asia and did not support the AMF.[17] China tends to associate Japanese initiatives in the region with Japan's attempts to create a Greater East Asia Co-Prosperity Sphere in the past, and this always makes China sceptical about Japan's goodwill in its regional policy (Breslin 2001). In addition, China basically wants neither Japan nor the US to dominate the region. If a regional framework does exist, such as in the case of APEC, China has to participate in order to prevent Japan or the US from dictating, but sees no reason to positively support the creation of a new organisation, in which Japan or the US could exert influence (Breslin 2001).

Hong Kong was reluctant to give its support to the proposal as well. It was reported that it had difficulties building a domestic consensus for the AMF, as the government had had a hard time dealing with the parliament's opposition to the country's US$1 billion contribution to the Thai rescue package in August 1997.[18] Also, according to one newspaper, China and Hong Kong preferred to hold on to their foreign reserves as the currency peg of Hong Kong remained under pressure, rather than commit to a larger framework.[19] Meanwhile, Australia was also negative about the AMF plan, explaining that it would be difficult to get domestic support for contributing to the fund.[20]

As far as the IMF was concerned, the AMF would be just an awkward institution, which could undermine its authority and the effectiveness of its activities and could reduce its influence in East Asia. As argued before, some Japanese officials hinted that the AMF would not simply be a subset of the IMF, but retain some autonomy. Also, the Malaysian Prime Minister asserted that the AMF should be completely independent of the IMF. Those remarks made IMF officials very cautious about the idea. They claimed that such a regional fund was not only unnecessary, but also harmful, as a fund that was readily and easily available during any crisis could lead to poor banking and business management, namely it would create moral hazard. They also feared that the IMF would have difficulty in getting countries to accept its conditionality and to agree about the reforms it demanded. European countries were relatively indifferent to the matter, but there was no reason why they should support the establishment of an organisation that could reduce the importance of the IMF, which traditionally had had a close relationship with Europe.

The US opposed the AMF proposal giving the same reasons as the IMF, namely the duality of function between the IMF and the AMF and the possibility of creating moral hazard. However, another problem with the AMF, as far as the US was concerned, was that the US was not a member of the proposed organisation. It seems that there was some concern about its declining influence in East Asia while Japan looked increasingly dominating, particularly after the conclusion of the Thai rescue package, where Japan had played a central role and the US had failed to contribute. Sakakibara writes that he had a phone call from the then Deputy Treasury Secretary Lawrence Summers on 14 September, and Summers's worries were that the US was not supposed to be a participant in the AMF, and the AMF could act independently of the IMF (Sakakibara 2000: 185). Sakakibara further states that the US seemed to have taken the AMF as Japan's challenge to US hegemony in Asia (Sakakibara 2000: 186).

Furthermore, the US has never been able to accept the formation of any organisation that could weaken IMF influence, because the IMF is a very important and convenient channel for US foreign policy. There are a number of reasons why the IMF is so important to US foreign policy. First, the US and the IMF share the same ideology of economic management, namely the neoclassical orthodoxy, as discussed in Chapter 3. The US can consequently spread what it believes to be correct via the IMF's policy.

Second, the US can push its agendas on its foreign policy more smoothly and with less conflict via the IMF than independently. Cohen points out that the IMF is a convenient conduit for US influence, because:

[A]ny effort by Washington itself to impose unpopular policy conditions on troubled debtors would undoubtedly have fanned the flames of nationalism, if not revolution, in many countries. But what would be regarded as intolerable when demanded by a major foreign power might, it seemed, be rather more acceptable if administered instead by an impartial multilateral agency.

(Cohen 1886: 229)

Similarly, Kahler writes that the US utilises the IMF 'as a buffer in awkward bilateral relations, imposing economic conditions that the United States would find it hard to impose bilaterally' (Kahler 1990: 110).

Third, given that the US public interest has shifted from international to domestic matters after the end of the Cold War, bailout through the IMF is much more likely to get the support of the American people, as well as that of Congress, than bilateral assistance. In particular, the US government has been increasingly constrained by Congress from committing to international initiatives financially, as observed in the Thai bailout package in August 1997. Although the US government has been facing the difficulty of Congress opposition to the increase of the IMF quota, any bilateral rescue would be even more difficult domestically.

Fourth, the US can simply shift some costs of any bailout to other industrialised countries through the IMF. In the case of the East Asian financial crisis, given the size of the economic stakes that American firms had in East Asia (lower than the stakes for Japanese firms operating there, though), the US could not be indifferent to the region's trouble. IMF packages are quite convenient means for pushing a part of the cost of any bailout onto other countries. Also, it could be said that under the IMF umbrella, it is more feasible to involve more countries in a rescue package.

Finally, the US is traditionally in a position to pursue its own favourable policy through the IMF. It enjoys a dominant influence on the decision-making process in the IMF, where it keeps the largest share in the quotas among all the member countries, although this has declined in the last few decades.[21] The US dominance in the IMF may also come from what Jagdish Bhagwati calls a Wall Street–Treasury Complex, that is, 'a definite networking of like-minded luminaries among the powerful institutions – Wall Street, the Treasury Department, the State Department, the IMF and the World Bank', which arises from the fact that the members of this elite go back and forth among these institutions. Bhagwati argues that this powerful network is 'unable to look much beyond the interest of Wall Street', and 'the IMF has been relentlessly propelled toward embracing the goal of capital account convertibility' (Bhagwati 1998: 10–12). In short, IMF policy could easily tend to favour US national or domestic interests. Also, as mentioned in the previous chapter, with respect to IMF policies towards the East Asian financial crisis, Wade and Veneroso document the influence of the US Treasury Department and Wall Street on the IMF policies, arguing that the IMF 'bail-outs' with the combination of massive devaluations, the IMF pushed financial liberalisation, and the IMF facilitated recoveries are equally 'bails-ins' for foreign corporations and the multilateral institutions, where US firms would benefit greatly, while these policies are likely to cause far-reaching damage in Asia (Wade and Veneroso: 1998).

What made Japan interested in a regional financial mechanism?

Although it may look as if Japan's proposal for the AMF was simply an unexpected response to the East Asian crisis, strengthening financial cooperation for the sake of financial stability in the region, or even creating some regional financial framework, had been on Japan's agenda for some years, which probably enabled Japan to put forth the AMF proposal very promptly.

Some efforts for closer regional cooperation had been already made before the crisis. In particular, the Mexican crisis in 1994 gave some concern to the Japanese monetary authorities, the MOF and the Bank of Japan (BOJ), and made them take some actions to assure financial stability in the region and put forward some regional mechanisms (Yamamoto 1997: 224). Japan signed an agreement for entrustment intervention with Hong Kong and Singapore in February 1996. Subsequently, in April 1996 the Japanese monetary authorities agreed on the repurchase (repo) arrangements of US dollar government securities to provide liquidity on a bilateral basis with seven countries in the region, namely Australia, Hong Kong, Indonesia, Malaysia, the Philippines, Singapore and Thailand.[22] These repo arrangements were not directly linked to Japan's proposal for the AMF, but later developed into more networked arrangements called the Chiang Mai Initiative,[23] which were agreed on in May 2000, as discussed in the next chapter.

Even before the Mexican crisis, the BOJ initiated an unofficial forum for the region's central banks (Australia, China, Hong Kong, Indonesia, Japan, Malaysia, New Zealand, the Philippines, Singapore, South Korea and Thailand) in 1991, which is called the Executive Meeting of East Asia–Pacific Central Banks (EMEAP). Its primary objective is to strengthen the cooperative relationships among its member countries and to exchange opinions about each other's financial policy and the like. For the first six years it held Deputies' meetings twice a year, but since 1996 Governors' meetings and various working/study groups have been held on a regular basis. The BOJ has provided the secretariat function since its inception. Although the US has shown an interest, it is not a member, probably because ASEAN countries have opposed US membership (Tadokoro 2000: 65).

Moreover, some informal discussions about further financial mechanisms in the region were going on before the East Asian financial crisis. Even the idea of the AMF itself had been nursed at a private level by some Japanese officials, such as Haruhiko Kuroda, Chief of the International Finance Bureau at that time, supported by some Japanese intellectuals, such as Hajime Shinohara.[24] Also, it was reported that prior to the Thai crisis some MOF officials had considered establishing a regular meeting of East Asian Finance Ministers and Central Bank Governors, which would be held three times a year in order to discuss frankly the macro-economic performance as well as the monetary policies of their countries and to take collaborative action when necessary.[25] Furthermore, in an EMEAP Governors' meeting, where Japan naturally has a large influence, held in July 1997 in Shanghai prior to the Thai rescue conference, they agreed to investigate some kind of financing facility among the EMEAP member countries to support the economic policies of their countries, in cooperation with the IMF.[26]

Although these policies and discussions prior to the crisis were not necessarily concerned with Japan's proposal for the AMF directly, it is noteworthy that there was a mood in the MOF to consider a regional framework. The Thai crisis provided an opportunity for Japan to advance such an idea. In fact, Sakakibara writes that he and other officials thought that they should take advantage of the atmosphere that arose in the Thai conference and use it as a driving force to advance the agenda (Sakakibara 2000: 182). It could be argued that this background helped Japan propose the AMF so speedily in September.

Although the interest of Japan in closer financial cooperation in East Asia is partly due to the lessons learnt from the Mexican crisis as well as past policies and discussions during the 1990s, there are also various underlying factors at play in this interest of Japan. One apparent reason for Japan's interest in creating a regional mechanism is the deepening economic interdependence in East Asia. As discussed in Chapter 2, East Asia has become considerably more important to Japan economically because of Japan's closer economic ties with the region. From a microeconomic point of view, a sound East Asian economy has been vital for Japanese firms and financial institutions. East Asia is an important trading partner as well as a foreign direct investment destination. Also, the Japanese financial institutions have massive exposure to East Asia, much larger than the American and European financial institutions have. Financial instability in the region could be a serious blow to the Japanese economy. In addition, the disturbance of the East Asian financial system, and subsequently that of the international financial system, could damage Japan's macroeconomic condition through the fluctuation of the yen and the plunge in the value of the stock markets. Therefore, it can be argued that Japan's interest in East Asian financial regionalism and its positive attitude towards it has been consistent with its national interests.[27]

In addition, a political factor, namely Japan's willingness to assume a greater political role in the region, has also contributed to Japan's turn towards regional financial cooperation. We will come back to this point in the next chapter, but here it should be noted that the financial area is one of the areas where Japan's initiatives are quite feasible. In other areas, particularly security, its positive policies are still quite limited due to Japan's extraordinary dependence on the US as well as the history of its colonisation of the region, although, as argued in Chapter 2, even in the security field, Japan has gradually showed a more positive stance than before.

It could also be argued that Japan's interest in financial regionalism or a regional financial mechanism has been in a sense a reflection of its dissatisfaction with the existing international economic system that centres on the Washington Consensus. As argued in Chapter 3, there has been an ideological divergence, which has lasted throughout the 1990s, between the Washington Consensus institutions and the Japanese government, particularly the MOF, concerning economic development and systemic transition. Japan has increasingly become sceptical about the effectiveness of what Washington has promoted, such as structural adjustment policy, and its inclination to implement the same policy universally in any country. The previous chapter also argued that this ideological disparity led to their different interpretations of the causes of the crisis. These differences have made Japan dissatisfied with IMF policies towards the crisis, although Japan failed to oppose the arguments about the efficacy of financial openness and deregulation in the East Asian developing economies before the crisis, as discussed above. Sakakibara clearly made this point when he said that he and other finance officials in charge were very dissatisfied with IMF policies towards the crisis, and according to them the IMF, led by the US, imposed unreasonable structural reforms on crisis-hit countries. He continues, by proposing the AMF and later by advancing regional financial cooperation, he together with other finance officials consciously tried to challenge the existing international system; the strong US opposition to the AMF was couched in terms that indicate that the US officials sensed such an intention from Japan.[28] Strictly speaking, when it proposed the AMF, Japan had not had a clear idea about the causes of the crisis, and only the later policies towards closer regional financial cooperation reflected to a greater extent these differences of interpretation and interest in relation to the East Asian crisis. However, as Sakakibara's remarks show, even the proposal of the formation of the AMF may be considered in the context of these ideological disparities.

Moreover, Japan's dissatisfaction with the establishment in Washington is not limited to their ideological differences: Japan's influence in the existing international organisations is quite limited, and it is difficult to get Japanese views reflected in their policies, despite the fact that Japan is now one of the main contributors in most organisations.[29] This is partly because Japan is a latecomer to these organisations. Also, Japan's voting share in the international organisations is not high, considering the amount of its contributions.[30] Moreover, the number of the Japanese staff in these organisations is small, particularly in some of the key posts, and it is said that the Japanese officials that are stationed there on temporary posts feel uncomfortable and helpless in the Western dominated organisations. A MOF official, who had actually been stationed in the IMF, comments that Washington's language is neoclassical economics, and thus influencing Washington's policy is hard for Japan, who does not share the language.[31] It can be argued that these situations have made MOF officials interested in establishing 'their' organisations,[32] which has indirectly contributed to Japan's assertive policies towards the crisis and the regional financial cooperation.

At the same time, there is some awareness among the MOF officials about the risk of relying solely on the international organisations. They think that, due to their US-centred nature, these organisations are limited in their ability to deal with East Asian issues because of their access to a limited volume of available resources and information. A MOF official comments that the MOF does not take the stance that the IMF is unnecessary, and when problems emerge, its existence is crucial. However, he continues, the IMF cannot be expected to resolve future crises on its own, and, in fact, the IMF alone was not able to provide sufficient funds for the East Asian financial crisis.[33] The fact that the US has been less willing to commit to East Asian matters, as revealed in its reluctant attitude towards the Thai rescue package, gives another reason for this position of the MOF officials. In short, the MOF officials have come to believe strongly that it is essential to establish some self-help mechanisms in East Asia to supplement the existing international system for preventing and preparing for any future financial disturbance.

It is not true that Japan is moving away from the existing international organisations. It has been traditionally a supporter of the international organisations and, in fact, tried to cooperate with the IMF in the early stages of the East Asian financial crisis, as argued above. Japan has made an effort to raise its position in the existing organisations and to voice its views on their policies. This has been consistent with what Japan has been doing throughout the postwar period, namely enhancing its international status. Nevertheless, Japan's dissatisfaction with the international organisations should not be overlooked. As discussed below, this dissatisfaction became more conspicuous as the crisis spread and deepened.

Finally, it may be possible to think about Japan's positive attitude towards closer financial cooperation in the region from the viewpoint of Japan's domestic policy-making process. At the risk of over-generalisation, it can be said that the MOF tends to be less constrained by US relations in its policy and to be in a position to assert the importance of East Asian relations more, compared with the MOFA. Of course this is not to say that the MOF tends to neglect the importance to Japan of US relations, but sometimes the MOFA has been too cautious about US relations, which has prevented the ministry from taking positive East Asian policies in the past (Hook *et al.* 2001: 43–5). These differences can be attributed to the MOF's character as an economic ministry as against the MOFA, which is a diplomatic ministry. It may also be that due to the MOF's historical tie with the ADB, there have been more 'Asianists' in the MOF than in the MOFA, while the decade-long ideological discussion of development issues has possibly been an opportunity for MOF officials to become motivated to display a measure of assertiveness towards the US and to learn how to do it. It can be argued that the differences in mandate and orientation of the MOF and the MOFA are one of the reasons why Japan's interest in regional cooperation became conspicuous in the financial area.

The failure of the AMF proposal and its replacement with the Manila framework

Although Japan continued to make an effort to realise the idea of the AMF and discussed the issue with some ASEAN countries bilaterally even after the meeting in Hong Kong on 21 September 1997, the deepening and spreading of the crisis made the situation difficult for the pursuit of this project. The currencies of Thailand, Malaysia, Indonesia and the Philippines, which had been under strong pressure since July, continued to fall, and on 8 October, Indonesia finally appealed to the IMF, following Thailand and the Philippines.[34] Furthermore, the crisis reached Taiwan in the middle of October, when the Taiwan dollar plunged, which triggered a speculative attack against the Hong Kong dollar. Overnight interest rates in Hong Kong rose from 7 per cent to nearly 300 per cent on 22 October, while the stock market fell by 10.4 per cent the following day. Then, the crisis spread to South Korea at the end of October, leading to a sharp drop of the Korean won. Japan experienced two large bankruptcies of financial institutions in November and its stock markets and the currency plummeted, although it is arguable that Japan's difficulty at that time could be regarded as the result of the contagion of the crisis. Under these circumstances, the impetus for the AMF was lost rapidly.

The AMF proposal was finally replaced by a different framework for regional cooperation, called the Manila Framework, at a meeting of the finance and central bank Deputies in Manila on 18–19 November. Fourteen countries (Australia, Brunei, Canada, China, Hong Kong, Indonesia, Japan, Malaysia, New Zealand, the Philippines, Singapore, South Korea, Thailand and the US) attended the meeting, along with the IMF, the World Bank and the ADB as observers. They agreed on four broad principles, on which the framework was based:

1 A mechanism for regional economic surveillance to complement global surveillance by the IMF.
2 Enhanced economic and technical cooperation particularly in strengthening domestic financial systems and regulatory mechanisms.
3 Measures to strengthen the IMF's capacity to respond to financial crises.
4 A cooperative financial arrangement that could supplement the IMF resources.

The Manila framework is different from what Japanese officials had envisaged in the AMF proposal. There is no specific pooling of resources by member countries, and no standing staff or secretariat. Moreover, the framework does not have any room to act independently of the IMF, being completely subordinated to the IMF. The Manila framework has primarily a monitoring and supervisory role, although, if necessary, funds could be provided on a case-by-case basis after a program and conditionality are agreed between the IMF and a country threatened by a crisis.

What has to be noticed here are the reasons why Japan finally gave up the AMF. It is generally recognised that the US and the IMF opposition forced Japan to abandon the idea, together with Japan's domestic financial problems that surfaced in the autumn of 1997. They were certainly crucial factors. An official comments that it is unlikely that, under the opposition of not only the US and the IMF, but also international society in general, Japan and East Asian countries could advance regional cooperation.[35] However, this should not be taken as another example of Japan behaving as a reactive state. What is important is the influence that the US had on other East Asian countries. In particular, ASEAN countries did not want to risk their economic and security relations with the US by supporting the Japanese plan, even though they were discontented with the US negative attitude and the slow movement of the IMF towards the Thai rescue plan. Eric Altbach points out that it 'quickly became clear that there was little appetite in Asia for a confrontation with the United States and the IMF amidst plummeting currencies and stock markets' (Altbach 1997: 10). Although some countries, like Malaysia, still strongly supported a fund independent of the IMF, other countries moderated their positions in the face of strong US opposition and the deepening crisis. In addition, no country other than Japan was willing, or able, to contribute to the proposed fund. As stated before, China, Hong Kong and Australia, who were possible contributors to the fund given the level of their foreign reserves, were not positive from the onset. Also, the Singaporean government was beginning to feel public pressure domestically against giving assistance to troubled countries after extending US$1 billion to Thailand and later US$5 billion to Indonesia. In short, Japan did not maintain a regional support large enough to press forward with its proposal under US opposition. Furthermore, some officials stress that China's reluctance was a fatal blow to the AMF proposal.[36] Japan has increasingly come to take China's stance seriously in its foreign policy decisions, as the country has grown as a regional power in the 1980s and particularly since the 1990s. Also, without China's participation, East Asian regionalism could have only limited significance.

Furthermore, perhaps the fact that there was not sufficient consensus even within Japan might be another reason that made it difficult for Japan to advance the AMF proposal. It seems that there was broad agreement within the MOF about pressing forward with the AMF. Even the Budget Bureau, which is usually reluctant to increase its disbursements, did not disagree.[37] Sakakibara also obtained the Prime Minister's consent.[38] However, according to MOF officials, the MOFA, which does not have jurisdiction over international and regional financial issues, was not positive about the MOF's plan[39] or continued to be indifferent, at best,[40] partly because the MOFA tends to be more anxious about US relations than the

MOF, as argued above, and partly because the MOFA, which is the chief ministry with responsibility for the assistance to East Asia through ODA, technical assistance and so on, does not want to lose its dominant position on this matter.[41] The AMF proposal was abandoned before comprehensive discussions with other ministries took place.[42]

The AMF proposal and the implications for Japan's policy style

A series of Japanese policies over the AMF proposal have significant implications for one of the arguments of the book, namely the style of Japanese foreign policy. This will be the main subject of Chapter 6, and here it is outlined only briefly to draw attention to the relevance of this issue for the manner in which Japan acted towards the East Asian financial crisis.

Japan's unsuccessful attempt to establish the AMF is seemingly considered as a reflection of its lack of ability to take an independent initiative in East Asia, let alone the world. Several newspaper articles reported that Japan had lost to the US and the IMF, or that Japan bowed to US pressure. A Japanese daily even wrote that Japan had been defeated in the struggle for currency hegemony in Asia.[43]

However, as will be discussed later in detail, the AMF proposal was not necessarily a failure from the perspective of Japanese MOF officials, nor was the Manila Framework merely a compromise for Japan. Rather, these policies should be considered in the context of Japan's longer-term policy goals as well as its style in pursuing them. In other words, it is possible to see Japan's proposal for the AMF and the advancement of the Manila framework as a step towards the long-term policy goal of closer financial cooperation in East Asia. In fact, the discussions on regional financial cooperation have survived thereafter. The AMF proposal contributed to advancing such a long-term goal by initiating intense regional discussions about closer financial cooperation, and it actually led to the regional swap arrangements, as discussed in the next chapter. Also, in supporting the establishment of the Manila Framework, there was an implicit motive among Japanese officials to keep on with regional dialogues and maintain momentum for further regional cooperation. Inada notes that the Manila Framework is not a fund that the AMF was supposed to be, but still establishing a framework was a significant step for regional financial cooperation (Inada 2001: 30). It can be argued that these policies are quite consistent with Japan's style of foreign policy, namely to pursue its goals gradually and in a low-profile, less contentious manner. This point will be elaborated in Chapter 6, together with more evidence from the rest of this chapter and the next chapter.

The spread of the crisis to Indonesia and Japan's policies towards it

The crisis in Thailand soon spread to Indonesia, as mentioned above. The Indonesian government was forced to float its currency, the rupiah, on 14 August

1997 after it had plunged due to speculative attacks. Thereafter, despite various measures taken by the technocratic ministers in the government, the currency and the stock market continued to drop, and on 8 October, Indonesia announced that it was seeking IMF assistance.

With respect to the content of the IMF program for Indonesia, there was clear divergence of opinions between Japan and the IMF, although Japan eventually had to give in and cooperated with the IMF to organise a rescue package. The IMF insisted on an overall, and ambitious, structural reform of the Indonesian economy, which included the cancellation of the national car project, the reduction of government subsidies and the drastic restructuring of the banking system in a short period of time. On the other hand, Japan stressed that the pressing need was to stabilise the rupiah through concerted intervention as the crisis centred on confusion on the foreign exchange markets, although Japan accepted that the restructuring of the economy was necessary as a long and medium-term goal. There was a heated discussion between Sakakibara and the chief of the IMF mission, Vijian Agebri, on 16 October, but Japan failed to win concessions in the end (Sakakibara 2000: 196–7). On 31 October, the IMF and the Indonesian government reached an agreement for a US$23 billion package, and detailed measures for reforms were announced immediately, including the closure of 16 ailing banks.

Although Japan was not satisfied with the content of the agreement, it had no choice but to try to make the program successful, once the IMF and Indonesia had agreed to it.[44] On 1 November, Japan discussed bilateral assistance with Singapore and Indonesia, which would be supplementary to the assistance from the IMF and other multilateral institutions. This effort of Japan led to additional assistance as the second line of defence (Japan and Singapore contributed US$5 billion each, the US, US$3 billion, and others, about US$3 billion altogether). This brought the total amount of the package to US$39 billion.

Despite this considerable assistance, far exceeding the US$17 billion package for Thailand, the rupiah continued to fall throughout the rest of the year. The fall was greatly affected by the South Korean financial problems as well as the uncertainty over President Suharto's health. In addition, the closure of the 16 banks, without providing a safety net, implemented under the IMF agreement, exacerbated the situation by causing a run on banks and panic selling of the rupiah. In January 1998 the problem worsened. The national budget, unveiled on 6 January, disappointed the markets, as it was 31 per cent expansionary despite the fact that Indonesia was under the IMF austerity policy and the markets regarded this as evidence that Indonesia did not intend to implement the IMF program. Although Suharto and the IMF signed a new agreement on 15 January, the government had lost market confidence completely by this time, which led to a further sharp drop of the currency to a level that had been unthinkable previously.

It is debatable what made the crisis in Indonesia more prolonged and more severe than in other countries. For one thing, it was said to be a problem of the political institutions, or Suharto himself. For instance, Andrew MacIntyre argues that 'the unfettered power of the presidency and the resulting uncertainty about his policy commitments was highly destructive of investor confidence in the context of a regionwide economic crisis' (MacIntyre 1999: 155). On the other hand, Japan overtly stresses the mismanagement of the IMF. A report of the Subcommittee on Asian Financial and Capital Markets under *Gaitame Shingikai* in the MOF reads:

> [T]he IMF agreement with Indonesia which contained numerous terms address-ing structural issues invited questions and criticism . . . the question remains as to whether these issues had to be addressed in the midst of a currency crisis. The attention of the market was directed toward the resolution of structural issues because this was presented as the central issue in re-establishing con-fidence. As a result, confidence in the rupiah was further eroded when it became clear that the Indonesian government was not prepared to rectify quickly its structural issues.
>
> (Subcommittee on Asian Financial and Capital Markets 1998: 25)

It should be noted that Japan's discontent with, and distrust of, the IMF policies over the crisis began to increase from around this time. Japan did not accept the IMF policies towards Indonesia despite contributing to the IMF program, and the fact that the IMF policies could not help the crisis situation but rather worsened it, at least in the view of Japanese officials, let Japan begin to criticise the IMF policies publicly, as discussed below.

The South Korean crisis and Japan's policy towards it

Following the economic turmoil in Southeast Asia, the South Korean currency, the won, came under attack in the middle of October 1997. Since early 1997, various problems of the South Korean economy had come to be recognised publicly, and there had been some collapses among the chaebol, South Korea's large diversified conglomerates. Under the circumstances, South Korea easily became another target of currency speculation. The won dropped sharply, and by early November this process accelerated. The South Korean government first sounded out Japan and the US about the possibility of bilateral assistance, but the US quickly made it clear that it did not have any intention to assist the South Korean economy bilaterally.[45] Japan also declined the request, since, as Sakakibara argues, the effect of Japanese assistance alone would have been limited: private financial institu-tions, Japanese, US, and European, were withdrawing funds from South Korea at a rapid speed, and there was no choice but to coordinate with the IMF and the US (Sakakibara 2000: 203). On 21 November, South Korea announced a request for loans from the IMF, and on 3 December, it signed the agreement for the US$55 billion bailout package (later increased to US$58 billion), which also included US$10 billion from Japan and US$5 billion from the US as a second line of defence.

Nevertheless, the agreement with the IMF was little help in regaining the confidence of the markets and the won continued to decline. This was because, in addition to speculation that the situation of South Korea's foreign reserves was worse than reported, foreign bankers questioned the government's commitment to undertaking the IMF reforms.[46] In addition, Sakakibara argues that South Korea's request to the IMF was regarded as an announcement of a sort of defeat, and also the credibility of the IMF program had deteriorated, as the Indonesian reforms did not look to be going well (Sakakibara 2000: 204). He also stresses that the IMF's insistence on structural reforms, as was the case for Indonesia, threw the South Korean economy into disorder, and the announcement of the closure of nine merchant banks and the liquidation of two commercial banks, subsequently leading to the failure of the settlement operations in other eight merchant banks, seriously damaged the financial system (Sakakibara 2000: 204–5). By mid December, foreign banks rolled over only 20–30 per cent of South Korea's short-term debt as each tranche expired.[47] South Korea was on the verge of bankruptcy.

Under the circumstances, South Korea negotiated with the IMF and the G7 countries the accelerated disbursement of the next instalment of assistance funds[48] in return for agreeing to a new set of proposals that would speed up economic reforms, including the rapid opening of the financial markets to overseas investors. Simultaneously, the G7 requested the creditor private financial institutions to roll over their loans to South Korea. The negotiations did not go smoothly, but finally on 24 December, a new agreement including the acceleration of payments was reached among the IMF, the G7 and South Korea, while a meeting of the creditor foreign banks was held in New York, and the rolling over of their loans to the South Korean banks was granted. Thus South Korea overcame the critical situation.

Japan made every effort to assist in the rescue of the South Korean economy within the framework set by the IMF and tried to make the IMF package successful. A MOF official who was directly involved in this issue at that time argues that, when the negotiations among the IMF, the G7 and South Korea seemed to break down, Japan helped them to find a way to reach an agreement by presenting various schemes, and provided a bridge loan until IMF funds were disbursed (Kimura 1998: 17). He also writes that MOF officials really tried hard to help South Korea not only because the plight of the South Korean economy was seen to have the potential to affect the Japanese economy negatively, but also because they genuinely wanted to lend a hand to their neighbouring country (Kimura 1998: 17).

Although South Korea's crisis was abating due to the successful involvement of the private creditor financial institutions, Japan's discontent with the IMF was increasing. As discussed above, Japan criticised the demand for drastic structural reforms in the midst of a crisis, and in fact the initial IMF policies towards South Korea were not able to contain the crisis effectively. In particular, the IMF demanded extensive structural reforms, which included not only financial restructuring and financial opening, but also trade liberalisation, the restructuring of cooperate governance and reforms in labour markets. Kenji Aramaki points out that the content of structural reforms became more comprehensive as the crisis spread (Aramaki 1999: 119). Wade and Veneroso also argue that the IMF program for South Korea (and to the same extent, for other East Asian countries, too) goes beyond standard IMF programs (Wade and Veneroso 1998). These factors further increased the divergence of opinions between Japan and the IMF with respect to crisis management.

The New Miyazawa Initiative

Although in the first half of 1998 the exchange rates of most East Asian countries gradually regained some stability and the stock markets showed signs of recovery, these economies were still in a serious state of disarray. In particular, the reconstruction of the financial systems and the decline in the growth rates had to be grappled with urgently. It was also pressing to build up social safety nets as a large increase in poverty and unemployment could cause social unrest. Against this background, Japan announced the New Miyazawa Initiative in October 1998.

The New Miyazawa Initiative was a package of various support measures totalling US$30 billion, half of which was made available for the medium to long-term financial needs for economic recovery in East Asian countries,[49] and the rest was set aside for their possible short-term financial needs during the process of implementing economic reforms.[50] The countries that the initiative was intended for were Thailand, Indonesia, South Korea, Malaysia and the Philippines. It was politically controversial to include Malaysia in the program, as the country had overtly criticised the way the IMF had conducted the rescue operations and had introduced capital controls while enforcing an expansionary policy domestically in defiance of the IMF. However, the Japanese government decided to support Malaysia within the framework of the New Miyazawa Initiative, holding the view that the Malaysian policy of capital controls was justified in the situation in which Malaysia had been put (Doi 1999: 27). Various measures were employed under the New Miyazawa Initiative including not only the traditional direct official financial assistance, such as yen loans through the Export-Import Bank of Japan, but also indirect ways to support East Asian countries in raising funds from international financial markets, such as the provision of guarantees. Further-more, Japan later established 'a fund' within the ADB, called the Asian Currency Crisis Support Facility (ACCSF), as part of the New Miyazawa Initiative.[51] This facility has the following three instruments: (1) interest payment assistance grants which are applied to interest payment for ADB loans or official or commercial co-financing of ADB-assisted projects; (2) technical assistance grants; and (3) guarantees to co-finance loans with the ADB and bond issues by the affected countries.

It should be noted that the New Miyazawa Initiative implicitly stated that Japan was still aiming at establishing a regional financial mechanism. Although the Initiative itself is a bilateral framework, not the multilateral fund that the AMF was supposed to be, it leaves open the possibility that it could develop into a multilateral framework in the region, like the AMF. Specifically, the MOF officials thought that the above-mentioned ACCSF could lead to a multilateral framework in the future. The New Miyazawa Initiative reads: The ACCSF will be an open facility in which all countries are welcome to take part. Shuhei Kishimoto, the then Director of the Asian Currency Office in the MOF, who was involved in implementing the New Miyazawa Initiative, explained that Japan was considering that the ACCSF could move forward to a regional organisation, although at this stage Japan was the sole contributor (Kishimoto 1999: 42–3). For instance, he continued, it may be possible that some countries could establish the same sort of agreement with the ADB as Japan did, and those separate agreements could be reorganised into an independent regional fund, something like an East Asian regional guarantee institution, which would help East Asian countries issue bonds by giving guarantees (Kishimoto 1999: 43). The New Miyazawa Initiative also reads: it is hoped that in the long run the establishment of an international guarantee institution with a prime focus on Asian countries will be seriously considered. This confirms that Japan's motive behind the New Miyazawa Initiative involved the creation of some kind of regional framework. Notably, Kishimoto further maintains that this East Asian guarantee institution should develop into the AMF in the future (Kishimoto 1999: 43).

The New Miyazawa Initiative also indicates the change in the nature of Japanese foreign policy in the sense that Japan overtly broadcast its policies, rather than keeping a low profile, as it had done in the case of the AMF proposal. In fact, the announcement of the New Miyazawa Initiative was quite effective, and not only regional leaders, but also the public in the region, have become aware of the Japanese assistance to the region. A MOF official said that the Japanese government tried to publicise its assistance as much as possible through the local media, which had not been done before.[52] Furthermore, the Japanese bureaucrats were more positively and assertively involved in the implementation of the assistance given under the New Miyazawa Initiative than in the past. Japanese aid policy is generally based on a request from recipient governments (*yosei shugi*). Orr argues that as 'the aid program was initiated in Southeast Asia, the *yosei shugi* approach was undertaken to allay fears of the recipients of an incipient reemergence of Japanese imperial policy' (Orr 1990: 60). However, the Japanese officials were more actively engaged in the implementation of the New Miyazawa Initiative. Japan dispatched emergency missions to the five countries that were the beneficiaries of the Initiative from the end of October to the end of December, and they discussed with the recipient governments how to implement the economic reconstruction plans through the New Miyazawa Initiative (Doi 1999: 28). Also, after the programs began to be implemented from the middle of December, Japan remained involved in discussions with the recipients.

The New Miyazawa Initiative was largely welcomed and appreciated not only by the recipient countries, but also the US, which had opposed the AMF proposal a year before. The US support for the New Miyazawa Initiative was partly because the Initiative was a bilateral scheme, which in a sense could be regarded as an extension of past Japanese ODA policy. In addition to that, with the spread of the crisis beyond East Asia to Russia and further to Latin America, the claim of the US and the IMF that the economic and social systems peculiar to East Asia, such as crony capitalism, had caused the crisis was losing support. Furthermore, facing the need to cool down the instability in Latin America and to prevent the crisis from expanding further whatever the cost, the US policy seemed to shift from imposing structural reforms on the affected countries to stabilisation through strengthening public credit lines (Tadokoro 2000: 11). Japan also sounded out China about the New Miyazawa Initiative beforehand, as Japanese officials thought that China's understanding was important to the success of the proposal. In fact, Sakakibara was sent to Beijing in secret to explain Japan's proposal.[53]

In the process of drafting and implementing the New Miyazawa Initiative, not only the MOF, but also the MITI and the MOFA were heavily involved. A MOF official states that there were close exchanges of opinions and discussions with the MITI and the MOFA about making the proposal.[54] This means there were various motivations involved behind Japan's proposing the scheme.

First, the MOF and the MITI had to address pressing issues to do with the condition of the Japanese economy. As discussed earlier, due to the increasing economic interdependence between Japan and the East Asian countries, the instability of the regional economy was a considerable blow to Japan's already sluggish economy. Green points out that one driving force behind the New Miyazawa Initiative was the desperate situation of the Japanese banks, whose loans were tied up in long-term FDI that affected the Japanese trading, construction and auto companies that had large exposure to the stagnant Japanese economy (Green 2001: 254–5). Also, in the words of an official from the MOF, the New Miyazawa Initiative was one part of a broader set of measures to resolve the financial turmoil in Japan.[55]

Second, the New Miyazawa Initiative can be considered as a reflection of the growing importance of the political and diplomatic relations with regional countries, as already discussed. After giving up the proposal for the AMF and with the deepening of the regional economic problem, East Asian countries became sceptical about Japan's commitment to the region as well as its ability to take the lead there. This could have seriously undermined Japan's overall East Asian relations, which it had made such an effort to cement during the previous decades. The New Miyazawa Initiative was aimed to, and actually was able to, change this perception and maintain, or probably strengthen, Japan's influence in the region, which could, in turn, enable Japan to take more initiatives there. It could be argued that the size of the sum of itself, i.e. US$30 billion, showed Japan's large commitment to East Asia and its recovery, particularly given the situation that Japan had economic problems domestically, and that it had already committed US$43.5 billion before announcing the New Miyazawa Initiative.[56] Eventually, Japan's total assistance offered in response to the East Asian financial crisis reached approximately US$80 billion by March 1999.[57] This is an extraordinary contribution even when the size of the Japanese economy is taken into account. A MOFA official argues that Japanese foreign policy has been criticised sometimes as merely chequebook diplomacy but without this money countries could have collapsed, and that East Asian countries realised that no country or organisation, other than Japan, would pay such a large sum for regional matters.[58]

Third, the New Miyazawa Initiative can be seen as a reflection of Japan's discontent with IMF policies. The IMF was, in the view of Japanese officials, particularly MOF officials, too obsessed with market mechanisms and imposed on countries hasty, inappropriate, measures for structural reforms, which sacrificed economic stability and resulted in social disorder. After the strict economic restructuring plans were implemented in accordance with the IMF programs, the economies of the crisis-hit countries suffered from severe recession. The New Miyazawa Initiative was largely aimed at revitalising these economies and to help them get out of the severe economic downturn and resume healthy economic development by creating employment as well as expanding their social safety nets. A Japanese official argues that the New Miyazawa Initiative was significant for its feature of quick disbursement, and for trying to get some results straight away and to maintain employment during the process of economic restructuring.[59] It can be argued that what the Japanese officials believed to be necessary was to give these countries time to take a breath and regain market confidence. In this context, the New Miyazawa Initiative can be regarded as Japan's tacit criticism against the IMF policies.

Conclusion

This chapter has discussed how Japan was positively engaged in resolving the East Asian financial crisis. Japan's contribution to organising the Thai rescue package involved a great deal of diplomatic effort, as well as contributing funds, and the subsequent proposal of the AMF was, despite the fact it was not realised then, an ambitious attempt to create a new regional framework aimed at financial stability in the region. Also, Japanese policymakers were positively and assertively involved in proposing and implementing the New Miyazawa Initiative, which represents a departure from the traditional aid policy-making. Furthermore, Japanese policymakers became able to articulate Japan's stance overtly and to criticise IMF policy towards the crisis publicly, although on the whole Japan tried to cooperate with the IMF and the US. These proactive policies of Japan have continued and have contributed to the current momentum in financial regionalism, which is one of the main subjects of the next chapter. Furthermore, this chapter also highlighted the specific policy style characteristic to Japan, namely its low-profile and incremental style of policy, as it tried to establish a financial framework in the region by taking into account the long-term perspective. It has been argued that the AMF proposal was not necessarily a failure from the viewpoint of Japanese policymakers, nor was the Manila Framework merely a face-saving effort. Moreover, the New Miyazawa Initiative has the potential to lead to a regional framework, possibly the AMF. These points are also relevant for the discussions on the style of Japanese foreign policy in Chapter 6.

5 Japanese policy towards East Asian regionalism

The previous chapter documented Japan's interest in financial regionalism in East Asia. This chapter expands the subject from the financial area to East Asian regionalism in general, as the last case study of the book. The chapter analyses how East Asian regionalism has developed since the late 1990s, how and to what degree Japan has contributed to that process, where Japan's interest in the new East Asian framework lies and what that means to its foreign policy as a whole. Building on the argument developed in the previous chapters, this chapter demonstrates Japan's increasing initiative in the region, along with its growing interest in East Asia. Also, the way in which Japan has contributed to the development of East Asian regionalism has great significance for the discussion about the style of Japanese foreign policy in the next chapter.

As discussed in Chapter 2, for the last few decades, specifically since the early 1990s, there have been two contesting conceptions of the Asian region, namely Asia Pacific and East Asia. The former was predominant until the mid-1990s, while the latter, specifically the idea of the EAEC, whose identity is constructed around the opposition between Asia and the West, has shown remarkable resilience in the face of strong US opposition in the early 1990s. Regions are cognitively constructed, and the concept of East Asia, which, Higgott and Stubbs (1995: 530) opined, 'is an exercise in invention, seen by leaders, who advance such notions, as a way of stemming the intrusion of Western cultural and moral values systems without rejecting the dynamic aspects of Western economic and technological modernization', has had consistent appeal. In fact, since the latter half of the 1990s, there has been a shift of emphasis from Asia Pacific, or APEC, to East Asia, or EAEC, although the former has never been completely dismantled.

The recent development of East Asian regionalism is indeed striking, considering that until recently the East Asian region was regarded as a market-driven, as opposed to state-led, economic integration, or regionalisation. A formal framework in East Asia was regarded as unrealistic largely due to the US's strong opposition and the lack of regional leadership, as shown in the failure of the EAEC proposal in the early 1990s. In particular, Japan, the region's economic power, did not look ready to lead the potential region, while its initiative would not be eagerly accepted by neighbouring countries mainly as a result of its colonialism in the past. Given such a condition in the region, the current development in East Asia makes us wonder what has prompted the shift in the region's political economy.

This chapter's focus on Japan's role and motivation on this matter is justified because its policies have had a great deal of impact on the political economy of East Asia due to its economic dominance in the region. Without Japan's positive participation, East Asian regionalism would be less viable and much less significant, if not completely impossible. Thus, carefully examining Japan's role and interest is vital in analysing the political economy surrounding the new East Asian cooperation and integral to understanding what is happening in East Asia.

Furthermore, the investigation into the sources of Japan's interest in the new regional framework has important implications for the study on Japanese foreign policy as a whole. There are various economic and political reasons behind Japan's growing interest in East Asia, which reveals that the shift in Japan's policy towards regional cooperation represents fundamental changes in its foreign policy, arising from the transformation of its diplomatic situation in the last decade. Specifically, the considerable changes in the world political economy, largely brought about by the end of the Cold War and the forces of globalisation, have been pushing Japan to move out of its old postwar framework, epitomised by the Yoshida Doctrine. What this means is that East Asian regionalism is not just a buzzword among Japanese policymakers, and that Japan's interest in East Asia is based on substantial changes in their beliefs and way of thinking with respect to the way national interests are pursued.

The chapter certainly does not intend to argue that Japan has a single-minded trajectory uniquely towards East Asian regionalism. As stressed before, the bilateral relationship with the US has been, and still is, the core of Japanese foreign policy. Also, Japan has continuously put great emphasis on other multilateral frameworks, both international and regional. In fact, its positive support for the East Asian framework does not mean a decision to disregard APEC, or to exclude the US or the Oceanian countries from East Asia. On the contrary, Japan wants to keep those countries in the region as much as possible. It is noteworthy that when Prime Minister Junichiro Koizumi, in his Singapore speech in January 2002, proposed a 'community' that acts together and advances together, making the best use of the framework of ASEAN + 3, he included Australia and New Zealand as core members of the community. This book stresses that what Japanese policymakers are trying to do is to establish a new framework to complement the traditional ones in East Asia, and to have multiple options, so that they can pursue Japan's political and economic interests in the post Cold War era.

The initial development of the ASEAN + 3 meeting and background forces behind the new trend in East Asia

East Asian regionalism has developed out of ASEAN's invitation to three Northeast Asian countries, China, Japan and South Korea, to attend its informal and formal meetings. The first meeting of what is now called 'ASEAN + 3' was held in December 1997 in Kuala Lumpur. It was actually a meeting of the same countries that constitute the EAEC, and the leaders of these countries had already met in February 1996 for the first time as part of the ASEM process.[1] Despite the symbolic meaning of the ASEAN + 3 framework, the meeting in Kuala Lumpur did not attract much attention from the press or the public. Even the US, who had been a strong opponent of the EAEC, did not interfere. Instead, there was actually an atmosphere of gloom and tension, as the meeting took place in the midst of the financial crisis.

Whilst holding the meeting of the East Asian leaders in itself was highly significant, there was little substance in the first ASEAN + 3 meeting. It was reported that issues concerning the currency crisis occupied most of the agenda.[2] Although the joint statements of the meetings between ASEAN and each of the three additional countries, China, Japan and South Korea, were publicised, that of the ASEAN + 3 meeting itself was not announced. Also, the leaders did not agree at that stage that this sort of meeting would be held on a regular basis, although the summit meeting later evolved into the current trend of regional cooperation in East Asia, as discussed below.

The initial impetus for the Kuala Lumpur meeting can be traced back to the beginning of 1997, to the visit of the then Japanese Prime Minister Ryutaro Hashimoto to ASEAN countries, when Japan proposed holding regular talks between the Japanese and the ASEAN leaders. This visit to ASEAN had particular significance for Japan, as Hashimoto was aiming at a diplomatic breakthrough during the trip, and revealed during his speech on the visit the 'Hashimoto Doctrine' that would replace the Fukuda Doctrine as the basis of Japanese policy towards ASEAN. Hashimoto emphasised the importance of ASEAN in Japanese foreign policy and the necessity of 'broader and deeper exchanges between Japan and ASEAN at the top and on all the other levels.' The proposal to hold regular meetings between Japan and ASEAN was the focal point of his speech. However, the response of ASEAN countries to this proposal was not enthusiastic. Indonesian President Suharto was reportedly positive, but the Malaysian Prime Minister did not give a definite answer to Hashimoto.[3] Instead of giving Japan a direct answer, ASEAN announced at the end of May 1997 that it would invite the leaders of three countries, China, Japan and South Korea, to its informal summit scheduled in December 1997. The three countries accepted the invitation, and the meeting was held as planned.

What has to be noticed here is the fact that, although the current enthusiasm for East Asian cooperation is seen to have grown out of the financial crisis in 1997, the first meeting of the ASEAN + 3 countries, which became a stepping stone for the recent trend in East Asia, was set up before the crisis occurred. What this implies is that, while the crisis has been a driving force in the development of East Asian regionalism as discussed later, regionalism in East Asia has been developing in a larger context.

It is noteworthy that the concept of East Asia has been nurtured throughout the 1990s through the gradual process of increasing interaction of East Asian officials on various occasions, which is probably a crucial element of East Asian regionalism to be developed. Specifically, ASEAN members continued to discuss the need for an East Asian framework at a number of summit and ministerial meetings, and this greatly helped the East Asian concept become increasingly acceptable to them (Terada 2003: 251–77). ASEAN also tried to have unofficial dialogues on EAEC with the three northern countries, China, Japan and South Korea. Meetings were held between the ASEAN Secretary-General and officials of those respective countries in November 1993 (Leong 2000: 61), and then, ASEAN invited the foreign ministers of the three countries to an informal luncheon meeting during the ASEAN Ministerial Meeting (AMM) in July 1994, which was followed by the same meetings during AMMs in 1995 and 1996. Also, as mentioned before, their leaders met unofficially in February 1996 for the first time as part of the ASEM process. Takashi Terada points out, the increasing awareness of the East Asian concept and a shared new identity (which have both been gradually developed by the above interaction among regional countries) are the preconditions of the current development in East Asia (Terada 2003: 251–77). It can be argued that the proposal for the formation of the EAEC, which did not receive an enthusiastic response when Prime Minister Mahathir of Malaysia introduced it in December 1990, was not in fact abandoned completely. Indeed, the idea has gradually become more acceptable to the countries of East Asia.

One of the forces behind the growing interest in East Asia among the regional countries has been the increasing economic interdependence in the region, which has made regional countries more aware of each other's importance. The economic regionalisation, which has been progressing since the 1980s, has made regional leaders think about the necessity of cooperating with each other for stability and further economic prosperity. Ohba argues that the emergence of East Asian regionalism in the form of ASEAN +3 was based on the confidence of the East Asian countries backed by the economic boom in East Asia as well as the increasing interdependence of their economies (Ohba 2001: 276). As discussed later, the crisis has strengthened the sense of closeness of the economies in East Asia.

In addition, the region's increasing interest in East Asian cooperation is, to a great extent, a reaction to stagnation in APEC. The formation of APEC as a government-level economic forum in 1989 was a landmark event in the region, and it had a momentum in the 1990s particularly during the term of the Clinton administration. However, it seems that the impetus for APEC has been declining since the late 1990s, which even Japanese senior officials in the MOFA and the Ministry of Economy, Trade and Industry (METI, the name changed from MITI) admit.[4]

There are various reasons for this stagnation. As APEC has developed, the various discords among member countries have increased, particularly with regard to the speed and extent of the institutionalisation of APEC as well as the imposition by the US of its liberal economic norms and social standards. Some East Asian countries were concerned about the US dominance of APEC, which has made them resist Washington's agendas. Ellis Krauss argues that, as APEC rests on several different interests of its major players and is pulled in different directions simultaneously, if it goes primarily in just one of these directions, it will lose the interest and cooperation of the other players.[5] Also, several MOFA officials note that it has become difficult to discuss a complicated issue and reach an agreement in APEC due to the increasing number of member countries (21 countries as of February 2005) particularly after the inclusion of the Latin American countries and Russia.[6] In addition, some argue that now that the WTO deals with the global rules of trade between nations, the

APEC way of advancing liberalisation voluntarily has become outdated (Kimura 2000, Ohba 2001: 278–9). It could be argued that all these factors have contributed to a loss of impetus in APEC, if not its virtual disintegration, and have motivated East Asian policymakers to turn to alternative options.

Japan's participation in the first ASEAN + 3 meeting, and its growing enthusiasm for East Asian regionalism, are relevant for the change of course in Japanese foreign policy explored in this book. In addition to the above factors underlying recent East Asian regionalism, Japan's increasing interest in East Asian cooperation stems to a great extent from the increasing importance that East Asian relations occupy in Japanese foreign policy. This, in turn, has been brought about by dramatic changes in the international and regional orders, as previous chapters discussed. In particular, the new diplomatic situation after the Cold War has made Japanese policymakers think that Japan has to demonstrate its ability and willingness to take more initiative beyond chequebook diplomacy and has to be more involved politically in the architecture of a new world order. This has greatly contributed to Japan's turn towards the region and consequently greater regional cooperation, as East Asia is naturally the place where Japan's political initiatives are more likely to be directed for historical, geographical and economic reasons. It can be argued that Japan is eager to consolidate the regional basis and create a new regional order that allows it to establish its influence there and play a greater political role.

In addition, Japan's positive stance on East Asian regionalism is, in part, related to the strong belief of a wide range of Japanese policymakers that East Asia should have a self-help mechanism as an alternative option to ensure the stability and prosperity of the region and that of Japan. The end of the Cold War has prompted Japan's interest in East Asian regionalism in the sense that it has made Japanese policymakers think that East Asia has to reinforce its own frameworks, or initiate a self-help mechanism, to prepare for a possible US withdrawal from the region in the long term. The disappearance of the Cold War order has made it likely that the US forces will have to withdraw from East Asia to a certain extent if not in the immediate future, and this will be accompanied by the reduction of its political presence. This is not what Japanese policymakers wish, nor are they trying to exclude the US from the region. However, in the long-term the US cannot be expected to maintain the same policy towards East Asia as it did during the Cold War, a situation which Japanese and East Asian officials have to accept. The following comment of a senior MOF official confirms that high-ranked Japanese officials particularly in the MOF, the MOFA and the METI have shared the view that East Asia has to prepare for this eventuality:

It is inevitable that the American commitment to Asia will decrease in the future in terms of both security and economic issues, considering the change in the international system resulting mainly from the end of the Cold War. Therefore, Asia has to prepare for the US's gradual withdrawal from the region by starting to work for a regional framework, and this sort of consideration seems to be shared by a quite large number of high-ranked officials across key ministries.[7]

This fresh understanding of Japanese policymakers motivates them to promote Japan's greater political and security commitment to regional affairs so as to compensate for the possible decline in the US presence. In other words, the changing international situation after the Cold War has forced Japanese policymakers to cultivate new regional relations in order to expand its policy channels so that Japan can offset the importance of the US and enhance its political influence without damaging US relations. Saori Katada, focusing on the financial area, argues that Japan is trying to counterweigh US influence by resorting to regional institutions while at the same time collaborating with the US (Katada 2004: 176–97). This orientation seems to be a more general feature, beyond the financial field, of Japanese foreign policy at present.

Considering the above background behind Japan's interest in East Asian cooperation, the change of its stance from the ambiguous attitude towards the EAEC proposal to the positive participation in the ASEAN + 3 framework may not be a huge surprise. When Japan was sounded out about joining the ASEAN's informal summit, it would have been difficult for Japan to decline the invitation from ASEAN without causing offence, which Japanese policymakers wanted to avoid at any cost. As mentioned before, Hashimoto's visit to ASEAN was more than merely a diplomatic visit, and the invitation from ASEAN to its informal summit in December was in a sense a response to Hashimoto's proposal during the visit. Also, ASEAN announced that it would have meetings with China, Japan and South Korea individually (and separately from the meeting of the ASEAN + 3 countries) thus responding to Hashimoto's request.[8] A MOFA official stated that Japan did not have any hesitation in attending the meeting, and it accepted ASEAN's proposal in May immediately.[9]

Furthermore, other conditions were also favourable to Japan's participation in the meeting. For one thing, as argued before, the concept of East Asia or EAEC has come to be more acceptable for the prospective members, and it does not sound as foreign to them as before and therefore the conditions are easier for Japan to more readily support the new framework. When the Malaysian Prime Minister proposed the EAEC, Japan was cautious about the attitude of other regional countries, who were not necessarily positive about the idea. However, this time there was a consensus within ASEAN, as the invitation to the commemorative Kuala Lumpur summit that would mark its thirtieth anniversary came from ASEAN as a group. It can be argued that the growing consensus held by regional leaders and officials about the usefulness of their own regional framework has created more favourable conditions for Japanese policymakers to promote the idea. In addition, as a diplomatic signal to other countries, the meeting was less problematic than convening a conference for setting up the EAEC or having an East Asian summit. The three northern countries were invited to what could be presented as a regular ASEAN summit, and thus could avoid possible conflict with non-Asian countries, particularly the US.

The second meeting of ASEAN + 3 in December 1998

Although the leaders of the ASEAN + 3 countries did not promise during the first meeting to meet on a regular basis or to have a second meeting in the next year, the leaders of the same countries got together in December 1998 in Hanoi. This time the meeting was more fruitful and showed that there was a growing tendency towards closer economic cooperation among the participating nations. The economic issue was again the main focus of the meeting, as East Asian countries were still struggling with the after-effects of the crisis, but it is noteworthy that ASEAN clearly demonstrated its interest in closer cooperation with the three northern countries, and proposed to hold an ASEAN + 3 summit once a year. Also, responding to South Korea's proposal, the East Asian Vision Group was initiated to discuss the long-term possibility of East Asian cooperation in a wide range of fields, including political, economic, social and cultural, among academics of the ASEAN + 3 nations.[10]

As for Japan, the then Prime Minister Keizo Obuchi gave an important policy speech in Hanoi before the summit titled 'Towards the Creation of a Bright Future for Asia'. It is particularly noteworthy that he stated in his speech that this summit meeting among the ASEAN + 3 countries was aimed at realising 'region-wide cooperation in East Asia'. This was indeed the first speech in which the Japanese leaders referred to East Asian, as opposed to Asia Pacific, cooperation on an official occasion, and can be regarded as Japan's endorsement of the growing trend of East Asian regionalism. Obuchi also argued that in order to uphold this objective the network of dialogue among the three countries of China, Japan and South Korea must be strengthened as well.

Furthermore, China proposed to hold a regular forum of the Finance Deputies of the ASEAN + 3 countries to exchange opinions about financial issues. It is important to note the change in China's stance towards regionalism. Ruan Wei points out that, although China had been reluctant to form alliances with other countries since it fell out with the former Soviet Union in the 1960s, 1997 marked a turning point in its policy, and it is now engaged in forming regional frameworks (Wei 2002). She identifies several factors behind China's inclination towards regionalism. First, having witnessed the chain reaction of the East Asian financial crisis, China now understands that a stable external environment is indispensable for its economic growth. Second, it recognises that most major countries are participating in free trade agreements. Third, it acknowledges that the stability and advancement of the ASEAN economy would lead to increased Chinese exports to the region. Fourth, it hopes to dispel the anxiety of its neighbours about the competitive pressures created by the Chinese economy by promoting regionalism and encouraging other participants to jointly reap the benefits of trade and cooperation. Finally, it is hopeful that forming a regional framework with ASEAN would pre-empt any US attempts to besiege China (Wei 2002).

ASEAN was positive about China's idea of holding a forum for Finance Deputies, and its response was very quick. ASEAN soon invited the Deputies of the three northern countries to a meeting with its ASEAN counterparts in March

1999, which was followed by the first Finance Ministers' meeting among these members in April of the same year. These meetings of Finance Ministers and Deputies were a significant step towards further cooperation in East Asia. A Finance Ministers' meeting was held again in the subsequent year, when there was important progress in terms of East Asian financial regionalism, as discussed later, although there was little substance in the first 1999 meeting itself.

The mission for the revitalisation of the Asian economy (the Okuda mission)

In June 1999, two years after the currency crisis had begun, and East Asian countries were starting to show signs of recovery, Prime Minister Obuchi announced that in August he was going to dispatch a mission, called the Mission for the Revitalisation of the Asian Economy (the Okuda Mission), to six East Asian countries (South Korea, Vietnam, Thailand, Malaysia, Indonesia and the Philippines). The mission consisted of eight members, including business leaders from Japanese leading companies and influential academics, with Hiroshi Okuda, the then Chairman of the Board of Toyota Motor Corporation and the then Chairman of the Japan Federation of Employers' Association (*Nikkeiren*) as the head of the mission. The aim of the mission was to study the issues and needs facing East Asian countries and to identify, in the light of the crisis, the issues that East Asia must address to safeguard its prosperity in the twenty-first century and the role that Japan has to play in addition to the assessment of Japan's assistance to the countries hit by the crisis.

It is worth discussing the contents of the report of the mission briefly because it was dispatched at the direct request of the Prime Minister, and its recommendations were taken into account in later regional policymaking, although it was not an official statement of the Japanese government. In fact, some of the recommendations took shape as concrete policies, such as the Chiang Mai Initiative. Also, a large part of this report is directly reflected in the Obuchi plan that was announced during the third ASEAN + 3 summit in November 1999, and was highly appreciated by ASEAN countries, as we will discuss later.

In addition, it could be argued that the emphasis on East Asia and East Asian cooperation in the report indicates that the concept of East Asian cooperation had become more broadly accepted within Japan. The members of the mission not only included influential private people and academics, but also a number of high-ranking officials of the four prestigious ministries of the MOFA, the MITI, the EPA and the MOF as observers. The report was the result of their intensive discussions based on almost 200 interviews with East Asian leaders, high officials and business leaders.

First of all, the report clearly states the necessity to build a new relationship with East Asian countries. It argues that, although the currency crisis was an unfortunate event, it clearly showed where reforms were needed. Also the report states that the fact that the crisis hit many East Asian countries almost simultaneously indicates that East Asian countries are developing into a community; they are no longer just a collection of individual countries. More significantly, the report reads that the formation of regional economies that has taken place in Europe and North / South America needs to take place in East Asia as well, although the form may be different. Furthermore, it suggests, in making a regional effort to address past failures, which caused the crisis in 1997, Japan's larger role will bring substantial benefits to Japan as well as East Asian countries.

Subsequently, the report makes specific recommendations in the areas of people, goods, money and information. With respect to people, it emphasises three points: (1) the cooperation for human resources development in East Asia; (2) the opening of Japan to the East Asian people; and (3) assistance for the socially vulnerable. As far as goods are concerned, the report addresses the issue of what is necessary for the development of manufacturing in the region as well as what roles Japan can take on, including the importance of opening Japanese markets. Furthermore, it is noteworthy that the report supports the idea of regional free trade agreements, arguing that such an agreement is one way to strengthen and deepen economic relations between Japan and the East Asian countries, particularly South Korea and ASEAN. It suggests that the talks for a bilateral free trade agreement with South Korea can be supplemented by studies of similar agreements with Singapore and other countries that are enthusiastic about the idea. In the field of money, the report suggests that five issues should be addressed: (1) the stabilisation of East Asian currencies; (2) the internationalisation of the yen; (3) the development of East Asian bond markets; (4) the establishment of early warning systems to prevent currency crises in the future; and (5) the standardisation of corporate accounting according to an international criteria. The report holds that appropriate foreign exchange regimes and concrete schemes for emergency regional financing should be discussed at regional forums such as the ASEAN + 3 meeting. It is noticeable that this point was taken up in Japan's initiative in the Chiang Mai Initiative (Kishimoto 2000). Finally, regarding information, the report made various recommendations including the enhancement of information networks in East Asia.

The third meeting of ASEAN + 3 in November 1999

The third summit in November 1999 made great strides towards further East Asian regionalism. A joint statement on East Asian cooperation was announced by the participating nations for the first time, and the heads of the countries pledged further deepening and broadening of cooperation. They stressed the importance of co-operation particularly in the following eight areas: (1) economic cooperation, including trade, investment and technology transfer; (2) monetary and financial cooperation; (3) social and human resources development; (4) scientific and technical development; (5) culture and information; (6) development cooperation; (7) politics and security; and (8) transnational issues. It is noteworthy that they agreed to expand cooperation to the political and security fields and beyond economic issues. In order to achieve cooperation in these areas, the leaders instructed the relevant ministers to oversee the implementation of the joint statement through existing mechanisms. Japan also proposed to hold an ASEAN + 3 foreign ministers meeting, and the joint statement included a commitment to this. In addition, a meeting of the leaders of China, Japan and South Korea (separately from the ASEAN + 3 meeting) was held for the first time in history during the session.[11]

It should be noted that a further shift in Japan's stance concerning regional cooperation was observed during the year between the second and third meetings. This is reflected in the MOFA's account of Japan's objectives at the ASEAN + 3 summit.[12] With respect to the second meeting in 1998, the MOFA stressed the importance of the meeting for strengthening the dialogues between Japan and ASEAN. However, the Ministry evaluated the 1999 meeting, which it called a virtual 'East Asia Summit', as a valuable opportunity for the Japanese Prime Minister to build up relations with his counterparts in East Asian countries, who were important economic as well as political partners for Japan. In addition, the MOFA declared that Japan had the intention to play a positive role to advance East Asian cooperation in accordance with the Joint Statement, and that Japan attached great importance to the ASEAN + 3 summit as a meeting designed to enhance a sense of solidarity among East Asian countries and to advance regional cooperation. In short, the MOFA's interest in East Asian cooperation became much more explicit at the 1999 summit than in the previous year.

This shift in the MOFA's stance on regional cooperation can also be observed in the Blue Book, which is Japan's official account of its foreign policy by the MOFA. While the 1999 Blue Book, which deals with policies implemented in 1998, does not even refer to East Asian cooperation or the ASEAN + 3 summit at all, there is an independent section titled 'Japan-ASEAN relations and regional cooperation in East Asia' in the 2000 Blue Book. The 2000 Blue Book acknowledges that by taking into account lessons learnt from the crisis, a trend to strengthen regional cooperation in East Asia has grown among the countries concerned, and it recognises that it is important to implement the policies proposed in the Joint Statement of the 1999 ASEAN + 3 summit. These changes in the stance of the MOFA are indeed surprising, considering its indecisive attitude towards the EAEC in the early 1990s.

In addition to its increasing interest in East Asian cooperation, Japan has come to show its willingness to take on a larger role beyond economic assistance. During the ASEAN + 3 summit in 1999, Prime Minister Obuchi announced 'a comprehensive plan for enhancing human resources development and human resources exchanges in East Asia', which President Estrada of the Philippines, the host of the meeting, suggested calling the Obuchi Plan. The plan was based on the report of the Okuda Mission. Obuchi explained that, given that the East Asian economies had largely overcome the crisis and were on track for recovery, the plan focused on people for the purpose of working together to prevent the reoccurrence of a future crisis and to build a foundation for medium to long-term stable economic development. In addition, Obuchi said that Japan was willing to advance the dialogue between Japan and ASEAN, which was one of the major economic and political partners for Japan. He stressed that Japan was prepared to enhance and expand its assistance to ASEAN in order to redress the economic disparities within ASEAN and enhance its organisational capacity. In this way, Japan committed itself to the region by expressing publicly what it intended to do for it in the future, as the crisis was abating.

The Chiang Mai Initiative

In response to the joint statement on East Asian cooperation issued in November 1999, there was a further move to advance cooperation in the financial area. The third Finance Deputies' meeting of the ASEAN + 3 countries was held in March 2000, when they agreed to consider a more concrete framework for financial co-operation to prepare for any possible future financial crisis.[13] While thinking that a new permanent fund would be a remote possibility, they looked at expanding the existing currency swap arrangements in the immediate future. These arrangements had been set up among the five ASEAN founding countries of Indonesia, Malaysia, the Philippines, Singapore and Thailand (totalling about US$200 million), but had the potential to include China, Japan, South Korea and the other ASEAN countries and this extension was agreed.[14] Subsequently the ASEAN Finance Ministers' meeting endorsed this decision of the ASEAN + 3 Deputies. The ASEAN Ministers also backed the Deputies' decision to examine a possible mechanism to facilitate regional surveillance in East Asia.

On 6 May, the ASEAN + 3 Finance Ministers announced the Joint Ministerial Statement after their second meeting in Chiang Mai. They backed the decision of their Deputies, and endorsed efforts to strengthen East Asian financial cooperation. The statement reads: we agreed to strengthen our policy dialogues and regional cooperation activities in, among others, the areas of capital flow monitoring, self-help and support mechanisms and international financial reforms. With respect to self-help and support mechanisms, they formally proposed region-wide swap arrangements, which were dubbed the Chiang Mai Initiative, to supplement the existing international facilities. This fell short of the establishment of a fund which Japan had originally targeted as a goal in 1997. Its main limitations are that it is a bilateral framework, as against the multilateralism of the AMF, and it cannot be put into effect automatically during a crisis; to be activated negotiations have to take place between a recipient and a supplier nation. Also, it is not large enough as an emergency regional financial mechanism. Nevertheless, it can be argued that the swap arrangements were indeed a significant step forward for financial cooperation in East Asia. The *Financial Times* writes: '[the agreement on the swap arrangements] has advanced regional co-operation well beyond pre-crisis levels. It cements growing and valuable links between east and south-east Asia'.[15] Also, the ASEAN + 3 Finance Ministers decided to meet each other twice a year on a regular basis, which could raise the expectation of further cooperation in East Asia.

Japan took the initiative behind the scenes, conducting negotiations with the countries concerned very cautiously in order to avoid falling in the same trap as they had done with the AMF. In particular, the MOF took great pains not to give the US grounds for suspicion that Japan was trying to exclude the US from East Asian matters.[16] The Japanese Finance Minister emphasised at the press conference just after the ASEAN + 3 Finance Ministers Meeting that the initiative was not linked to the AMF, a gesture that can be regarded as an attempt to circumvent US concern about Japan's intentions. Also, Japan conducted a number of negotiations with the regional countries at the deputy, as well as lower, levels, prior to the announcement of the Chiang Mai Initiative.[17] The ASEAN countries and Korea backed Japan's proposal overall. China also showed a very positive attitude this time, quite different from its stance on the Japanese AMF proposal in 1997. Some finance officials comment that the success of the Chiang Mai Initiative was largely due to the change of China's stance.[18] Wei notes that China is coming to accept that Japan has to play a certain role in the region, as it now believes that, without the participation of Japan, no regional economic organisation can be complete, given Japan's economic power (Wei 2002). Furthermore, Japan persuaded the member countries to agree that a recipient country can receive only 10 per cent of the limit through the swap arrangements without linkage to the IMF loans: a compromise to reconcile both sides, namely ASEAN nations, with Malaysia in particular, insisting on no linkage to IMF loans, and China and South Korea, potential donors, favouring closer linkage to IMF programs to minimise the risk that funds lent are not repaid (Amyx 2004: 212–16).[19]

It is particularly important to note that the MOF's interest in pushing the regional swap arrangements demonstrates that the ministry is still aiming to establish a regional fund, more specifically the AMF. In other words, some key officials are still driven by their initial vision of establishing the AMF, albeit in the very long term; they believe that such swap arrangements could be a step towards this goal. A senior finance official, who had been a central figure in the MOF's effort to advance regional swap arrangements, commented that he and other MOF officials wanted to enhance regional surveillance by encouraging regional policy discussion. According to him, it is very difficult to establish a surveillance system (even the IMF does not have a perfect one), but he insists that having an effective surveillance system is essential to realising the AMF in the long term.[20] Another official states that by advancing the Chiang Mai Initiative, Japan wanted to maintain the momentum of regional financial cooperation, which had grown since the crisis occurred.[21] The then Vice Finance Minister Kuroda, who suggested that the AMF is Japan's medium-term, not long-term, agenda, is reported to have said at a meeting with Malaysian Prime Minister Mahathir that he would not give up the AMF. He opined that the shortest way towards the AMF is to expand the swap arrangements and to establish a surveillance system.[22] In short, although MOF officials think that it is difficult to push the AMF at this stage and that the Chiang Mai Initiative may not necessarily lead to the AMF directly, it can at least keep alive, and even advance, the discussion on financial cooperation among East Asian countries. Also, if such a mechanism begins to work well and encourages regional surveillance, it will lead to closer financial relations among East Asian countries, which can create a more favourable environment for the AMF. An official states that the MOF has been continuously considering a multilateral framework since the crisis, as it would be more effective than bilateral agreements in terms of the impact on markets.[23]

Additionally, behind the MOF's initiative concerning the East Asian swap arrangements, there is increasing support in East Asia for closer regional financial cooperation, and the AMF in particular. Shuhei Kishimoto, one of the main figures to implement the New Miyazawa Initiative, writes that after the abandonment of the AMF in 1997 East Asian countries continued to tell Japan they hoped to establish a framework for regional financial cooperation, although the support for the AMF varies from country to country (Kishimoto 2001: 304). The then Malaysian Prime Minister Mahathir consistently supported the AMF, while his Deputy suggested, at a symposium on ASEAN–Japan relations in Tokyo in September 2000, that the Chiang Mai Initiative would not be sufficient to meet the challenges ahead, and that it could and should be expanded to become part and parcel of the AMF.[24] It was reported that, at the conference the 'Future of Asia' in June 2000,[25] there were discussions about the AMF.[26] For instance, the Secretary of Foreign Affairs of the Philippines stressed that the country was supporting the East Asian Swap Arrangements, the AMF and the internationalisation of the yen, while Lee Kuan Yew, the Senior Minister of Singapore, commented that, although he was not against the AMF, it had to be subsidiary to the IMF, as it is not possible to ignore the way the world is structured. He also said that bitter medicine has to be administered from outside. Also, the ASEAN–Japan Consultation Conference[27] recommended in October 2000 on a private level that ASEAN and Japan should study the establishment of the AMF that is consistent with global governance.[28]

South Korea, who originally supported the AMF in 1997, had kept silent about the idea, but seemingly have begun to be more positive. The then Prime Minister Kim Jong-pil surprised many when, during a meeting with the Japanese Prime Minister in November 1998, he proposed the creation of an Asian version of the IMF, the size of which would be around US$300 billion. The South Korean government failed to endorse the Premier's remark at that time, saying that it was not the government's official position. Nevertheless, in the following year he was again reported to be reiterating his call for the creation of the AMF.[29] Still there was little support from the country. However, it appears that the government was not entirely negative about the AMF. A senior finance ministry official said that regional countries would first need to establish bilateral guarantees, followed by a multilateral agreement, before the AMF could take root.[30] Also, an official even said that the launching of a monetary fund was critically important to Korea, as Korea's recovery from financial and economic woes was closely inter-linked with its East Asian trading partners.[31]

As discussed earlier, China's increasingly positive attitude towards East Asian cooperation is striking. Although China failed to support the AMF proposal in 1997, there have been more positive responses from China to the idea. Angang Hu, a politically influential Chinese scholar and a member of the Chinese Academy of Science, stated at the conference on the 'Future of Asia' (mentioned above) that the view that it was necessary to support the AMF was gaining ground in China. Also, the then Premier Zhu Rongji was reported as saying that he wanted to support an 'East Asian Monetary Fund' during the meeting with the Malaysian Prime Minister in November 1999.[32] In fact, with respect to the swap arrangements, China has shown quite a positive attitude. China was actively involved in drafting an outline of the swap arrangements together with Japan and South Korea. Indeed, during the ASEAN + 3 Finance Ministers meeting in September 2000 in Prague, the Chinese Minister repeatedly emphasised that the swap arrangements should be put in place as soon as possible.[33] Also, as discussed earlier, it was China who proposed to hold a Finance Deputies meeting among the ASEAN + 3 countries, which eventually led to the Chiang Mai Initiative. Yoichi Funabashi commented that without Japan and China sharing a similar, or the same, concept about the region, regionalism in East Asia was going to be difficult to develop.[34] In this sense, the change in China's stance is quite significant for the development of East Asian regionalism, and the AMF in particular.

The fourth meeting of ASEAN + 3 in November 2000

There was another step towards closer cooperation in East Asia before the turn of the century. The ASEAN + 3 leaders met in November 2000 for their fourth meeting, and agreed to set up an East Asian Study Group to consider two remarkable ideas, namely an East Asian summit and an East Asian free trade zone. The former idea, which was proposed by Malaysia, is an attempt to replace the present form of the ASEAN + 3 meeting, to which ASEAN invites the northern three countries, with a forum where each country attends as a member of East Asia although the forum consists of the same countries. Additionally, Thailand proposed the latter idea of an East Asian free trade zone. The leaders also agreed that, in addition to the trade area, the study group will investigate the possibility of creating a free investment area as well.

Despite the difficulties that these two ideas would face, it is noteworthy that the establishment of the study group that will work on these ideas was agreed on by the leaders and there was no particular opposition to it, contrasting with the negative reactions to the EAEC proposal in the early 1990s. As for ASEAN, Malaysia and Thailand were very positive about the two ideas, while Singapore was more guarded and stressed a gradual approach to them.[35]

As far as Japan's stance is concerned, the then Japanese Prime Minister Yoshio Mori suggested, after the meeting, that Japan would like to deepen the discussion about an East Asian summit with ASEAN,[36] although Japan seemed to be more cautious about a free trade area. The then Foreign Minister Yohei Kono said that the idea of a free trade area would not be easy and would need further investigation among regional officials as well as ministers.[37] South Korea, who had proposed more wide-ranging cooperation that included cultural issues, was reportedly supportive about both ideas. In fact, in early November, when the then Japanese MITI Minister visited South Korea, President Kim Dae-jung told the Minister that he thought East Asia needed a framework for regional cooperation that is equivalent to the EU and NAFTA.[38] Also, the president's aides were reported to be in favour of promoting his vision for transforming the ASEAN + 3 grouping into an economic community eventually.[39]

The Chinese officials at first refrained from articulating China's stance on the two ideas. It seems that China was a little bit embarrassed by the proposal about an East Asian free trade area, as it originally suggested the possibility of a free trade area among the ASEAN countries and China (not among East Asian countries) before the summit. However, China began to accept cooperation that includes Japan and Korea, although, at the same time, it continued to make an effort to form a free trade area with ASEAN. During the summit meeting, the Chinese Premier declared that China would advance cooperation with ASEAN together with Japan and South Korea, while China agreed that the leaders of the three Northeast Asian countries, China, Japan and South Korea, would meet regularly on the occasion of the ASEAN + 3 summits, despite previous opposition.

The stance of the US on East Asian regionalism

It must be noted that the current advancement of East Asian regionalism would have had difficulty in progressing without a change in the US stance. The US has not opposed the development of regionalism in East Asia, in contrast to its hostile attitude towards the EAEG in the early 1990s and the AMF in 1997. The US failed to respond to the Joint Statement of the ASEAN + 3 Summit in November 1999, while its attitude was surprisingly positive with respect to the proposal for the East Asian swap arrangements in May 2000. The then Treasury Secretary Lawrence Summers was reported as saying that he would give maximum support to the agreement.[40]

There appear to be a few reasons for this change in the US stance on East Asian cooperation. For one thing, although the US may not like these developments, it finds it difficult to find an appropriate way to respond to them. Its strong opposition to the AMF proposal in 1997 as well as its policy towards the East Asian financial crisis generated the negative reaction of East Asian countries. This has made the US more sensitive in its attitude towards the recent movement in East Asia. It may be argued that the US wants to avoid being seen to interfere with what East Asian countries are eager to advance. Also, the fact that even within the US there are criticisms against the government's opposition to the AMF has made the US more cautious about its position. Furthermore, Sakakibara considers that East Asian regionalism has not been seen as threatening to the US so far, for instance, the swap arrangements are linked to IMF policies almost completely.[41]

The crisis and the momentum of East Asian regionalism

It has been shown so far that the trend of East Asian regionalism in the late 1990s can be explained by a range of long-term factors. Also, Japan's various interests in supporting East Asian cooperation, and financial cooperation in particular, have been considered in this chapter and previously in Chapter 4. These arguments contradict the popular view that it was the East Asian financial crisis that triggered the development of regionalism in East Asia, and that Japan's interest in regional financial cooperation has stemmed solely from the crisis. Instead, it has been argued that such changes in East Asia and in Japanese policy should be considered in a longer-term and deeper context.

Nevertheless, the impact of the crisis on East Asian regionalism should not be overlooked. In fact the crisis in 1997 and 1998 accelerated this trend greatly.

A senior Japanese MOFA official, who was deeply involved in the process of East Asian cooperation, stated that the impact of the crisis on the East Asian economies, and in turn on their policies, was immense, far more than generally recognised. He also said that the event intensified the growing trend to strengthen East Asian cooperation for peace and prosperity in East Asia.[42] This section explores how the crisis has affected the trend of East Asian regionalism.

First of all, the crisis has not only made the regional countries realise more clearly their economic interdependence, but it has also given them a considerable shock. It revealed to them the fact that they could be vulnerable to the negative effects of globalisation, a process they had previously thought to be entirely beneficial to them. When the currency crisis happened in Thailand in July 1997, no one could expect that the crisis would spread to such a large part of the region so rapidly. This contagion of currency devaluations and the fall of stock markets were actually caused by the global movement of capital and speculation, but the economic interdependence of the countries involved, which had been developed by the regional networks of trade and investment, affected the views of these markets, and eventually allowed the currency crisis to lead to the region-wide economic crisis. In some countries, a lot of what they had achieved economically in the previous decades, and which had given pride and confidence not only to the policymaking elite but also to their people, was lost overnight. Also, the extent of the crisis affected China's stance on regionalism, and China came to recognise the significance of regional cooperation, as discussed earlier. This change in China's position is an essential factor if East Asian regionalism is to advance forward. Thus, it can be argued that ASEAN + 3 was, in a sense, developed out of the need to overcome the shock of the crisis. The East Asian countries came to be more aware of their economic interdependence and the necessity of some self-help measures to protect their economies against the forces of globalisation.

In addition, during the course of the crisis, the disappointment with the US stance on East Asia grew significantly, which reinforced the trend for East Asian regionalism. The East Asian countries began to feel that East Asia was really too distant for the US, and also that the US was less willing to engage in East Asian matters. The prompt US policy towards the crises in Russia and Latin America following the East Asian crisis presented a clear contrast to its reluctant involvement in the Thai crisis, when it failed to contribute, and its relations with the East Asian countries subsequently became awkward. Also, the US did not provide any actual money for bilateral assistance to the crisis-hit countries in East Asia, although it contrived to form a second line of defence in the rescue packages for Indonesia and South Korea and put its name on the list of contributors. A MOF official comments that there is no doubt that the crisis generated a sense that the affected countries had to help themselves, and that self-help was the only alternative, and this has contributed greatly to the region's interest in further financial cooperation.[43]

Meanwhile, the IMF policies towards the East Asian financial crisis, which demanded radical structural reforms and austerity policies, were not regarded as effective or convincing by East Asian countries. Instead, the IMF policies left a bitter taste in the mouth for the region and even resentment (Higgott 1998a). The IMF failed to prevent the crisis from spreading, and in Indonesia the financial crisis even led to a political crisis. In other countries, too, it took quite a long time to get their economies back on track. As indicated earlier, some have even discussed a conspiracy involving the US and the IMF. Also, Japan's dissatisfaction with the IMF in particular heightened as the crisis deepened, especially after the disagreement over the rescue package for Indonesia between the MOF and the IMF. Furthermore, as the crisis spread outside East Asia and the blame the US and the IMF had apportioned to the region's crony capitalism for causing the crisis was seen to be largely unfounded, East Asian countries began to criticise the present international financial system, which allowed global capitals and specifically hedge funds to destroy their financial systems. Considering these factors, there is no wonder that the East Asian countries became increasingly discontented with the Washington Consensus, which reinforced their belief that self-help was the only alternative.

Furthermore, the crisis has created a more favourable environment for Japan's larger role in the region. It was after all Japan who provided most of the necessary funds to address the crisis. The announcement of the New Miyazawa Initiative was effective and timely, and the regional countries deeply appreciated it. As mentioned before, Japan's total assistance during the East Asian financial crisis eventually amounted to US$80 billion. In addition, a senior METI official emphasised that, despite a decline in the number of new Japanese direct investments in East Asia after the East Asian financial crisis, Japanese firms that had already invested locally rarely withdrew, nor did they lay off their employees in large numbers, and this convinced the East Asian leaders and people that Japan was taking its commitments towards them seriously.[44] On the other hand, the crisis revealed the limitation of ASEAN to protect its economy by itself. This seems to make more countries and more policymakers in ASEAN favour the expansion of their framework of cooperation to the Northeast Asian countries as a strategy to restore its economic vigour and to have a larger voice in the world. Also, even South Korea, which has been historically suspicious of Japan's dominance in the region, has become very interested in a regional framework, largely due to its humiliating experience during the crisis and a growing sense of the vulnerability of its economy in the world. In short, an East Asian mechanism, in which it is essential for Japan to assume a major role, has become more acceptable in the region.

The crisis also increased the opportunities for policymakers in the region to work together. The Thai rescue package was the first significant event in which East Asian countries showed their commitment to resolve a regional issue together, feeling a sense of community. As the crisis spread to a large part of the region, the regional officials were deeply involved in various meetings throughout 1997 and 1998 in a search for ways to cope with the problems. For instance, there were various intensive discussions concerning the AMF in 1997 among regional policymakers. Japan sent some missions to East Asian countries, including the missions for implementing the New Miyazawa Initiative and later the Okuda Mission, to discuss with the countries involved how to reconstruct their economies and to determine how Japan could help them. Some new bodies for regional dialogue, such as the

Manila Framework and the ASEAN–Japan Finance Ministers as well as Finance Deputies meetings, obviously increased the opportunity for top-level interactions among East Asian countries. In order to deal with the increasing level of communication among East Asian officials, the Japanese MOF set up a new office named the Asian Currency Office (later the Regional Financial Cooperation Division) under the International Bureau of the Ministry in July 1998. An official working in the Office commented that the number of meetings related to the East Asian issues increased dramatically after the crisis, and there was always somebody from the Office on an official trip to some regional country.[45] It can be argued that these opportunities afforded by the crisis for the improved communication among East Asian countries has further expanded their collective activities in the region, and has led to further extensive efforts to build the East Asian networks of cooperation, particularly in the financial area. All of these activities have contributed to the recent momentum towards regionalism in East Asia.

It follows from what has been argued that the crisis has greatly contributed to the advancement of East Asian regionalism by forcing some significant changes in the mind-set of East Asian policymaking officials. The crisis gave East Asian countries a common lesson concerning the risks and defects of the global capital markets as well as the existing international economic system. They also learnt the necessity of self-help, particularly in the financial area. Furthermore, the crisis definitely increased communication among regional countries. Masayuki Tadokoro points out that the common bitter experiences and shared memories of working together to overcome the crisis among central bankers and financial officials in the region undoubtedly enhanced the sense that Asians are all in the same boat (Tadokoro 2000: 18). This awareness has been an essential element in advancing the recent development of regionalism in East Asia. Given all this, it is reasonable to argue that the current momentum of East Asian regionalism is not merely a short-lived fad. These changes in the mind-set of the East Asian policymakers may be significant enough to be characterised as cognitive learning as opposed to tactical learning,[46] although how East Asian regionalism will develop in the future remains to be seen.

Further development after the 2000 meeting

The ASEAN + 3 framework has been making a sure and steady progress since. In addition to the development in the financial area discussed above, it is noteworthy that the two remarkable ideas of East Asian summits and an East Asian free trade area have been moving forwards. The East Asian Study Group (established at the summit meeting in November 2000) submitted its final report to the same meeting in November 2002, when the leaders agreed on the report's claim that, in the long term, the ASEAN + 3 framework should evolve into East Asian summits and an East Asian free trade area. Notably, at the summit meeting in 2004 the member countries agreed to hold an East Asian summit in Malaysia in 2005. Also, the 2004 meeting endorsed the idea of setting up an expert group to conduct a feasibility study on an East Asian free trade area.

Although it still remains to be seen how the idea of an East Asian free trade area will develop in the future, it is noteworthy that a movement of bilateral and sub-regional Free Trade Agreements (FTAs) among East Asian countries has been gaining impetus since the late 1990s. Japan's initial interest in FTAs with Singapore as well as with South Korea triggered the interest of regional countries, particularly China, in bilateral and regional FTAs, which in turn facilitated Japan's FTA policies further. Also, ASEAN has come to actively engage in negotiations with external countries, and has been playing a pivotal role in FTAs in East Asia. These may become the building blocks for the establishment of a region-wide free trade area.

As touched on earlier, China has been particularly keen on cementing its ASEAN relations, and has eagerly pushed forward an FTA with ASEAN by showing plans to liberalise its agricultural market and to support the development of under-developed countries, such as Vietnam, Laos and Cambodia. It made an agreement with ASEAN to enter the negotiations on an FTA between them in November 2001 with a target of establishing it for the next ten years; they concluded the Framework Agreement in November 2002, which included the target, the coverage and the schedule. China also proposed an FTA to incorporate China, Japan and South Korea in November 2002, while pushing the agenda of an East Asian free trade area at the ASEAN + 3 summit meetings.

In the face of China's aggressive stance, particularly towards ASEAN, Japan's FTA policy has been accelerating. Since around late 1998, the Japanese government has been shifting its trade policy to diversify its options and embrace bilateral as well as regional trade arrangements, instead of relying exclusively on the multi-lateral framework centred on the WTO. This shift in Japan's trade policy comes partly from closer economic relations with East Asian nations, and partly from a sense of fear that it might be left out (given that most major countries have joined some sort of trade arrangement, regional or bilateral), together with unease about the future of the WTO. Since the FTA with Singapore came into force in November 2002, Japan has entered negotiations on an FTA with South Korea, Thailand, Malaysia and the Philippines. Additionally, when visiting ASEAN countries in January 2002, Prime Minister Junichiro Koizumi proposed an Initiative for 'Japan-ASEAN Comprehensive Economic Partnership', which included elements of an FTA. Japan and ASEAN signed a framework for this initiative, and have agreed to enter negotiations from April 2005. South Korea also has agreed to begin negotiations with ASEAN in early 2005.

Considering the abundant movements of bilateral and regional FTAs above, it is expected that a web of FTAs will cover East Asia in the next ten years. This may possibly lead to a region-wide free trade area eventually. Indeed the current picture of the region offers a great contrast to the past without FTAs; before the FTA between Japan and Singapore coming into effect, there was no FTA in East Asia except the ongoing project of the ASEAN Free Trade Area (AFTA).

At the same time, cooperation in the financial area has been further strengthened through regular dialogues between officials in the region. While the swap network under the Chiang Mai Initiative has gradually expanded,[47] the development of regional bond markets has become another important focus of regional cooperation (although this trend is not actually confined to the ASEAN + 3 framework). The need to foster regional bond markets came to be widely recognised after the crisis. Many argue that one of the fundamental causes of the East Asian financial crisis was the double mismatch, namely the currency and maturity mismatches in financing: abundant regional savings were directed not to the regional banking sectors, but to the international financial centres in the US and Europe, and they flew back to the region as foreign currency denominated, short-term loans, on which regional firms and banks relied too much. It is also argued that the crisis revealed the regional problem of over-reliance on the banking sector. Against this backdrop, discussions on regional bond markets have proceeded in various places including the ADB, APEC, EMEAP and ASEAN + 3. The issue actually came to hold centre stage when Prime Minister Thaksin of Thailand called for the development of such markets in 2002.

There has been important progress within the framework of ASEAN + 3. Japan proposed the Asian Bond Markets Initiative in December 2002, which was endorsed by the ASEAN + 3 Finance Ministers in August 2003. It is stated that the initiative aims to develop efficient and liquid bond markets in the region, which would facilitate better utilisation of regional savings for regional investments and would enable regional firms and banks to raise financing without the currency and maturity risks. So far, six voluntary working groups on the following issues have been established to address issues considered to be obstacles in promoting Asian bond markets: new securitized debt instruments, credit guarantee and investment mechanisms, foreign exchange transactions and settlement issues, issuance of bonds denominated in local currencies by multilateral development banks, foreign government agencies and Asian multinational corporations, rating systems and dissemination of information on Asian bond markets, and technical assistance coordination.

Another important initiative worth mentioning here is the one called the Asian Bond Fund (ABF) Initiative, instigated by EMEAP, a forum of central banks and monetary authorities in the region. It must be noted however that its member countries are different from those of ASEAN + 3 (Australia, New Zealand and Hong Kong are involved). This is a fund to which member central banks contribute their foreign currency reserves. EMEAP established the first stage of ABF (ABF1) in June 2003, which invests in a basket of dollar denominated sovereign and quasi-sovereign bonds in EMEAP economies (other than Japan, Australia and New Zealand). This extension to include bonds denominated in local currencies has been studied and the group announced the launch of the second phase of ABF (ABF2) in December 2004.

To sum up, the above discussions essentially indicate that East Asian cooperation has been gradually consolidated. Holding an East Asian summit in 2005 was hardly conceivable in the past, and may prove to be a landmark decision for the East Asian region. The ASEAN secretary-general is reported as saying that having an East Asian summit might not be just a simple change of name and had other implications.[48] The progress has been substantial and most prominent in the fields of finance and economics. However, as expected in the 1999 joint statement, the areas of cooperation have expanded to politics and security, labour, agriculture and forestry, tourism, energy and environment.

Conclusion

This chapter has shown how East Asian regionalism has developed since the late 1990s and the role Japan has played in that development. East Asian regionalism has grown out of ASEAN's invitation of the three Northeast Asian countries to its annual meeting, and thus ASEAN has assumed a prominent role. Significantly, Japan has also played an important role behind the scenes. While Japan's economic resources themselves are essential for the East Asian regional frameworks, particularly for the financial frameworks, Japan has not been passive diplomatically and politically. Indeed it has been actively engaged in the development of such frameworks. The chapter argued that the behind the scenes initiatives of Japan, together with its economic resources, have greatly encouraged the development of East Asian regionalism. This low-profile style of Japanese policy is the subject of the next chapter, where it will be examined more comprehensively in the longer-term context of postwar Japanese foreign policy.

6 The style of Japanese foreign policy

A low-profile and incremental approach

While looking at what Japan actually did in dealing with the East Asian crisis and its moves towards East Asian regionalism, and considering the factors that led to these policies, the previous two chapters noted how Japanese policymakers have tried to promote their policy agendas, namely East Asian cooperation in general and East Asian financial regionalism in particular, by taking into account the long-term perspective. This chapter reconsiders these issues, placing them in the context of the style of Japanese foreign policy.

The style of Japanese foreign policy in the postwar period

Among the various policies Japan implemented during the East Asian financial crisis, the AMF proposal in September 1997 deserves special attention. The proposal was, as Altbach points out, atypical of traditional Japanese foreign policy in the sense that Japan assertively articulated a policy and tried to take an independent initiative to bring the idea to fruition. He is correct to argue 'the [AMF] plan represented one of the most ambitious foreign economic policy proposals to come out of Tokyo in the postwar period' (Altbach 1997: 2). As argued so far, Japan has gradually begun to show its willingness to take more initiative in the region as well as in the wider international society, and in fact, the AMF proposal can be seen as evidence of this change in the nature of Japanese foreign policy. However, what gives this proposal particular significance is the way Japan proposed the idea: it tried to take an overt and assertive initiative in the region, which looks like a departure from the usual manner in which Japan has traditionally pursued its aims. Indeed, despite the fact that the proposal was not realised, it provides us with important insight into Japanese foreign policy.

As touched on in previous chapters, it can be argued that Japan has avoided taking an obvious and dominant leadership role throughout the postwar period, even in the region, where its economic superiority is overwhelming. This has often led to the criticism that it is reluctant to play a role, or to assume the leadership, that reflects its economic ability in the region, let alone in wider international circles, and that may have contributed to the image of Japanese foreign policy as immobilism or Japan as a reactive state. This may be correct if leadership is taken to mean merely 'hegemony' or dominant actions by one or more countries to compel others to go along with their preferred agendas.[1] However, this book argues that Japan has carried out its policies in a different style from what the dominant international relations circles usually expect: Japan has preferred to keep a low-profile approach while quietly and incrementally carrying out its policies to pursue policy objectives. In fact, considering the domestic, regional and international constraints imposed on it, that style of Japanese foreign policy has been quite effective. In other words, Japan has tried to avoid being regarded as taking the lead in a dominant fashion, but has taken some initiatives behind the scenes, successfully having steered the situation in a direction favourable to Japan's national interests.

This low-profile and incremental style of Japanese policy has been referred to in several places in the previous chapters. The following section re-examines the discussions, considering how Japan has effectively achieved its policy goals in the postwar period.

Japan's low-profile diplomacy in the postwar period and its regional relations

Japan's basic policy stance after the Second World War, based on the Yoshida Doctrine, namely the separation of economic matters and political matters, the concentration on economic development and minimalist diplomatic as well as security policy, can be considered in the context of the discussion on the style of Japanese policy. It is true that this policy has come at a large political cost. As discussed in Chapter 2, Japan's heavy economic as well as security dependence on the US has greatly constrained Japanese policy, and at times has forced Japanese policymakers to conduct diplomacy cautiously and to compromise quite often with US requests. However, in a long-term perspective the Yoshida line has undoubtedly favoured the postwar Japanese economy and has greatly affected Japan's later political economy, laying the foundation for the current international and regional position of Japan. In fact, its one-sided dependence on the US was actually what Japan chose. It was Japanese policymakers' clever way of pursuing national interests in the peculiar international situation of Cold War bipolarity and its devastated economy after the war. In particular, the conclusion of the US–Japan Security Treaty after the Second World War, to which Japan's dependence can be largely attributed, was the result of Prime Minister Yoshida's skilful strategy. It is fair to say that this policy of Yoshida, accompanied by generous access to US markets (which Japan also obtained by choosing to support US Cold War strategies), greatly contributed to Japan's quick recovery from the postwar economic ruin and led to remarkable development thereafter throughout the 1960s and 1970s by allowing it to concentrate on economic issues. Also, this security relationship based on the treaty between the US and Japan was significant domestically as well, as it accommodated the Japanese people's pacifism and anti-militarism after the war.

This policy line has also contributed to the development of Japan's postwar regional relations, in the sense that the US–Japan Security Treaty has helped to lessen the fear of the neighbouring countries that Japan might re-emerge as a dominant military power. The US engagement in East Asia through the security treaty has been regarded as a deterrent to Japan's militarism by East Asian countries, and thus has given them reassurance. This guarantee of Japan's good conduct and US engagement in East Asia through the security treaty has laid the foundation to allow Japan to conduct a regional policy, albeit in a low-profile way. This has eventually contributed to recovering relations with its neighbours, so that Japan has been able to successfully expand its role in the region throughout the postwar period.

In addition to what the US–Japan Security Treaty has contributed to Japan's regional relations, Japan's economic power has gradually affected neighbouring countries throughout the postwar period and has helped Japan to build closer relations with them. This has led to the consolidation of Japan's economic and political position, and has eventually begun to allow Japan to take more initiative regionally. Although its regional policy was very limited in the 1950s and 1960s, Japan started a low-profile diplomacy within the region through aid, which developed into one of Japan's core policy tools towards East Asia, thereby making the region increasingly reliant on Japan. Also, successive Japanese leaders have tried to address East Asian relations, and it has become almost a custom that they make official visits to Southeast Asian countries and make policy speeches, usually pledging new economic assistance. The Fukuda Doctrine adopted in 1977, in particular, contributed greatly to the subsequent development of Japan-ASEAN relations. With respect to its relations with China, even before the normalisation of diplomatic relations in 1972, Japan maintained economic channels with China under the *seikei bunri* policy. After the normalisation, Japan has dealt with China very cautiously through formal and informal networks, or 'politics behind politics' (Zhao 1993), and has been the largest aid donor to China. Furthermore, particularly since the 1980s, Japan's private and public capital has flown into the East Asian economy. This has not only triggered the regionalisation of the East Asian economy and has moulded a new regional economic order, but has also raised Japan's profile in the region, contributing to ever closer relations between Japan and East Asian countries. This has eventually enabled Japan to lead from behind, having gradually created Japan's long-term influence, initially economically but increasingly more politically, and having developed a regional climate that allows its larger, albeit limited, role there.

This leading-from-behind argument may have to be qualified to a certain extent, as it is fundamentally the private sector and its economic needs that have triggered the changing economic order in East Asia, rather than government policies. Nevertheless, it should not be overlooked what the government has done, either. The Japanese government and the private sector, without doubt, have a much more intimate relationship than is usually seen in Western economies, and government 'has penetrated business, and business has penetrated government' (Hatch and Yamamura 1996: 116–17). For instance, in spite of the fact that the ratio of aid tied or partially tied in the total Japanese aid has been significantly reduced and is now substantially lower than the OECD average, in reality Japanese firms have won 40 or 50 per cent of contracts for projects paid with Japanese untied aid (Inada 1989: 200). Weiss stresses that 'relocation to the region [of certain parts of the Japanese production system] was much more a publicly coordinated effort than an *ad hoc* response by individual firms acting alone' (Weiss 1998: 206). Furthermore, Japan's aid itself has great significance in this process, as discussed in Chapter 2. Therefore, while it would be an exaggeration to say that what has been happening in the East Asian economy in the last few decades is solely the result of the strategies of the Japanese government, it can be said that at least their policies have contributed to the changes in the East Asian economy to a significant extent. Hook *et al.* note, 'Japan, through a policy of careful re-engagement and quiet diplomacy with East Asian states in the post-war era, has undoubtedly succeeded in manoeuvring itself into a position whereby it has regained the ability to construct and lead a latent East Asian region' (Hook *et al.* 2001: 227).

Japan has used its economic resources for diplomatic purposes not only in its bilateral relations: by contributing to international organisations Japan has tried to enhance its international position in the long term, and indirectly to increase its regional influence (Yasutomo 1995: 62–3). Despite the ideological difference between Japan and the Washington Consensus, as discussed in Chapter 3, Japan has never neglected its role in international organisations. Indeed, contributing to international organisations has become one of the mainstays of Japanese foreign policy. Japan is now the second largest contributor to many international organisations, including the UN and the World Bank, and the largest to the ADB, together with the US. Drifte points out that 'international organisations provide an environment where Japan can take on certain leadership functions without being perceived as an obvious leader and without sacrificing too much political capital' (Drifte 1998: 134). He goes further on this point and notes the 'catalytic' nature of Japanese foreign policy, where Japan chooses to cooperate and make coalitions with other states, transnational institutions and private sector groups to achieve its goals rather than taking on the traditional type of leadership. Drifte calls this incremental and low-profile type of leadership Japan's 'leadership by stealth' (Drifte 1998: 171–3).

It can be argued that this incremental and low-profile style of Japanese policy has built an environment that has allowed Japan to play a larger role even in the area of security. As discussed in Chapter 2, there has been a shift in Japan's attitude towards the country's security policy since the early 1990s due to the end of the Cold War, and specifically because of the severe international criticism of Japan's failure to make a military contribution to the UN operation during the Gulf War. Although the majority of politicians, bureaucrats, influential academics and business leaders still strongly favour a US military presence in Japan and East Asia, an increasing number of people now accept the wider, albeit limited, role of the SDF (as the poll presented in Chapter 2 shows). Japan also began to voice its views on regional security matters, being more positive about regional security dialogues, an attitude which could not have been imagined before. This new move of Japan since the early 1990s has become possible and less controversial regionally as a result of Japan's approach throughout the postwar period that built up regional relations based on economic resources under the US–Japan Security Treaty. Although not all the regional countries are supportive of Japan's larger security role, the fear that Japan will resort to military means again as it did more than half a century ago has gradually abated, if not completely disappeared. Furthermore, while Japanese policymakers have avoided taking a bold and visible decision about its security policy, Japan has successfully strengthened its military by taking careful account of both internal and external pressures. It has incrementally and quietly reinforced its military capacity, and its SDF force has now become an ultra-modern fighting force (Hook *et al.* 2001: 72).

It is probably worth mentioning here that the shift in Japan's stance on security issues since the early 1990s has actually been a very incremental development. Japan's ability to take relatively quick action after the terrorist incidents on 11 September 2001 in New York and Washington and the fairly wide domestic consensus about the possible dispatch of the SDF on limited logistical missions in wartime for the first time, which can be seen as a major development in Japan's security policy considering the government's past hesitant attitude towards dispatching the SDF overseas even for PKO, were possible against the background of this step-by-step process of gradually shifting Japan's security stance since the early 1990s. Japanese policymaking agents and intellectuals as well as the public have gone through various stages of extensive discussion about Japan's security framework throughout the 1990s. This started in 1990 during the Gulf War through the passage of the PKO Bill in June 1992 and the deliberation over the revised Japan-US defence cooperation guidelines from September 1997 to September 1999. In addition, even the discussion about revising the constitution has been gaining momentum since the early 1990s. Based on these developments in the 1990s, Japan finally was able to dispatch the SDF during the actual military action in Afghanistan following the 11 September incident, although it was limited to providing logistical and non-combat support. Stockwin points out that in 1960 the revision of the Security Treaty, which forced the Prime Minister out of office, eventually passed through Diet, and despite the political crisis subsequent to the government's failing to deal with the Gulf War, the debate over the Gulf War crisis led to the passage of the PKO Bill a year and a half later. All this is proof that 'immobilist politics does not, in the Japanese case, mean a total inability to effect political change, rather that a cumbersome process of consensus-building and of exhausting all possibilities has to be gone through for change to eventuate' (Stockwin 1999: 215). Similarly, Hook and McCormack argue:

> Unlike the dramatic and sudden changes in Eastern Europe and the Soviet Union symbolized by the collapse of the Berlin Wall and the break-up of the West's nuclear antagonist throughout the Cold War period, in Japan change only began to gather momentum after a prolonged period of unravelling, fatigue and uncertainty, during which the framework and direction imposed by Cold War politics and the growth economy dissolved slowly. The call on Japan to make a military contribution to the resolution of the Gulf War made the search for a new way forward all the more imperative, but it was only when it was clear that old ways no longer worked that the national debate slowly turned to focus on the options available for Japan in the emerging new world order.
>
> (Hook and McCormack 2001: 3–4)

To sum up, Japan has gradually improved its regional relations over the last few decades in a very cautious way. Some difficulties still remain, particularly in its relations with China and the Korean Peninsula, but it is noteworthy that there is now a much better climate in which Japan's greater initiatives, not only economically but also politically and even on security issues, are better received than before. There are various factors behind this change, as discussed before, such as the end of the Cold War and more recently the East Asian financial crisis. However, it can be argued that Japan's incremental and low-profile policies towards the region throughout the postwar period and the use of its economic resources under the Yoshida Doctrine have greatly contributed to this situation.

Asia Pacific Regionalism and Japan's behind the scenes initiatives

While Japan has improved and strengthened its regional relations through the low-profile and incremental policies, its policies towards regional cooperation, specifically Asia Pacific cooperation, are also relevant to the discussions on Japan's policy style. Since the 1960s Japan has embarked on a project to establish regional frameworks. However, Japan has not led from the front and instead has tried to advance this agenda behind the scenes. As discussed in Chapter 2, Japan, in fact, tried to take some initiative for the construction of regional multilateral frameworks in the 1960s, such as the ADB as well as MEDSEA, but these initiatives were not very successful. Japanese policymaking agents learnt from these experiences that the countries of the region did not welcome Japan's high-profile initiatives, and that Japan had to show its neighbours that it was not trying to dominate them. Thereafter, Japan began to take more cautious and low-profile approaches and tried to avoid overt initiatives in advancing regional frameworks.

This de facto failure of Japan in promoting an independent regional initiative in the 1960s made it turn to the idea of Asia Pacific cooperation. Although originally nurtured among academics, this concept received increasingly more attention from Japanese policymaking agents since the 1960s, as they considered that this was actually a very convenient concept for Japan. Namely, in this larger framework, Japan could not only incorporate both its relationships with the US and East Asia, which it had tried to coordinate throughout the postwar period, but could also appear to dilute its influence and could advance regional cooperation without provoking open hostility.

The then Foreign Minister Miki espoused the concept of Asia Pacific cooperation at the official level for the first time in 1967. This, as argued in Chapter 2, laid the foundation for the future development of Asia Pacific regionalism based on the longer-term perspective. With little enthusiasm from other countries, government level interest in the concept became dormant, and instead it lived on mainly in academic circles, such as the PAFTAD and the PBEC, until the end of the 1970s. However, these private organisations became an important vehicle for the later development of the idea of Asia Pacific cooperation. Chapter 2 also argued that Miki seemed aware that it was necessary to take a long-term approach to advance Asia Pacific cooperation by first creating an atmosphere favourable to this cooperation.

After Prime Minister Ohira expressed his support publicly for the idea of Pacific Basin cooperation in the late 1970s, official level involvement in the regional process of cooperation increased greatly. However, again Japan's policy was very cautious. For one thing, Japanese policymakers preferred the quasi-private framework of PECC, as Ohira's study group as well as MOFA officials considered that it was essential to take a cautious and gradual approach for advancing Pacific cooperation because of the complicated regional situation. Furthermore, Japan hesitated to promote this agenda openly on its own, and instead proposed it jointly with Australia and let Australia take a major public role. Japan wanted to avoid being regarded by its East Asian neighbours as controlling the region or creating a second Greater East Asia Co-prosperity Sphere, and also to avert US concern that Japan was building an exclusive East Asian block.

The Asia Pacific cooperation process eventually culminated in the establishment of APEC in 1989. Japan again kept a low-profile presence in the initiation of APEC. The MITI played a more than supportive part in the process of launching APEC, although Australia also took a crucial lead. However, the MITI persuaded Australia to assume the public role, while sticking to a behind-the-scenes role, partly because of its domestic rivalry with the MOFA, and partly because of the concern that there could be an unfavourable reaction from East Asian countries towards Japanese leadership.

In short, as far as Japan's approach towards Asia Pacific cooperation is concerned, there has been a quite consistent pattern of long-term and behind the scenes policymaking. Japanese policymakers have been very cautious in advancing this agenda, and until the formation of APEC they preferred to use private mechanisms, trying to nurture the idea of Asia Pacific cooperation by taking into account the long-term perspective. Also, Japan has tried to avoid taking the lead from the front so that it could appear to dilute its influence in the region. The above policies are not entirely a reflection of Japanese policymakers' strategic thinking. For instance, the rivalry of the MITI and the MOFA in the process of establishing APEC was referred to above. However, it is also true that subsequent Japanese policymakers shared the view that a regional framework that includes the US and Australia would contribute to Japan's national interest. At the same time, they had strong reservations about the extent of Japan's visible role, being aware that the best way to achieve their policy goal of such a mechanism becoming established was to proceed cautiously and take a long-term approach.

Factors in the low-profile and incremental style of Japanese policy

Then, why has Japan exhibited such a style of policy particularly in its regional relations? How effective is this style of policy for Japan in advancing its policy agendas, and how does it compare in effectiveness with the alternative style, i.e. taking the lead openly? Some points have been already mentioned so far, and here they are recapitulated from international, regional and domestic angles.

Internationally, Japan's relationship with the US is an important reason for the low-profile and incremental style of Japanese foreign policy. As discussed before, this book does not agree that Japan is merely reacting to US policies, but it is true that sometimes Japan has had to compromise with US requests because of Japan's heavy dependence on the US in economic as well as security matters. In addition, other East Asian countries are closely linked with the US as well, and do not want to risk their relations with the US. In the light of this, it is quite unlikely that they would support a Japanese policy of strong opposition to the US. Such a situation has made it difficult for Japan to take a position independent of the US, and has made Japan show sensitivity to the US position, and conduct regional policies very cautiously. This has made Japan's dynamic, as opposed to incremental, policy-making difficult to implement and therefore quite unlikely. In fact, although the US does not oppose Japan's economic engagement in the region, it does not want Japan to dominate the region, as the case of the AMF proposal, presented in Chapter 4, suggests. Krauss rightly points out that, although the US at times requests Japan to take more responsibility for international affairs and to take a leadership role commensurate with its economic power, the US 'would like Japan to play a "leadership" role when it accords with American interests and strategy', and the 'American definition of "leadership" for Japan . . . sometimes has tended to be rather a form of followership to accomplish American goals with Japanese resources' (Krauss 2000: 485). In this sense, the incremental and low-profile style of Japanese policy has been effective for Japan as it has allowed it to pursue its objectives without giving the US grounds to suspect that it is trying to dominate the region, or perhaps to challenge the US in terms of hegemony in East Asia.

Japan's regional relations have been the most important factor that influenced the choice of a low-profile foreign policy style. Due to the legacy of Japanese colonisation of its neighbouring countries, Japan's attempts to take any leadership in the region tended to cause disquiet for East Asian countries, as shown in the case of the ADB as well as MEDSEA. Any such attempt arose the suspicion that Japan intended to move towards the Greater East Asian Co-prosperity Sphere again. Although countries in the region have become, in time, less worried about a repeat of what happened in the early twentieth century, some are still wary of Japan's intentions, and, even recently, Japan's overt leadership has not been entirely welcome in the region. China, in particular, is highly sensitive to Japan's activism in East Asia. This is partly due to its rivalry with Japan over regional leadership, in addition to historical reasons, although, as argued in Chapter 5, it seems that even China has come to accept that Japan has a certain role to play in the region especially since the crisis. A number of Japanese policymakers admit that the relationship with China is currently the biggest factor that constrains Japan's regional initiative and that they must always give careful consideration to China's stance.[2] ASEAN countries and, to a lesser extent, South Korea may be increasingly ready to accept Japan's larger role in the region, and policymakers in these countries have begun to acknowledge the necessity and importance of Japanese regional initiatives. However, they still do not want to see dominant leadership from Japan and welcome its low-profile initiatives a lot more. This is partly because it is difficult for Japanese initiatives to be accepted by the general public in these countries, which is particularly true in South Korea. In short, Japan is in a very delicate position in East Asia and Japanese policymakers must handle this regional situation very cautiously.

Finally, there are some domestic reasons for this style of Japanese foreign policy. For one thing, some cultural[3] factors, such as the consensus-based system of Japanese society, where people generally do not criticise others publicly, avoid causing them to lose face, and try to negotiate behind the scenes in pursuit of self-interest, might contribute to this style. This book cannot provide clear evidence of any causal relationship between culture and Japanese policy, as such an analysis lies outside the scope of the book, nor does it argue that cultural factors can explain a major part of Japanese foreign policy. As discussed in the Introduction, this book adopts the stance that policymakers' considerations about various interests (national, organisational, domestic and personal) are important. Also, it seems that such cultural factors fail to explain, for instance, why the prewar Japan, which presumably had much the same society and culture, took a more proactive approach. Nevertheless, cultural factors are not so insignificant that they can be excluded from the analysis of Japanese foreign policy completely, contrary to the claims of some scholars who embrace rational choice theory.[4] Without overemphasising the peculiarity of Japanese society, it is reasonable to assume that cultural factors have some effect on the behaviour of Japanese policymakers. In addition to cultural factors, as discussed in the case of the formation of APEC, domestic politics such as bureaucratic turf battles have sometimes prevented Japan from taking decisive action. In fact, it is interesting to note that, in the case of the discussions on the AMF, when those involved were limited to MOF officials (and it was abundantly clear who was in charge), we see Japan taking a quite different approach from the usual style of its policy.

In short, considering these constraints on Japan's diplomacy, its policy style looks a very effective way to achieve its policy goals. It is the smoothest way to advance the country's agendas, causing the least controversy with the US and regional countries and fitting well in its domestic society.

The implication of Japan's policies towards the East Asian crisis and East Asian regionalism for the style of Japanese foreign policy

If this is the case, the proposal for the formation of the AMF in 1997, which can be regarded as Japan's attempt to take an independent and explicit initiative for a regional financial mechanism, is a major innovation. This raises the question of why Japan proposed the AMF in such an extraordinarily bold manner. For one thing, the dramatic success of the Thai rescue package encouraged Japan to go beyond its usual style and voice its policy more assertively. MOF officials sensed an unusual atmosphere in the Thai meeting, which made them think that they should take advantage of this impetus and show Japan's willingness to take the lead in the region whenever necessary. Interestingly, Japan's initiative was not deemed completely objectionable by regional countries, which certainly was a very different reaction from that of a few decades ago. Also, MOF officials were frustrated with the response of the IMF and the US to the crisis, which was probably compounded by the MOF's decade-long ideological disagreement with Washington. In fact, as mentioned in Chapter 4, to some MOF officials the AMF proposal meant a challenge to the Washington-based international system, and this strong feeling made them respond to the excitement created by the success in regional cooperation that lay behind the Thai rescue package. Also, the strong character of Eisuke Sakakibara, who was quite distinctive among the MOF and the Japanese bureaucracy more generally, also greatly affected the behaviour of the Japanese officials.[5]

It remains to be seen whether the style exhibited in Japan's proposal of the AMF implies the possibility of a shift in Japan's policy style. In fact, Japan did not press the proposal further after the Hong Kong meeting in September 1997, and resigned itself to forming the Manila Framework, which was a compromise for both Japan and the US (and the IMF). Importantly, Sakakibara later reflected that the way Japan proposed the AMF was a more American-style approach, the style in which the US advances and realises its foreign policy goals. He continued, however, that he should have been more aware of the fact that Japan was in a different situation from the US (and, it would be difficult for Japan to adopt the same style as the US) (Sakakibara 2000: 186).

However, there are some factors that might cause a change in the style of Japanese foreign policy. It may be that the current quiet diplomacy has become less accept-able domestically. Because of the tight budgetary situation of Japan under the prolonged stagnation of the economy, the Japanese government cannot afford to maintain the budget for ODA, which has been its main diplomatic tool for decades. At the same time, how effectively ODA is used diplomatically has come under closer public scrutiny. A MOFA official comments that the government has been urged to show the public how ODA has enhanced Japan's national interests, although that will possibly appal recipient countries.[6] An editorial of the *Nihon Keizai Shinbun* reads: Japan has provided China with a total of 3 trillion yen of ODA in the last 20 years, which is more than half of what China has received bilaterally, but such a fact is hardly known by the Chinese public and the relations between the two countries have actually deteriorated.[7] This perspective probably reflects the views of an increasing number of Japanese intellectuals and the public. In this sense, it is noteworthy that when the Japanese government announced the New Miyazawa Initiative, it overtly publicised the policies specifically through the East Asian media, rather than keeping a low profile. Also, it was more positively involved in the implementation process of the assistance measures under the New Miyazawa Initiative, in contrast to the passivity of the past aid policy based on the *yosei shugi*. In short, the image of Japan as the party whose role was reduced to merely writing a cheque is losing domestic support, and the government increasingly has to show more explicitly how the country's resources are effectively used for its national interests. This might become incompatible with the quiet style of policy.

Also, as discussed so far, Japan has increasingly tried to obtain a voice in international society and to re-establish its international status particularly after the end of the Cold War. This sometimes has persuaded Japan to articulate its policy more assertively, leading to its more visible roles. Take a look at a recent example. It may be possible to consider Japan's quite conspicuous policy of hosting a ministerial conference for the reconstruction of Afghanistan in January 2002 as a sign that Japan has taken on a more high-profile role. With respect to the hosting of this international conference, the *Financial Times* said that Japan is 'hoping to persuade the world that it has outgrown its customary role as the globe's cheque-book diplomat'.[8] This might be affecting the style of Japanese policy in the near future.

Nevertheless, this book considers that Japan's style of foreign policy and its initiative-taking are not necessarily incompatible. The way in which Japan takes initiatives still exhibits the above-discussed style of policy, although in a sense it may be less low-profile than before. More recent Japanese initiatives, such as the New Miyazawa Initiative and the hosting of the international conference for Afghanistan, are still very cautious (rather than dominant or intrusive), despite being more high-profile than usual. Japan has made every effort to create a consensus with East Asian countries as well as with the US behind the scenes. It does not have any intention to defy the US, or to influence regional countries forcefully through the deployment of its economic resources. In this sense, it probably does not necessarily follow in the light of these recent initiatives that Japan has been going beyond its usual style of foreign policy, and its relationships with the US as well as East Asian countries have still constrained Japanese foreign policy to a large extent.

Furthermore, it is noteworthy that, since the AMF proposal became a regional agenda in 1997, the regional project to establish a financial cooperation mechanism has been making steady progress. In other words, the AMF proposal and the manner in which it was discussed during the latter half of 1997 became a springboard for regional discussions concerning regional financial cooperation. It can be argued that, by proposing the AMF, Japan, as a consequence, was able to initiate regional dialogues about matters that some Japanese officials had been wanting to bring to the table for some time. Chapter 4 discussed their recognition of the need to strengthen financial cooperation for the sake of the region's financial stability and their interest in a regional financial framework even before the crisis, although this had not been considered very pressing at that time. The AMF proposal actually advanced this agenda. The interest of East Asian countries in the AMF looked to have diminished and the idea was regarded as spent when Japan dropped it in 1997, but, contrary to some expectations, the idea of the AMF and the discussions about a regional financial framework actually survived. An increasing number of East Asian leaders and officials are currently supporting the idea of the AMF, as discussed earlier. The increasing regional discussions, in fact, have led to the current momentum of regional financial cooperation. In short, despite its apparent failure, the AMF proposal has contributed to a lasting discussion on East Asian financial regionalism among regional leaders and intellectuals. In this sense, the AMF proposal and the subsequent Japanese policies during and after the crisis still exhibit some elements of the quiet and gradual policy style.

In fact, although the AMF did not come into being, it seems that Japanese officials do not necessarily regret having proposed the idea. A finance officer comments that, when Japan put forward the idea, they did not necessarily intend to establish the AMF coercively.[9] In addition, the formation of the Manila Framework was not, contrary to what some may argue, simply a face-saving attempt by Japan after abandoning its original idea. Although the Manila Framework falls short of the AMF, it at least provides more opportunity for regional leaders to meet and discuss with each other, which Japanese officials thought to be important in order to keep alive the regional dialogues for further regional cooperation originally triggered by the AMF proposal. Sakakibara states that Japan's motivation in advancing the formation of the Manila Framework was that it did not want to lose the momentum that had been generated by the AMF proposal and wanted to prevent the proposal from being buried completely (Sakakibara 2000: 189).

It is not that Japanese policies towards the AMF and the establishment of the Manila Framework are solely the result of Japanese policymakers' strategic thinking on future regional financial cooperation. Although the AMF proposal triggered regional discussions, this was probably not what Japanese policymakers exactly planned when they originally proposed the idea. In fact, Chapter 4 discussed various factors, economic as well as political, that led to the AMF proposal, other than their grand strategies on the future regional monetary architecture. Also, in the face of the failure of the AMF proposal and the prolonged crisis in late 1997, it is doubtful that MOF officials had a very clear vision about what the ministry had to do, although it does seem that they shared a sense of emergency.

Nevertheless, it should not be overlooked that these policies of Japan certainly involved strategic thinking on the part of Japanese policymakers, specifically MOF officials, on Japan's future role in East Asia as well as its national interest. They were aware of how Japan should advance its policy agenda under its international and regional constraints and how they should act when opportunities present themselves. Adachi and Shiroyama point out that MOF officials, in particular, are educated within the ministry to serve national interests after they start their career in the ministry as new graduates, which has greatly contributed to their stronger commitment to national interests than bureaucrats in other ministries (Adachi and Shiroyama 1999: 247–8). Also, it is noteworthy that some senior ex-MOF officials have recognised how Japan should advance its agenda in its relations with East Asian countries as well as with the US. For instance, Eisuke Sakakibara comments that Japan should take regional initiatives in terms of offering ideas and money, but should do this cautiously and not in a dominant way.[10] Likewise, Isamu Kubota states that Japan does not have to take a visible leadership role like the US, and that it is more than satisfactory for Japan to take a long-term view and realise its goals eventually.[11] In fact, it was discussed in Chapters 4 and 5 that key MOF officials, such as Sakakibara, Kuroda and Kishimoto, have considered that any regional monetary framework, specifically the AMF, should be pursued, and they were fully aware of the necessity of longer-term strategies to achieve that goal. This orientation of Japanese policy has become more apparent in the subsequent policies.

The New Miyazawa Initiative, which, in a sense, was an extension of past aid policies, also implicitly contributed to the advancement of regional financial cooperation. The policy greatly helped the crisis-hit countries to relieve their economies, and impressed East Asian countries, particularly as Japan was beset by its own difficult economic problems. This could help restore Japan's reputation and the confidence of the regional countries in Japan after their disappointment over Japan's withdrawal of the AMF proposal in 1997. In fact, this policy of Japan seems to have dramatically improved its relations with ASEAN countries and South Korea not only for the moment but even from the middle and long-term perspective.[12] It has possibly made Japan more welcome as a regional power and has created a more favourable environment for Japan to advance the agenda of forming a regional financial framework. In addition, as argued in Chapter 5, Japan's positive attitude and commitment to resolve the crisis has made ASEAN countries recognise anew the necessity to deepen their relations with Japan, and with the other Northeast Asian countries, China and South Korea. It has also given them some confidence that it is worth considering the formation of a regional framework in East Asia. This understanding of ASEAN policymakers has led to their more positive attitude towards cooperation with the north even beyond the financial area, and has contributed to the current momentum in East Asian regionalism.

Another significant factor of the New Miyazawa Initiative, relevant to the discussion here, is that there was an implicit message in this policy that Japan still desired to create some form of regional financial framework or the AMF in the long term. Specifically, Japan established the ACCSF in the ADB as part of the New Miyazawa Initiative in the hope that it could develop into a regional mechanism in the future. The New Miyazawa Initiative actually states that in the long run a multilateral organisation that provides guarantees for East Asian countries should be seriously considered. Japanese officials even hoped, in drawing up the New Miyazawa Initiative, that such a mechanism would evolve into the AMF in the future.

In addition, the establishment of the region-wide swap arrangements can be regarded as another step towards closer financial cooperation in East Asia, although the swap arrangements themselves are a collection of bilateral arrangements, in fact the expansion of existing agreements, and should be distinguished from the AMF. The new swap arrangements may actually have only limited significance economically, as they are not large enough in size to work as a regional emergency financial mechanism, and cannot be activated automatically. However, given that there are few financial frameworks in the region, such a new framework could play a certain, albeit limited, role in preventing and preparing for a future crisis, practically as well as by giving assurance to the markets. Furthermore, it should make future regional discussions on the AMF much easier, in that an East Asian financial framework can be seen as a more natural idea, or as a fait accompli to some extent, rather than something completely new.

Japanese officials evidently see the swap arrangements as a way towards realising the AMF in the future. In other words, Japan's interest in advancing this agenda stems, to an important extent, from their strategy to establish a regional fund in the long term. While the support for the AMF within Japan has increased, Japanese officials have thought that it is not the right moment to put forward the AMF proposal again and that they need more time to create a consensus among East Asian countries, the US and the IMF before proposing it again. For the time being, by proposing the swap arrangements they wanted to show that Japan was still working towards closer regional financial cooperation in order to maintain the momentum and to keep regional countries interested in it,[13] while expecting these arrangements to develop into a multilateral framework in the future. As mentioned in Chapter 5, the then Vice Minister Kuroda, in promoting the swap arrangements, is said to consider that the establishment of the AMF should be Japan's middle-term policy objective, which was to be advanced step by step, and that extending the regional swap arrangements would be a significant move towards it. Also, Japan tried to make the member countries agree that a recipient country can receive only 10 per cent of the limit through the swap arrangements without linkage to the IMF loans. This was partly the result of taking into account US interests. Japanese officials, particularly Kuroda, thought that some compromise with the US had to be made as the priority was to establish a regional mechanism and not to lose the current impetus for regional financial cooperation.[14]

It is also worth noting the way Japan proposed and pushed forward the regional swap arrangements. As discussed earlier, the MOF took the lead behind the scenes to advance the idea, but it did so very cautiously and not in a dominant way in order to avoid receiving the same reaction as it had done when proposing the AMF. Prior to making public the plan to establish the swap arrangements, Japanese officials conducted a number of negotiations with the regional countries; after the consensus among the ASEAN + 3 countries was created, the Chiang Mai Initiative was announced for the first time as a statement of the ASEAN + 3 Finance Ministers in May 2000. Importantly, this time it was China who took a quite important and visible initiative to promote this mechanism. Also, the MOF did not neglect to assure the US that Japan was not trying to dominate the region nor exclude the US from East Asia, as referred to above.

To sum up, despite the failure of the AMF proposal in 1997, Japan has continued to advance the agenda of regional financial cooperation. It is not leadership from the front, nor has Japan overtly articulated what it wants to do. Japan has not directly promoted the regional fund that it is aiming to establish, neither. Yet a series of its policies after the crisis have gradually moved the region towards deeper financial cooperation, although this is still limited. They have also contributed to a revival of the discussions about the AMF among East Asian officials and have increased support for the idea in Japan and other East Asian countries. To be sure, the current momentum of financial cooperation stems from various factors, as discussed in Chapter 5. However, it is also true that Japan's low-profile, long-term oriented policies have effectively contributed to the present development.

How unique is the style of Japanese policy?

As we have discussed, Japan's policy style particularly in regional matters can be considered as exhibiting a somewhat different character from that of other major countries. But how unique is this style compared with that of other countries?

As suggested above, Japan's policy style seems to be quite different from the way in which the US advances its agenda internationally or regionally. Both countries possess a certain amount of material resources, although in the case of Japan such resources are predominantly economic. However, they clearly differ in the way they transform their resources into bargaining leverage: compared with Japan's low-profile style, the US tends to use their resources more directly, and often unilaterally and coercively, through threats and promises, overtly articulating what it wants to advance.

It is not difficult to find cases that illustrate the way the US implements its policy. For instance, the US relations with Latin America, a region of great significance to its national interests, are considerably different from the relations Japan has with its East Asian neighbours. Consider the US initiative to expand the NAFTA to the Western Hemisphere as a whole. Although this agenda has not necessarily been going smoothly, the US way of advancing it, starting with the announcement of the Enterprise of the Americas Initiative in 1990 and later through some important initiatives, notably hosting the first Summit of the Americas in Miami in 1994, makes a sharp contrast with Japan's behind the scenes initiatives in APEC or East Asian regionalism. Indeed, historically the strong foreign policy actions of the US 'condition the patterns of interaction not only in the [Latin American] system as a whole but also inside individual countries' (Nef 1994: 404). Also, the US forceful position, directly or through international organisations, can be often observed in East Asia as well. The hard line of US policy may not always work well in East Asia. For instance, despite its strong wish to propagate its liberal economic norms into East Asia, it is not easy for the US to impose them on the region.[15] Also, with respect to human rights issues, even though the US has made tough and forceful demands on China, it is by no means accurate to say that the Chinese government has made a full compromise so far. Nonetheless, East Asian countries' heavy dependence on US economic and security power has allowed, and will continue to allow, the US to adopt such a powerful and intrusive stance towards East Asia on a variety of issues.

Germany's policy style also contrasts with that of Japan's, particularly in the area of regional policy. Germany has a regional position akin to that of Japan in terms of its historical background as well as economic dominance, namely it failed to create an empire in Europe and was defeated in the war as was Japan and now is a prominent regional economic power as is Japan. However, it has taken a quite different regional approach to Japan since the end of the war, having taken much more explicit political initiatives in Europe than Japan has done in East Asia. Specifically it has taken the lead, together with France, in the development of a more unified Europe, and has played a conspicuous and visible role in the region. Katzenstein and Shiraishi contrast Germany's strong political commitment to the creation of an integrated European polity through influencing Brussels with Japan's economic engagement from behind the scenes in market integration in East Asia (Katzenstein and Shiraishi 1997: 341–81).

Furthermore, Japan's policy style seems to be quiet even when compared with 'middle power' countries like Australia. It could be argued that Japan's policy shares some common characteristics with that of these countries in the sense that they rely more on negotiating skills or consensus-making in advancing their agenda (Higgott, Cooper and Bonnor 1991, Higgott and Cooper 1990: 589–632), rather than taking dominant initiatives. However, Japan probably prefers to be more low-profile. In fact, it was shown above that Japan wanted Australia to take visible initiatives in advancing regional projects, most notably APEC, while supporting the ideas behind the scenes. The Australian policy style is different from the US unilateral approach, but is probably more visible than Japan's.

As far as the long-term and incremental nature of Japan's policy is concerned, some may argue that this point should not be overemphasised as being specifically unique to Japan. In general, policy in Western democratic countries tends to be incremental, and 'does not move in leaps and bounds' (Lindblom 1959: 84–5). However, there are reasons to believe that Japan's political economy tends to operate in a longer time framework than is the case in other countries because of domestic, regional and international factors, as argued above. Hook *et al.* refer to the long-term developmentalist goal of Meiji leaders, who successfully led the country to become a major industrial power within a century (Hook *et al.* 2001: 72). Over the last 50 years, Japan's postwar policies have also shown a remarkable degree of consistency and thus testify to the long-term nature of Japanese foreign policy.

Conclusion

It is reasonable to conclude, from what has been discussed so far, that Japanese policymakers have conducted foreign policy in a way that is different from other major countries, and that can be characterised as a low-profile and incremental style. Domestic factors, such as a consensus-based society, may have contributed to this style to some extent, but it is also certain that Japanese policymakers have recognised Japan's international and regional constraints, which has made them adopt this style of policy as a strategy to realise policy goals. This style of policy may give the appearance that Japanese foreign policy is reactive in nature, but it is important to note that, behind that picture of apparent reactivity, there are strategies with which Japanese policymakers have tried to advance the country's national interests.

7 Conclusion

We have considered Japan's new regional policy and relations by examining two arguments: (1) there has been a shift in the nature of Japanese policy, more precisely Japan has showed more interest in taking greater initiative independent of US policy, not only economically but increasingly politically; and (2) Japanese foreign policy has been characterised by a low-profile and incremental style, which makes for far greater effectiveness than often realised. As far as the latter is concerned, the last chapter comprehensively outlined the evidence presented in this book, and concluded that Japan has been quietly pursuing definite strategies, and that Japanese policymakers have acknowledged that this style suits Japan in realising its policy objectives given the various constraints imposed on it. This concluding chapter will review the results of the investigation of the former argument, followed by a conclusion about Japan's contemporary regional policy.

Conclusion on the nature of Japanese foreign policy

The book has dealt with the puzzling question of why there is a wide divergence of opinion on Japanese foreign policy. The two main points of disagreement are: (1) whether Japanese foreign policy can be characterised as reactive and opportunistic, or strategic and effective; and (2) whether its foreign policy priority is accommodating the US and its East Asia policy is therefore decided in accordance with US objectives, or whether East Asia has occupied a definite position in Japanese foreign policy. It is true that in the early postwar period Japan adopted a minimalist policy in terms of foreign affairs. Also, few would dispute that Japan's policy has been greatly constrained by its US relations. However, this book opposes the idea that Japan is just reacting to external pressures, and refutes the contention that US relations decide its foreign policy.

We have examined a range of empirical evidence on this point. Chapter 2 showed that even in the early postwar period Japan's policy reflected the thinking of Japanese policymakers about Japan's political and economic interests, rather than being purely dictated by US pressures. Even though Japan's regional policy was quite strongly influenced by the US Cold War strategies, Japanese policymakers also had their own agenda in regard to Japan's relations with the region. In fact, even in the early postwar period Japan showed its willingness to take some regional initiative, although it was not very successful at that time. Furthermore, although it is true that US policy greatly influenced, if not determined, Japanese policy, that was the cost that Japan had to pay in exchange for pursuing its postwar principle of the Yoshida Doctrine. In other words, as discussed in the previous chapter, Japan's economic and security dependence on the US after the war is what Japanese leaders chose as the path for realising their long-term policy objectives. Thus, the resultant apparent reactivity of Japan can be regarded as a strategy for pursuing its national interests. Moreover, as seen throughout the book, the nature of Japanese foreign policy has been changing from a minimalist political stance to more initiative taking, which has made the negative thesis on the nature of Japanese foreign policy increasingly inadequate. In short, the view of Japan as a reactive state or the interpretation of Japanese policy merely as an extension of its US policy is not only contradictory to the evidence presented so far, but also neglects what was stressed in Chapter 6, namely the way Japan has conducted its policy.

On the other hand, the positive thesis reviewed in the Introduction is not sufficient either, particularly when considering Japan's more recent policy after the end of the Cold War. This literature tends to stress the very positive nature of Japan's foreign policy in the economic sphere, but fails to fully discuss its increasing political initiatives independent of the US. The book has tried to provide more empirical evidence, and has considered the factors that have led to this change. Chapter 2 discussed how Japan's postwar regional policy has developed and how it came to assume significant roles in East Asia in a historical context. The chapter argued that the adoption of the Fukuda Doctrine in 1977 was a turning point in Japan's regional policy, but also that this policy has changed more significantly since the late 1980s. This argument is supported by Japan's direct involvement in the Cambodian peace process as well as its positive engagement in some regional frameworks such as APEC and ARF. Chapter 3 discussed Japan's ideological initiatives, looking at its consistent assertiveness over the development philosophy in the 1990s. Chapters 4 and 5 focused on specific issues, namely Japan's policies towards the East Asian financial crisis and East Asian regionalism, and discussed how and why Japan took independent initiatives on these issues. From the evidence discussed so far, it is fair to conclude that Japanese foreign policy has been changing throughout the postwar period in the direction outlined above. At the beginning of the twenty-first century, the nature of Japanese foreign policy is completely different from that of half a century ago. Nevertheless, sufficient attention has not been given to this point so far. Even recent studies conducted during the last decade tend to neglect this important change, and stress the economic nature of Japanese foreign policy.

In short, this book has tried to complement the literature on both the negative and the positive theses on Japanese foreign policy discussed in the Introduction, by demonstrating the occurrence of significant changes in Japanese foreign policy and by explaining the impact of a number of factors on these changes. Certainly, the book does not argue that Japanese foreign policy has been moving in a completely opposite direction. In fact, the fundamental part of postwar Japanese policy, namely the importance of US relations, has been still present. Nevertheless, the changes that have been observed are not trivial at all, and merit more attention in future research on Japanese foreign policy. On the whole, the discussions on the nature of Japanese foreign policy, made in the previous chapters, can be recapitulated as below.

The continuing importance of US relations

The fact that Japan has increasingly taken more initiative in East Asia does not mean that Japan is prepared to act against US interests or wishes. Japan is neither willing nor able to push through any agendas in defiance of the US, a fact which was evidenced in Japan's attitude towards the EAEC and the AMF proposals. In fact, Japan's recent initiatives are in any case not fundamentally against US interests. In most circumstances, Japan would have consulted with the US beforehand, trying to make it understand what Japan was going to do. In this sense, it may be argued that Japan's independent initiatives do not mean complete independence, and that 'Japan is conducting foreign policy with one eye carefully on Washington' still (Green 2001: 3).

This is because, in addition to Japan's close economic relationship with the US, even after the common enemy the Communist bloc had ceased to exist, the majority of Japanese policymakers and intellectuals consider that Japanese-US relations based on the security treaty are still at the core of Japan's security strategy. It seems that there has never been wider consensus about this issue than in the 1990s, when the Social Democratic Party of Japan, the main opponent of the treaty and the SDF during the Cold War period, accepted the legitimacy of the treaty and the SDF for the first time. In fact, security relations between the two countries were not diluted in the post Cold War era. The security treaty was reconfirmed by President Clinton and Prime Minister Hashimoto in 1996. Subsequently new Guidelines were agreed by the two governments in June 1997, and the related legislation was passed by the Japanese Diet in May 1999. Although Japan has increasingly become interested in multilateral security frameworks, such as the ARF, these are considered as supplements rather than substitutes to the existing bilateral frameworks. Thus, it is still strongly recognised among the majority of Japanese policymakers and intellectuals that the US security engagement in the region is indispensable not only for preparing to counter potential aggressions, but also as a deterrent to such incidents. Also, they believe that the US–Japan security treaty is a significant means for keeping a US military presence in East Asia. Tanaka argues that it is important to keep the US military presence in the region at least for some time, as it is too dangerous to deal with an issue such as the North Korean nuclear programme only among East Asian countries. He also claims the US may not really take an active part in a possible dispute in the South China Sea, but the presence of US forces itself will help prevent such an incident from occurring (Tanaka 1994: 139). Also, the security treaty between the US and Japan has had, and still has, a symbolic meaning: it guarantees that Japan will not threaten its neighbours and consequently its neighbours are reassured.

Considering all this, the centrality of the US in Japanese foreign policy has not changed, and will not change in the foreseeable future. Under the current relationship, it is the US that controls the security fate of Japan, and Japan is, after all, a junior partner to the US, even when Japan's economic influence over the US is taken into account. This situation has always made Japan pay attention to the US position when considering its policy, and sometimes Japan has inevitably had to compromise with the US. Furthermore, the US's structural power over international affairs, as suggested by Susan Strange, should also be considered. Even Eisuke Sakakibara, who is a strong advocate of a more independent Japanese foreign policy, notes that Japan will not be able to adopt any policy that could antagonise the US even in a few decades' time.[1]

The loosening of the framework of the Yoshida Doctrine

Nevertheless, despite this fundamental continuity, this book has stressed the occurrence of an important shift in Japanese foreign policy, which can be characterised as the loosening of the framework of the Yoshida Doctrine. The international, regional and domestic conditions under which Japan conducts its diplomacy have dramatically changed in the last few decades, and this has significantly affected its relations with regional countries as well as with the US. It has had a great effect on the framework of Japanese foreign policy as a whole, and it has been increasingly difficult for Japan to keep the Yoshida Doctrine as its main guiding principle for maintaining and enhancing national interests.

What the book has repeatedly emphasised is the increase in Japan's political initiatives. Japan was, on many occasions, quite reluctant to take positive action and avoided adopting political initiatives unless there were strong US pressures or direct economic interests involved. In this sense, it is particularly noteworthy that Japan has increasingly shown much more interest in assuming responsibility for independent political initiatives in the last one or two decades. It is also important to note that Japan has been more willing to participate actively in forging new international and regional frameworks, in marked contrast to its past passive stance.

In addition to this increasing interest in political initiatives, Japanese policy has shown some signs of change in the security area as well. Japan has gradually expanded the role of the SDF throughout the 1990s since the Gulf War, while having been more positive about regional security dialogues. It is noticeable that in January 1993, the then Prime Minister Miyazawa announced the Miyazawa Doctrine, which declared Japan's intention to participate actively in creating a regional political and security framework. These changes are particularly noteworthy, given Japan's past silence in this area, and are in contrast with the past stance of trying to avoid any military involvement by using economic means instead. Furthermore, even debates on a revision of the Constitution have arisen among intellectuals, the media and the public, although there has not been any consensus amongst them as yet. It seems that there have been an increasing number of voices not only among policymakers but also the Japanese public that Japan should cease to be a junior partner of the US. Considering the persistent pacifism of the Japanese public, it cannot be envisaged that any dramatic change in Japan's security policy in the foreseeable future will occur. It is quite unlikely that Japan will resort to military power as a major diplomatic tool. However, it is highly significant that there has been a gradual shift in its security stance since the early 1990s, accompanied by an expansion in the role of the SDF.

Greater emphasis on East Asian relations

In addition to Japan's increasing political and security activism, the book has also discussed another important change in Japanese foreign policy, namely the rise in significance of the position that East Asian relations have occupied in Japanese foreign policy over the last few decades. Asia has always been important to Japan. In the prewar days Japan's interest in Asia was manifested in the attempts to create the Greater East Asian Co-prosperity Sphere. However, for a couple of decades after the end of the war, Japan's regional policy was quite limited, and relatively little attention was paid to its regional relations. That was the era when Japan concentrated on its own economic development under the hegemony of the US. Since the 1970s, in accordance with various changes in the international environment, such as the growing economic interdependence in the region and the remarkable economic growth of many East Asian countries, Japan's emphasis on East Asia in its foreign policy has gradually been increasing. Economically, East Asian countries have become far more important partners for Japan rather than the mere suppliers of natural resources and importers of Japanese manufactured products that they used to be. In addition, East Asia has increased its importance for Japan's overall political strategy in the post Cold War era.

With the growing importance of East Asia, the positions taken by East Asian countries have increasingly influenced Japanese foreign policy, despite the fact that some believe that US pressures have largely dominated Japan's postwar policy. In fact, Japan's ambiguous attitude towards the EAEG proposal as well as its dropping of the AMF proposal were greatly influenced by the lack of consensus on these ideas among East Asian countries. Yamakage stresses that it is necessary for Japan to obtain the support of the ASEAN in order to realise its ideas (Yamakage 1999), which is also the case for other East Asian countries, notably China and South Korea. Japan has been very cautious about its regional relations throughout the postwar period, and despite the recent improvement in the relations between Japan and its neighbours, Japanese policy has been greatly constrained by them.

Conclusion on Japan's new regional policy after the Cold War

Finally, the questions with respect to Japan's regional policy and relations, raised in the introductory chapter, must be answered: what Japan has been doing in the region and what has caused the shift in its regional policy. The new character of Japanese regional policy, closely associated with the above changes in the nature of Japanese foreign policy, has been discussed in various places so far, and they can be summarised thus: Japan has begun to take on political and even security roles in East Asia beyond its customary economic role; and it has embarked on the project to advance a new regional framework, specifically East Asian cooperation. As discussed below, such a trend of Japan's regional policy is closely related to its overall foreign policy goals.

Japan's foreign policy goals have not changed throughout the postwar period. As presented in the Introduction, they are: (1) the political and security stability of its territory; (2) short-term and long-term economic prosperity; and (3) higher political status in the world. However, the ways of pursuing these three goals have been changing, as the diplomatic conditions surrounding Japan have changed due to the transformation of the international system since the 1970s (and more obviously since the late 1980s). Japan's new regional policy, along with the afore-mentioned changes in the nature of Japan's foreign policy, should be understood in this context.

First, the new character of Japan's regional policy is a reflection of the changing international conditions in which Japan has to pursue the stability of its territory, particularly after the Cold War. As discussed in Chapter 2, the end of the Cold War has made it more likely that the US forces will, at some stage, have to withdraw from East Asia to a certain extent, and this will be accompanied by the reduction of its political presence. This is not what Japanese policymakers want, nor are they trying to exclude the US from the region, but, as stated earlier, the US clearly has shown its intention to cease to be the world's policeman. The gradual withdrawal of the US from the East Asian region is highly likely in the long-term in the post Cold War era. Japanese high-ranked officials particularly in the MOF, the MOFA and the METI have shared the view that East Asia has to prepare for this eventuality. This has given Japanese policymakers enough motivation to promote Japan's greater political and security commitment to regional affairs so as to compensate for the possible future decline in the US presence. This is because political and security instability anywhere in the East Asian region would threaten Japan's stability. Under these circumstances, some regional frameworks have been seriously considered among Japanese officials, as they represent an important strategy for securing the political and security stability of Japan.

Second, Japan's increasing interest in political initiative as well as the creation of a new regional framework is concerned with Japan's economic interest as well. Due to the deepening economic interdependence of the regional economy, a large number of Japanese firms and banks have huge stakes in the region, and thus any economic instability in the regional countries would directly threaten Japan's economic interests. Furthermore, the East Asian financial crisis reminded Japanese policymakers of the closeness between East Asian economies, and has made them recognise the importance of economic, specifically financial, stability in East Asia for the Japanese economy itself. Also, the above concern of Japanese policymakers about the uncertain political and security situation in the region in the future due to the probable US withdrawal is also related to their thinking on economic issues as well, in the sense that any future political and security disturbance in the region would severely affect the regional economy, and in turn the Japanese economy. Japanese policymakers have become keenly interested in the health of the East Asian economy, and thus regional political stability. This has heightened the importance of regional matters in Japan's foreign policy to such an extent that the agenda for regional cooperation has become the focus of the policy.

Third, Japan's new regional policy, accompanied by the changes in the nature of Japanese policy, can be discussed in the context of the effort of Japanese policymakers, specifically MOF and MOFA officials as well as some politicians, to maintain and enhance Japan's political status in the world. As discussed in Chapter 2, the end of the Cold War and the resultant changes in the international system have raised a question of identity for Japan and have made its status in world politics more uncertain, while its traditional ways of contributing its economic resources, instead of political and military involvement, to international affairs have been criticised in some quarters as cheque book diplomacy. The Gulf War, in particular, had a considerable impact on the thinking of Japanese policymaking agents as well as the public. While Japan's huge economic contributions were not appreciated, the Japanese people learnt that its pacifism was not necessarily universally praised in international circles. Also, the decline of the Japanese economy since the 1990s has revealed the limitations of sole reliance on economic resources. For maintaining and enhancing its international status, Japanese policymakers believe that Japan has to show the world that it is willing to take a more active political role in the international system, other than contributing money, and for historical and geographical reasons East Asia has become the main venue where Japan can take certain political initiatives. This, in turn, has made it an urgent issue for Japan to establish firmer regional ties, and the increasing interaction of Japanese policymakers with their counterparts in East Asian countries since the early 1990s greatly reflects this point. This is also shown in Japan's current enthusiasm for East Asian regionalism.

In short, all the vectors concerned with Japan's policy goals have pointed in the direction of the changes in Japanese policy discussed so far, namely the interest in establishing closer relations with regional countries as well as some regional frameworks, accompanied by more political and security initiatives particularly for regional matters. They are useful to maintain the stability of the region, and hence that of Japan, considering the probable withdrawal of the US from East Asia in the long-term, if not in the foreseeable future. Also, they are concerned with Japan's economic interest, as political and security stability, and in turn economic stability, in the region have a significant impact on the Japanese economy. They are also the new ways in which Japan is enhancing its international status in the post Cold War period, a time when Japan needs to show more explicitly its political will. In other words, they are the effective ways to pursue Japan's national interests after the Cold War: they are the new ways, replacing the Yoshida Doctrine, of pursuing the policy goals of Japan under the changing international order particularly since the late 1980s. Japanese policymakers have come to believe that in the post Cold War period Japan must participate in establishing new international and particularly regional orders instead of simply trying to utilise existing ones for securing its national interests.

We have also discussed why Japan's main interest in regionalism has shifted from Asia Pacific to East Asia, specifically to the framework of ASEAN + 3, since the late 1990s. It has been shown that Japanese policymakers have been increasingly thinking that East Asia should have some frameworks for cooperation independent of the US. As stated repeatedly, this is not an attempt to exclude the US from East Asia, or to discard the frameworks of Asia Pacific cooperation, but it reflects the belief that East Asian countries should have their own frameworks as an alternative option, under the increasingly uncertain situation in the post Cold War period in addition to the existing international, regional and bilateral frameworks. This change is particularly interesting, as Japan has been consistently promoting some form of Asian Pacific regionalism since the 1960s. The concept of Asia Pacific is actually a very convenient one as it can help Japan manage its long lasting diplomatic issue of how to balance the relationship with the US and that with East Asia. The idea of Asia Pacific is also effective in that the Japanese influence is less conspicuous and therefore the concerns of its neighbours are reduced. It is important to think about what this shift in Japan's stance on regionalism means and what Japan is trying to do with the new framework of East Asian regionalism.

We have discussed various reasons for this question in previous chapters. Among them are East Asian countries' greater acceptance of Japan's larger role in dealing with regional matters, a more benign relationship between Japan and regional countries and the increasing number of 'Asianist' policymakers in Japan. Furthermore, there are additional factors that explain the shift in Japanese priorities in East Asia, and that depend on the area of discussion.

MOF officials, whose main interest is the stability of the Japanese financial markets, have been strengthening their belief since the early 1990s that East Asia should have some self-help mechanisms instead of solely relying on the assistance of the US and international organisations. To MOF officials, the existing inter-national organisations are limited in their ability to deal with East Asian issues in terms of the available resources and information. The financial crises in the late 1990s gave further credence to this interpretation, as not only was the IMF assistance not enough to ease the crisis situation, but also the crises revealed to Japanese (and East Asian) policymaking agents and intellectuals US double standards, in the sense that the US showed a lesser degree of commitment to the resolution of the East Asian crisis compared with their greater zeal in addressing the Latin American and Russian crises. This has made MOF officials believe that it is important to establish some self-help mechanisms in East Asia to supplement the existing system for preventing any future financial disturbance, and for preparing the ground for effective independent recovery if the worst happens.

Furthermore, a decade-long ideological disagreement between Washington and the MOF concerning the relevance of different models of economic management, as well as the dissatisfaction with the limited roles of Japanese staff in the existing international organisations and Japan's small voice there despite its huge financial contributions, have probably added momentum to the attempt of MOF officials to advance East Asian financial regionalism. In particular, these ideological differ-ences became even clearer during the crisis, which increasingly frustrated MOF officials and made them articulate their views more assertively. In this sense, it could be argued that MOF officials wish to have some regional framework that will not be influenced by Washington's policy. This does not mean that MOF officials want to decrease the US presence in East Asia, but rather that they wish to have another framework that can reflect their ideas more.

MOFA officials, who have a stronger interest in the country's political and security issues than other ministries, have a slightly different rationale attached to their advancement of East Asian cooperation. They share with MOF officials the view that East Asia has to prepare for the probable withdrawal of the US from the region in the long term by establishing some additional regional frameworks. Also, they have strongly felt that Japan has to show to the world its will to take the political initiative. Furthermore, the stalemate of the APEC processes encourages them to look for an alternative East Asian option. However, it is highly unlikely that Japanese (as well as East Asian) officials will pursue any self-help mechanism in the region in the foreseeable future in terms of security issues, as they still think that the US should remain a key player in the political and security matters of the region. What MOFA officials are currently doing is exploring multiple options. The ARF, which includes the US, is one, the political East Asian framework is another, and both could complement the traditional framework in East Asia.

This many-sided regional approach can be also effective in dealing with Japan's relations with China, which have been, and will be, increasingly important, albeit difficult, for Japanese diplomacy, given the perceived rise of China as an economic and military power and the two countries' traditional mistrust of each other. This multifaceted policy of Japan on regionalism is in part the result of an awareness of the issues involved in its engagement policy towards China and aims to encourage China's integration into regional and international society. Such a policy could contribute to a smoother relationship between the two countries as they begin to understand each other more, particularly since China is highly sensitive to Japan's dominance in the region and its intent in taking more political initiatives. In addition, drawing China into multifaceted regional and international frameworks could be an effective way to guard against any future increase in Chinese power, particularly military power, which might threaten and disrupt the international system.

Finally, METI officials' motivation to support the East Asian framework is obviously economic. While the US is still the most important economic partner for Japanese industries, East Asia has become another pillar as a trading and investing area. In this sense, APEC looked like a perfect mechanism for strengthening both relationships, and, in fact, the METI (then MITI) played an important role in establishing APEC. However, the stalemate of the APEC processes as well as the US establishment of NAFTA have gradually made METI officials look to bilateral as well as East Asian approaches because of the fear that Japan might be left out, when other major countries have joined their own regional and bilateral economic arrangements. Under the circumstances, they have been thinking that it may be wise to have several approaches, including bilateral and East Asian approaches, in addition to continuing its support for APEC and the WTO so as to secure Japan's economic interests.

It can be argued from the discussions above that, on the whole, Japan's interest in East Asian cooperation is the reflection of Japanese policymakers' thought that

Japan should broaden its options to pursue national interests so that Japanese foreign policy could have more diversity to offset the importance of the US. To Japan, the East Asian option is to complement the existing international and regional frameworks under the changing diplomatic conditions in the post Cold War period.

Last of all, it should be mentioned that the revised nature of Japan's regional policy has had a significant impact not only on Japanese and East Asian relations, but also on East Asian relations as a whole. It was discussed that Japan's economic power has gradually contributed to the creation of East Asia as an economic region throughout the postwar period, while its behind the scenes initiatives in the long-term perspective have advanced the process of Asia Pacific cooperation since the 1960s. In the same way, Japan has been leading a new project in East Asia since the late 1990s. It is true that other factors, particularly the East Asian financial crisis, have increased the momentum behind that project to a significant extent. However, it follows from what has been analysed in the book that the development of East Asian regionalism must also be discussed against the background of the shift in the orientation of Japanese foreign policy. The rise of Japan as a political power and the emergence of a new region are not a coincidence.

Notes

1 Introduction

1   This study defines East Asia as the ASEAN + 3 countries: the Association of Southeast Asian Nations (ASEAN) countries (Indonesia, Malaysia, the Philippines, Singapore, Thailand, Brunei, Vietnam, Laos, Cambodia and Burma), the People's Republic of China (hereafter China) and the Republic of Korea (hereafter South Korea). The term East Asia may sometimes include Hong Kong, the Republic of China (hereafter Taiwan) and Japan itself, depending on the context. The Democratic People's Republic of Korea (North Korea), despite being geographically located in the East Asian region, is excluded from the book's analysis, as Japan's relationship with that country is considerably different from the others and inappropriate to cover in a single volume.

2   See, for instance, Hook *et al.* (2001) and Pharr (1993: 235–62).

3   A total of 27 interviews were conducted in Tokyo over two periods (10 May–1 June 2000 and 27 March–4 April 2001). Among the interviewees were 12 bureaucrats, one politician, two academics and two journalists in 2000, and four bureaucrats, four academics and one employee of the World Bank in 2001. In addition, an interview with Eisuke Sakakibara, former Vice Minister of Finance for International Affairs, who is one of the key policymakers facing the crisis, was conducted in September 2001 in London. Seventeen interviews out of 27 were conducted with bureaucrats at various levels mainly in the Ministry of Finance and the Ministry of Foreign Affairs. This selection of interviewees was justified by the fact that these bureaucrats were considered to be the key decision makers in the cases covered in this book.

4   Cited in Grant (1997: 108).

5   He stresses the distinction between the studies of foreign policy and international politics, arguing that foreign policy cannot simply be the study of the way in which individual countries, treated as unified wholes, interact in the international system.

6   Argued in Hollis and Smith (1990: 117).

7   The capability of states also has been subject to intense discussion (Hanai 1998: 226–30).

8   Structural power is 'the power to shape and determine the structures of the global political economy within which other states, their political institutions, their economic enterprises and (not least) their scientists and other professional people have to operate' (Strange 1988: 24–5).

9   See Ikenberry *et al.* (1988: 1–14).

10 Inada, on the other hand, has a more reserved view in this respect, pointing out that, although it is true that the Japanese private sector has some impact on ODA, its influence has become limited; for instance, Japan's decision to promote the general untying of Japanese yen loans in 1978 was made despite strong opposition from business circles and the Ministry of International Trade and Industry (Inada 1989: 196–201).

2 Historical review of Japan's East Asian policy in the postwar period

1 The revised treaty stipulated the obligation of the US to defend Japan, and eliminated the article that had permitted the use of US forces to put down large-scale internal riots and disturbances in Japan, which had been highly controversial and antagonised many Japanese in the 1950s.

2 This amounts to around 10 per cent of Japan's annual defence budget (Hook *et al.* 2001: 134).

3 It reads: for the purpose of contributing to the security of Japan and the maintenance of international peace and security in the Far East, the United States of America is granted the use by its land, air, and naval forces of facilities and areas in Japan.

4 What constitutes the Asian region is a highly debatable issue. Regions are cognitively constructed, and so is the Asian region. It may include Australia and even Russia. Alternatively, the term Asia Pacific is sometimes used. Even within the Japanese government, the term has been used differently depending on the time and the issue. More recently, it has been used interchangeably with East Asia.

What the term 'Asia' stood for in the first blue book was not clearly stated, but the Japanese government generally thought of a more expansive area in the early postwar period than now, namely it was inclusive of South Asian countries like India. Also, when Japan referred to economic cooperation to Asia or Asian diplomacy in those days, China, the Korean Peninsula and Communist Indochina were left out. That is to say, Japan had to give up links with Communist countries in the region due to the Cold War reality. Also, Japan's relationship with South Korea, in spite of the fact that South Korea was part of the non-Communist world, was a thorny one because of deep animosity on both sides. The two countries' relationship was not normalised until 1965, when they signed the Treaty on Basic Relations. See Ohba (2001: 262) and Watanabe (1992: 89).

5 Cited in Watanabe (1992: 86–7).

6 The negotiations for reparations reached an agreement with Burma in 1954, with the Philippines in 1955, with Indonesia in 1958 and with South Vietnam in 1959. Japan also made agreements for economic cooperation with Laos (1958), Cambodia (1959) and Thailand (1962) (Hosoya 1993: 163–5).

7 Later the relationship between Japan and China was broadly based on the *seikei bunri* policy, whose implementation was occasionally disrupted, until they normalised their relations in 1972.

8 Okinawa was returned to Japan finally during Sato's premiership in 1972.

9 From around the mid-1960s, South Asia became excluded from Japan's focus with respect to its Asian policy, and Japan's interest turned more exclusively to non-Communist Southeast Asia (Ohba 2001: 264).

10 The Japanese government paid Japanese firms in yens for what Asian countries bought from them.

11 The following argument about the ADB draws largely on Yasutomo (1983).

12 The turning point of US policy came with Johnson's address at the Johns Hopkins University in April 1965. Since then the US supported Asian institutions by Asian initiatives (Yasutomo 1983: 67, Yamakage 1997: 19).

13 Since the establishment of the ADB, the Japanese have occupied the post of president.

14 ASEAN was founded in 1967 and was originally composed of Indonesia, Malaysia, the Philippines, Singapore and Thailand.

15 The MOFA was concerned about ASEAN's possible clash with the US bilateral security system in the region, while the MITI was worried about the possibility that ASEAN would turn itself into an economic block that could exclude Japan and the US. Also, they had a concern that the formation of ASEAN would have a negative effect on bilateral relations between Japan and the ASEAN countries (Hook *et al.* 2001: 186–7).

16 The yen appreciated against the dollar from 360 yen per dollar to less than 300 yen after it was floated in 1973.

17 The diplomatic use of its economic resources was not limited to East Asian policy. The substantial increase of aid to the Middle East is a case in point. The Arab oil embargo in 1973 had a huge impact on the thinking of Japanese policymakers, as Japan depended on the Middle East for a large part of its oil imports, which were the lubricant of the postwar Japanese development. That incident reminded them of the vulnerability of the Japanese economy in terms of natural resources, and forced them to reconsider the postwar strategy of Japanese foreign policy. In fact, Japan immediately acted to establish closer ties with oil-producing countries in the Middle East by using economic assistance as a means. Consequently, Japan's aid to this region increased significantly (the share of Middle Eastern countries in Japanese ODA increased from 3.6 per cent in 1970 to 10.4 per cent in 1980), and since then Japan has given special attention to this region specifically with respect to aid. It is noteworthy that this pro-Arab attitude of Japan was at odds with the US's pro-Israel stance.

18 The report, issued by the Department of Defense, confirmed the continued US commitment to the US–Japan Security Treaty as the basis of the US security policy.

19 *Nihon Keizai Shinbun*, 27 September 2001.

20 Article 9 declares: (1) Aspiring sincerely to an international peace based on justice and order, the Japanese people forever renounce war as a sovereign right of the nation and the threat or use of force as means of settling international dispute; (2) In order to accomplish the aim of the preceding paragraph, land, sea, and air forces, as well as other war potential, will never be maintained. The right of belligerency of the state will not be recognised (Hook and McCormack 2001: 191).

21 There are a number of arguments involved. For instance, *the Yomiuri Shinbun*, the conservative right, the most widely read newspaper in Japan, holds that several changes of the constitution are necessary, while *the Asahi Shinbun*, the liberal left, the second most widely read daily, opposes the idea. Also, Ichiro Ozawa, a conservative politician, favours revision and advocates the idea of Japan as a 'normal country'. On the other hand, Yoichi Funabashi of the Asahi Shinbun proposes a vision of Japan as a 'global civilian power'. (See, for detail of the debates on the constitution, Hook and McCormack (2001) and Finn (1997: 115–29).)

22 The share of Japanese FDI in the total investment in East Asia was 27.5 per cent (1990) and 16.5 per cent (1995), while the share of US FDI was 18.8 per cent (1990) and 12.2 per cent (1995) (JETRO 1997).

23 The flying geese model has not been unchallenged. For instance, Bernard and Ravenhill criticise the model, arguing that the pattern of industrialisation in East Asian countries has been dramatically different from that of Japan, as they remain highly dependent on Japanese capital goods and technologies. They also argue that the model also fails to capture the complexity of regionalised production networks, and focuses on the flow of specific products in isolation from others (Bernard and Ravenhill 1995: 171–209).

24 Japan was the largest donor in 2002 in the following East Asian countries: Indonesia, Vietnam, Cambodia, Thailand, China, the Philippines, Myanmar and Laos (MOFA homepage, <www.mofa.go.jp/mofaj/gaiko/oda/shiryo/hakusyo/04_hakusho/ODA2004/html/siryo/index.htm> (accessed 1 March 2005)).

25 See in more detail Hatch and Yamamura (1996: 115–29).

26 With respect to these debates, see Tanaka (1994: 132–5). He shows that the trend of new Asianism has risen due to the recognition on the part of influential politicians and business leaders that East Asia has to have a new mechanism to maintain regional security in the post Cold War period, together with the confidence that Japan's East Asian policy, specifically its aid policy, has greatly contributed to the remarkable development of East Asian countries in the 1980s and 1990s.

27 The third conference in 1983 was named PECC for the first time and the first and second conference were referred as PECC I and PECC II respectively (Korhonen 1998: 132).

28 The countries concerned were Australia, Canada, Japan, New Zealand, the US, the five

ASEAN countries, South Korea and South Pacific countries, which were joined by the representatives of PAFTAD and PBEC.

29 The following discussion about Japan's stance on this point draws on Kikuchi (1995: 110–36).

30 *Japan Economic Journal*, 8 April 1989 and 10 June 1989.

31 Cited in Terada (1998: 345–6).

32 Japan's military spending exceeded one per cent of GNP in 1987 (1.004 per cent), but went down below one per cent in 1990 (Japan Defense Agency various years).

33 The US basically took the same position as ASEAN in that it supported the tripartite coalition government, consisting of Prince Sihanouk's faction, Son Sann's faction and Pol Pot's faction (Khmer Rouge), against the Hun Sen's government in Phnom Penh. However, the US adopted quite a hard line policy as a part of its containment policy against the Soviet Union and also due to the consideration of its Chinese relations, while ASEAN took a softer approach, aiming at a more peaceful solution (Takeda 1995: 71–2).

34 In the previous meetings including the one in Paris in 1989, each of the factions in the tripartite coalition had an equal share with the Phnom Penh government, thus the share of the coalition government and the Phnom Penh government was 3:1.

35 Comment in a panel discussion featured in *Kokusai Mondai*, January 2001, p.12.

3 The Washington Consensus versus the Japanese approach and implications for the East Asian financial crisis

1 This term, coined by John Williamson (Williamson 1990), is used in this book as the view on desirable economic management based on the neoclassical orthodoxy, shared by Washington based international organisations, specifically the World Bank and the IMF, and major developed countries, particularly the US and the UK.

2 However, Kenichi Ohno comments that, unlike the US and the UK, the scholars that have supported the Japanese approach are on the side of the majority (Interview, 3 April 2001).

3 Shiratori is a former high MOF official and Executive Director of the World Bank on behalf of the Japanese government.

4 According to Chalmers Johnson (who is regarded as the founder of this school), those who point out that Japan has a political economy different from that of the Anglo-American countries in terms of institutions, the role of the state, and the weight of economic nationalism are said to be part of this school (Johnson 1995: 12).

5 Johnson himself considers the application of the Japanese developmental model to East Asian success as follows. Although none of the cases are identical to the Japanese model, the Japanese model has been successfully emulated by the four East Asian NICs, South Korea, Taiwan, Hong Kong and Singapore, but beyond those countries, the model does not exist (Johnson 1999: 40, Johnson 1998: 653–61).

6 By East Asia, Wade mainly means Japan, South Korea and Taiwan.

7 Wade argues that while Korea and Taiwan are examples of authoritarian corporatism, Japan illustrates a type of corporatism with characteristics between democratic and authoritarian, or soft authoritarian (Wade 1990: 27).

8 This does not mean that the deductive method is entirely dismissed by the Japanese officials and academics, of course. Rather, some of the Japanese scholars propose a middle way between the deductive and inductive approaches. For instance, Kenichi Ohno argues that researchers must continuously go back and forth between the neoclassical method and more inductive area studies (Ohno 1998: 19–20). Also see an interview with Kenichi Ohno in *Kokusai Kaihatsu Janaru*, January 1998, pp. 32–5.

9 MOFA homepage, <www.mofa.go.jp/policy/oda/summary/1999/ref1.html> (accessed 1 April 2002).

10 Cited in Inada (1995: 161).

11 However, Japan later announced it had reservations to the Bangkok approach, which reveals Japan's difficulty amid Asia and Western countries (Neary 2000: 85).
12 Kubota is a former high MOF official and was engaged in the discussion about development philosophy as a managing director in the OECF in the early 1990s.
13 *Far Eastern Economic Review*, 12 March 1992, and Shiratori (1998: 78).
14 *Nikkei Weekly*, 21 March 1992.
15 Ibid.
16 Johnson notes that Japan forced the World Bank to write the study as a condition for further Japanese funding (Johnson 1999: 35).
17 A comment by a Japanese official cited in Yasutomo (1995: 79).
18 World Bank Tokyo Office homepage, <www.worldbank.or.jp/11press/update/ P71.html> (accessed 12 December 2001).
19 Interview, 3 April 2001.
20 Ibid.
21 Ibid.
22 Ibid.
23 Ibid.
24 Shimomura was the then Director of the OECF's Economic Department.
25 Interview with Kenichi Ohno, 3 April 2001.
26 The World Bank took a quite different stance on the crisis from the IMF (World Bank 1998). In particular, Stiglitz aggressively criticised IMF policies.
27 For a comprehensive comparison between Japan and Washington concerning views on the crisis, see Aramaki (1999).
28 IMF homepage, <www.imf.org/external/np/exr/facts.asia.htm> (accessed 1 May 2001). These views of the IMF were slightly revised in the updated report issued in June 2000 (<www.imf.org/external/np/exr/ib/2000/062300.htm> (accessed 1 May 2001)). The new version argues that the crisis was caused partly by macroeconomic imbalances, and does not emphasise the governance problem in affected countries as a source of the crisis. It simply mentions that implicit government guarantees remained pervasive in an environment of large private capital inflow and rapid domestic credit expansion.
29 IMF homepage, <www.imf.org/external/np/exr/facts.asia.htm> (accessed 1 May 2001).
30 Speech at the Foreign Correspondents Club of Japan, 15 December 1998 (MOF homepage, <www.mof.go.jp/english/if/e1e057.htm> (accessed 1 May 2001)).
31 Japan's criticism of the IMF policies was backed by some prominent Western scholars, such as Jeffrey Sachs and Martin Feldstein.

4 Japanese policies towards the East Asian financial crisis

1 It lost 20 per cent of its value on the day of the announcement.
2 Interview with MOF official (International Bureau), 30 March 2001.
3 Interview with MOF official (International Bureau), 28 March 2001.
4 Only US$4 billion was available at most from the IMF then.
5 Also, interview with MOF official (International Bureau), 28 March 2001.
6 After the Mexican crisis in 1994, Congress put restrictions on US emergency funding to the Exchange Stability Fund. That restriction was close to expiring when the Thai crisis occurred, and the Treasury hesitated to ask Congress for an exemption for Thailand in order to avoid further restrictions on the fund (Green 2001: 245).
7 *Sankei Shinbun*, 19 August 1997 and *Nihon Keizai Shinbun*, 19 August 1997.
8 *Sankei Shinbun*, 31 August 1997.
9 Interview with MOF official (International Bureau), 12 May 2000.
10 Interview with MOF official (International Bureau), 12 May 2000. Also, Anthony Rowley notes that, according to some observers in Hong Kong, Tokyo was 'acting under the guise of supporting the so-called ASEAN initiative, which, after all, owed much of its genesis to Japanese thinking and behind-the-scenes persuasion' (Rowley 1997).

11 *Sankei Shinbun*, 9 October 1997.
12 Interview with MOF officials (International Bureau), 12 May 2000 and 28 March 2001.
13 Interview with Eisuke Sakakibara (Former MOF Vice Minister), 18 September 2001.
14 Interview with MOF official (International Bureau), 28 March 2001.
15 Interview with MOF official (International Bureau), 12 May 2000. The following account on the stance of ASEAN countries is largely based on the remarks of this MOF official who was posted in the Japanese embassy in Thailand then and was able to sound out informally ASEAN countries.
16 Nesadurai argues that IMF reforms were unacceptable to Malaysian leaders, because the IMF conditionalities could involve the eventual dismantling of the ethnic-based distributive policy that favours ethnic Malays. The political legitimacy of the current government is based on the continuation of this policy, which is also an essential element of the politics of patronage that is entrenched in the Malaysian political economy (Nesadurai 2000: 73–113).
17 Interview with MOF officials (International Bureau), 12 May 2000, 28 March 2001 and 30 March 2001, and Eisuke Sakakibara (former MOF Vice Minister), 18 September 2001. According to *Sankei Shinbun*, China and the US had conferred on the AMF behind the scenes and had agreed not to support it before the conference in September. It reported that the US used the card of the issue of WTO membership (*Sankei Shinbun*, 7 December 1997).
18 *Mainichi Shinbun*, 28 September 1997.
19 *South China Morning Post*, 21 November 1997.
20 Interview with MOF official (International Bureau), 12 May 2000.
21 It has declined from 38 per cent in 1946 to 17 per cent as of February 2005.
22 The arrangements placed the limit at US$1 billion. Before these arrangements, the five Southeast Asian economies of Hong Kong, Indonesia, Malaysia, Singapore and Thailand agreed on the same sort of transactions in November 1995.
23 Interview with MOF official (International Bureau), 12 May 2000.
24 Interview with Eisuke Sakakibara (former MOF Vice Minister), 18 September 2001.
25 *Sankei Shinbun*, 2 November 1997.
26 Interview with MOF official (International Bureau), 12 May 2000.
27 Some interviewees noted that the importance of the stability of the East Asian economies to Japan was behind Japan's interest in regional financial cooperation (interview with MOF officials (International Bureau), 12 May 2000 and 30 March 2001, and Eisuke Sakakibara (Former MOF Vice Minister), 18 September 2001).
28 Interview with Eisuke Sakakibara (Former MOF Vice Minister), 18 September 2001. Another MOF official also notes that the AMF proposal comes out of Japan's different stance on IMF policies towards the crisis (interview with MOF official, 27 March 2001).
29 Interview with MOF officials, 30 March 2001 and 27 March 2001.
30 Japan is in second place in the IMF and the World Bank (6.33 per cent and 7.91 per cent respectively), but this is still proportionally far behind the US (17.67 per cent and 16.49 per cent) (as of June 2000).
31 Interview with MOF official, 27 March 2001. He also stated that the organisational culture of the international organisations was quite different from that of Japan, or the MOF.
32 Yoichi Funabashi comments that MOF officials lack the ability to influence policy-making processes in the international organisations, and thus they tend to have parochial considerations and to do something by themselves, rather than make an effort to advocate their views internationally (interview with Funabashi (Asahi Shinbun), 1 June 2000).
33 Interview with MOF official (International Bureau), 28 March 2001.
34 The Philippines had been already under the IMF program, and it asked to expand IMF credit on 18 July.
35 Interview with MOF official (International Bureau), 28 March 2001.

36 Interview with Eisuke Sakakibara (former MOF Vice Minister), 28 September 2001, and MOF officials (International Bureau), 12 May 2000 and 30 March 2001.
37 According to a MOF official, the Budget Bureau preferred to appropriate a large one-off payment, rather than having to deal with a request each time a crisis arose (interview with MOF official (International Bureau), 12 May 2000).
38 Interview with Eisuke Sakakibara (former MOF Vice Minister), 18 September, 2001.
39 Interview with MOF official (International Bureau), 12 May 2000.
40 Interview with Eisuke Sakakibara (former MOF Vice Minister), 18 September 2001.
41 Interview with MOF official (International Bureau), 12 May 2000.
42 Interview with MOF official (International Bureau), 28 March 2001.
43 *Sankei Shinbun*, 7 December 1997.
44 Interview with Eisuke Sakakibara (former MOF Vice Minister), 18 September 2001.
45 *Financial Times*, 15 January 1998.
46 *Financial Times*, 15 January 1998.
47 *Financial Times*, 15 January 1998.
48 The IMF decided to finance the total amount of US$22 billion step by step, not altogether, while demanding severe conditions and trying to extract concessions by stages.
49 The New Miyazawa Initiative reads that East Asian countries affected by the currency crisis need medium to long-term capitals to implement the following policy measures for economic recovery: (1) support for corporate debt restructuring in the private sector and efforts to make financial systems sound and stable; (2) strengthen the social safety net; (3) stimulate the economy (implement public undertakings to increase employment); and (4) address the credit crunch (facilitate trade finance and assistance to small- and medium-sized enterprises).
50 The short-term facility takes the form of swap arrangements. Japan has established a facility for South Korea (up to US$5 billion) and that for Malaysia (up to US$2.5 billion).
51 The Board of the ADB approved the establishment of the ACCSF on 23 March 1999.
52 Interview with MOF official (International Bureau), 12 May 2000.
53 *Nihon Keizai Shinbun*, 1 December 1998.
54 Interview with MOF official (International Bureau), 12 May 2000.
55 Cited in Green (2001: 254–5).
56 The breakdown of this is: contribution to the international assistance package harmonised with the IMF (US$19 billion), assistance for private sector activities, facilitation of trade financing (approximately US$22.5 billion), assistance for economic structural reforms, human resources development (approximately US$2.3 billion) and assistance to the socially vulnerable (approximately US$0.15 billion). (MOFA homepage: <www.mofa. go.jp/policy/economy/asia/crisis0010.html> (accessed 26 April 2002)).
57 MOFA homepage: <www.mofa.go.jp/policy/economy/asia/crisis0010.html> (accessed 26 April 2002).
58 Interview with MOFA official (Asian Affairs Bureau), 12 May 2000.
59 Interview with MOF official (International Bureau), 12 May 2000.

5 Japanese policy towards East Asian regionalism

1 The foreign ministers meeting and that of the economic ministers were also held in July and September 1996 respectively. Also, East Asian senior officials meetings (SOM) under ASEM have been held as needed in order to coordinate the East Asian positions for ministerial and summit level meetings.
2 *Sankei Shinbun*, 16 December 1997.
3 *Mainichi Shinbun*, 12 January 1997.
4 Interviews with MOFA officials (Economic Affairs Bureau), 17 May 2000 and 16 May 2000, and METI (then MITI) official (International Trade Policy Bureau), 26 May 2000.
5 Comment from Ellis Krauss sent by email to the author in December 2000.

6 Interviews with MOFA official (Economic Cooperation Bureau), 11 May 2000 and MOFA official (Economic Affairs Bureau), 16 May 2000.
7 Interview with MOF official (International Bureau), 18 May 2000 (author's translation).
8 The meeting between the Japanese and ASEAN leaders was the first one in ten years. It was twenty years ago that a joint statement from them was adopted.
9 Interview with MOFA official (Asian and Oceanian Affairs Bureau), 29 March 2001.
10 The report of the East Asian Vision Group was submitted to the leaders at the ASEAN + 3 meeting in 2001.
11 When the Japanese Prime Minister proposed this meeting in the previous year, China was reported to have taken a very cautious attitude, but this time the then South Korean President, Kim Dae Jung, played a buffer role between the two countries, which led to the realisation of the meeting.
12 MOFA homepage, <www.mofa.go.jp/mofaj/gaiko/kaidan/s_obuchi/aseam99/shuseki. html> (accessed 27 October 2000).
13 The second meeting was held on 25 November 1999 during the ASEAN + 3 summit, and the Deputies agreed to advance a regional cooperation mechanism. On the same day, the ASEAN Finance Ministers meeting issued a joint statement that incorporated the following clause: '[w]e are considering with them [the East Asian dialogue partners] ways of cooperation by strengthening the institutional capacity for consultation and collaboration on monetary, fiscal and financial issues, including policy dialogue among the East Asian countries'.
14 Under the arrangement, a portion of each country's foreign reserves is pooled in a facility to prepare for possible short-term cash shortages in the balance of payments of any member.
15 *Financial Times*, 10 May 2000.
16 Interview with MOF official (International Bureau), 12 May 2000 and MOFA official (Economic Affairs Bureau), 17 May 2000.
17 Interview with MOF official (International Bureau), 30 March 2001.
18 Interview with Eisuke Sakakibara (former MOF Vice Minister), 18 September 2001, and MOF official (International Bureau), 30 March 2001.
19 The issue of the relationship between the regional facility and IMF assistance was decided as follows: assistance through the regional swap arrangements will be extended when a recipient country has already received an IMF loan, or is expecting to get it in the near future; however, when the countries who are giving credit consider that the recipient country is facing a short-term liquidity problem, the recipient country could obtain assistance through the arrangements of up to an amount of 10 per cent of its limit without linkage of the credit with IMF loans.
20 Interview with MOF official (International Bureau), 30 March 2001.
21 Interview with MOF official (International Bureau), 12 May 2000.
22 *Mainichi Shinbun*, 16 October 2000.
23 Interview with MOF official (International Bureau), 28 March 2001.
24 Ministry of Foreign Affairs Malaysia homepage, <www.kln.gov.my/english/ content/idx-speeches.htm> (accessed 1 April 2002).
25 The conference was sponsored by Nihon Keizai Shinbun, with the participation of East Asian leaders and business executives.
26 Nihon Keizai Shinbun homepage, <www.nni.nikkei.co.jp/FR/NIKKEI/inasia/future/> (accessed 20 March 2002).
27 An Eminent Persons Group that the then Prime Minister Obuchi proposed to establish, which consisted of 26 members including academics and executives of private companies from ASEAN and Japan.
28 Japan Institute of International Affairs homepage, <www.jiia.or.jp/pdf/e_nichi_ asean. pdf> (accessed 10 January 2005).
29 *Korea Herald*, 3 September 1999.
30 *Korea Herald*, 27 September 2000.

31 *Korea Herald*, 23 November 2000.
32 *Mainichi Shinbun*, 18 October 2000.
33 *Mainichi Shinbun*, 18 October 2000.
34 Interview with Yoichi Funabashi (Asahi Shinbun), 1 June 2000.
35 *Bangkok Post*, 26 November 2000, and *Straits Times*, 25 November 2000.
36 *Nihon Keizai Shinbun*, 25 November 2000.
37 *Nihon Keizai Shinbun*, 24 November 2000.
38 *Nihon Keizai Shinbun*, 4 November 2000.
39 *Korea Herald*, 27 November 2000.
40 *Nihon Keizai Shinbun*, 10 May 2000.
41 Interview with Eisuke Sakakibara (Former MOF Vice Minister), 18 September 2001.
42 Interview with MOFA official (Asian Affairs Bureau), 12 May 2000.
43 Interview with MOF official (International Bureau), 28 March 2001.
44 Interview with METI (then MITI) official (International Trade Policy Bureau), 26 May 2000.
45 Interview with MOF official (International Bureau), 12 May 2000.
46 According to Higgott, in tactical learning the behaviour of regional states changes in order to respond to domestically generated needs and interests, while cognitive learning is accompanied by value change, namely the change in 'regional values and aims, or more specifically the values of the individual regional states towards questions of economic autonomy, sovereignty and economic policymaking' (Higgott 1993: 103–17).
47 As of 25 January 2005, 15 arrangements (about US$37.5 billion) have been concluded. (MOF homepage, <www.mof.go.jp/jouhou/kokkin/frame.html> (accessed 1 March 2005).) Also, it is reported that the MOF is considering an increase in the limit of financing (Nihon Keizai Shinbun, 4 January 2005).
48 *Financial Times*, 30 November 2004.

6 The style of Japanese foreign policy: a low-profile and incremental approach

1 This understanding of the concept of leadership is close to what Oran Young calls 'structural leadership', namely the form of leadership derived from the possession of material resources, which is translated into bargaining leverage in negotiations in an effort to bring pressure to bear on others. On the other hand, the argument on the style of Japanese policy in this book is probably related to Young's 'entrepreneurial leadership', which is the use of negotiating skill to frame mutually acceptable deals and to persuade others to support them (Young 1991: 281–308).
2 Interview with MOF official (International Bureau), 30 March 2001. Also, interview with Eisuke Sakakibara (former MOF Vice Minister), 18 September 2001.
3 By culture, this book means, following the definition of Stockwin, those aspects of current practice which are influenced by relatively long-standing patterns of social interaction and by expectations about the behaviour of others conditioned by the norms and values of the society in which individuals operate (Stockwin 1999: 220–1).
4 See, Ramseyer and Rosenbluth (1993).
5 Green also notes the character of Sakakibara in Japan's proposing the AMF (Green 2001: 246–7).
6 Interview with MOFA official (Economic Cooperation Bureau), 19 May 2000.
7 *Nihon Keizai Shinbun*, 25 October 2001.
8 *Financial Times*, 18 January, 2002.
9 Interview with MOF official (International Bureau), 12 May 2000.
10 Interview with Eisuke Sakakibara (former MOF Vice Minister), 18 September 2001.
11 Interview with Isamu Kubota (former Director-General, MOF), 20 May 2000.
12 Makoto Iokibe, in a statement made at the Toshiba International Foundation Symposium

held at the British Museum on 17 September 2001. He also commented that, although Japan-South Korea relations seemed to have become difficult again due to disputes over a controversial history textbook and the Prime Minister's visit to the Yasukuni shrine, the attitude of South Korean officials and leaders was different from the past strong antagonism towards Japan, and they wanted Japan to make some gesture in order to calm the public down.

13 Interview with MOF official (International Bureau), 12 May 2000.
14 Interview with Eisuke Sakakibara (former MOF Vice Minister), 18 September 2001.
15 Nesadurai, in examining the process of APEC, questions that the US has the capacity to impose its economic agenda on the region (Nesadurai 1996).

7 Conclusion

1 Comment in a panel discussion featured in *Kokusai Mondai*, January 2001, p.16.

Bibliography

Publications in English

Allison, Graham T. (1971) *Essence of Decision*, Boston: Little, Brown.

Altbach, Eric (1997) 'The Asian monetary fund proposal: a case study of Japanese regional leadership', *Japan Economic Institute Report* 47A.

Amyx, Jennifer A. (2004) 'Japan and evolution of regional financial arrangements in East Asia', in Ellis S. Krauss and T.J. Pempel (eds) *Beyond Bilateralism: U.S.-Japan Relations in the New Asia Pacific*, Stanford: Stanford University Press, 198–218.

Arase, David (1993a) 'Japanese policy towards democracy and human rights in Asia', *Asian Survey* 33, 10: 935–52.

—— (1993b) 'Japan in East Asia', in Tsuneo Akaha and Frank Langdon (eds) *Japan in the Posthegemonic World*, Boulder: Lynne Rienner, 113–36.

—— (1995) *Buying Power: The Political Economy of Japanese Foreign Aid*, Boulder: Lynne Rienner.

Bernard, Mitchell and John Ravenhill (1995) 'Beyond product cycles and flying geese: regionalization, hierarchy, and the industrialization of East Asia', *World Politics* 47: 171–209.

Bhagwati, Jagdish (1998) 'The capital myth: the difference between trade in widgets and dollars', *Foreign Affairs* 77, 3: 7–12.

Blaker, Michael (1993) 'Evaluating Japanese diplomatic performance', in Gerald L. Curtis (ed.) *Japan's Foreign Policy After the Cold War: Coping with Change*, Armonk, New York: M.E. Sharpe, 1–42.

Breslin, Shaun (2001) 'Beyond bilateralism? the local, the regional and the global in Sino-Japanese economic relations', paper presented at German Institute for Japanese Studies conference, Tokyo.

Burchill, Scott (1996) 'Realism and neo-realism', in Scott Burchill *et al. Theories of International Relations*, London: Macmillan, 67–92.

Calder, Kent E. (1988) 'Japanese foreign economic formation: explaining the reactive state', *World Politics* 40, 4: 517–41.

—— (1993) *Strategic Capitalism: Private Business and Public Purpose in Japanese Industrial Finance*, Princeton: Princeton University Press.

—— (1997) 'The institutions of Japanese foreign policy', in Richard L. Grant (ed.) *The Process of Japanese Foreign Policy: Focus on Asia*, London: Royal Institute of International Affairs, 1–24.

Cohen, Benjamin (1986) *In Whose Interest?: International Banking and American Foreign Policy*, New Haven: Yale University Press.

Curtis, Gerald L. (1993) 'Introduction', in Gerald L. Curtis (ed.) *Japan's Foreign Policy After the Cold War: Coping with Change*, Armonk, New York: M.E. Sharpe, xv–xxvi.

—— (1999) *The Logic of Japanese Politics: Leaders, Institutions, and the Limits of Change*, New York: Columbia University Press.

Doner, Richard F. (1997) 'Japan in East Asia: institutions and regional leadership', in Peter J. Katzenstein and Takashi Shiraishi (eds) *Network Power: Japan and Asia*, Ithaca, New York: Cornell University Press, 197–233.

Drifte, Reinhard (1998) *Japan' Foreign Policy for the 21st Century: From Economic Superpower to What Power?*, London: Macmillan.

Dunne, Timothy (1997) 'Liberalism', in John Baylis and Steve Smith (eds) *The Globalization of World Politics: An Introduction to International Relations*, Oxford: Oxford University Press, 147–63.

Finn, Richard B. (1997) 'Japan's search for a global role: politics and security', in Warren S. Hunsberger (ed.) *Japan's Quest: The Search for International Role, Recognition, and Respect*, Armonk, New York: M.E. Sharpe, 113–30.

Fishlow, Albert and Catherine Gwin (1994) 'Overview: lessons from the East Asian experience', in Robert Wade *et al. Miracle or Design?: Lessons from the East Asian Miracle*, Washington, DC: Overseas Development Council, 1–12.

Fukushima, Akiko (1999) *Japanese Foreign Policy: The Emerging Logic of Multilateralism*, London: Macmillan.

Funabashi, Yoichi (1991/1992) 'Japan and the new world order', *Foreign Affairs* 70, 5: 58–74.

—— (1993) 'Asianization of Asia', *Foreign Affairs* 72, 5: 75–85.

—— (1995) *Asia Pacific Fusion: Japan's Role in APEC*, Washington, DC: Institute for International Economics.

—— (1998) 'Tokyo's Depression Diplomacy', *Foreign Affairs* 77, 6: 26–36.

Garten, Jeffrey E. (1992) *A Cold Peace: America, Japan, Germany, and the Struggle for Supremacy*, New York: Times Books.

Goldstein, Judith (1998) 'Ideas, institutions, and American trade policy', *International Organization* 42, 1: 179–217.

Goldstein, Judith and Robert O. Keohane (1993) 'Ideas and foreign policy: an analytical framework', in Judith Goldstein and Robert O. Keohane (eds) *Ideas and Foreign Policy: Beliefs, Institutions, and Political Change*, Ithaca: Cornell University Press, 3–30.

Grant, Richard L. (1997) 'Japan and Northeast Asia', in Richard L. Grant (ed.) *The Process of Japanese Foreign Policy: Focus on Asia*, London: Royal Institute of International Affairs, 107–22.

Green, Michael J. (1995) *Arming Japan: Defence Production, Alliance Politics, and the Postwar Search for Autonomy*, New York: Columbia University Press.

—— (2001) *Japan's Reluctant Realism: Foreign Policy Challenge in an Era of Uncertain Power*, New York: Palgrave.

Grieco, Joseph M. (1997) 'Systemic sources of variation in regional institutionalization in Western Europe, East Asia and the Americas', in Edward D. Mansfield and Helen V. Milner (eds) *The Political Economy of Regionalism*, New York: Columbia University Press, 164–87.

Haggard, Stephan (1997) 'The political economy of regionalism in Asia and the Americas', in Edward D. Mansfield and Helen V. Milner (eds) *The Political Economy of Regionalism*, New York: Columbian University Press, 20–49.

Hamada, Koichi (1999) 'From the AMF to the Miyazawa Initiative: observations on Japan's current diplomacy', *The Journal of East Asian Affairs* 8, 1: 1–32.

Harris, Stuart (2000) 'Asian multilateral institutions and their response to the Asian Economic Crisis: the regional and global implications', *The Pacific Review* 13, 3: 495–516.

Hatch, Walter and Kozo Yamamura (1996) *Asia in Japan's Embrace: Building a Regional Production Alliance*, Cambridge: Cambridge University Press.

Hellmann, Donald C. (1988) 'Japanese politics and foreign policy: elitist democracy within an American greenhouse', in Takashi Inoguchi and Daniel I. Okimoto (eds) *The Political Economy of Japan: Volume 2 The Changing International Context*, Stanford: Stanford University Press, 345–78.

Higgott, Richard (1993) 'Economic cooperation: theoretical opportunities and practical constraints', *The Pacific Review* 6, 2: 103–17.

—— (1994a) 'APEC – a sceptical view', in Andrew Mack and John Ravenhill (eds) *Pacific Cooperation: Building Economic and Security Regimes in the Asia–Pacific Region*, NSW: Allen and Unwin, 66–97.

—— (1994b) 'Ideas, identity and policy coordination in the Asia–Pacific', *The Pacific Review* 7, 4: 368–79.

—— (1998a) 'The international relations of the Asian economic crisis: a study in the politics of resentment', *New Political Economy* 3, 3: 333–56.

—— (1998b) 'The international political economy of regionalism: the Asia Pacific and Europe compared', in William D. Coleman and Geoffrey R.D. Underhill (eds) *Regionalism and Global Economic Integration: Europe, Asia and the Americas*, London: Routledge, 42–67.

—— (1999) 'The political economy of globalisation in East Asia', in Kris Olds, Peter Dicken, Philip F. Kelly, Lily Kong and Henry Wai-chung Yeung (eds) *Globalisation and the Asia–Pacific: Contested Territories*, London: Routledge, 91–106.

—— (2000a) 'Regionalism in the Asia–Pacific: two steps forward, one step back?', in Richard Stubbs and Geoffrey R.D. Underhill (eds) *Political Economy and the Changing Global Order (Second Edition)*, Ontario: Oxford University Press Canada, 254–63.

—— (2000b) 'Contested globalization: the changing context and normative challenges', *Review of International Studies* 26: 131–53.

Higgott, Richard, Andrew Fenton Cooper and Jenelle Bonnor (1991) 'Cooperation-building in the Asia–Pacific region: APEC and the new institutionalism', *Pacific Economic Paper* 199, Australia-Japan Research Centre.

Higgott, Richard and Andrew Fenton Cooper (1990) 'Middle power leadership and coalition building: Australia, the Cairns group, and the Uruguay round of trade', *International Organization* 44, 4: 589–632.

Higgott Richard and Richard Stubbs (1995) 'Competing conceptions of economic regionalism: APEC versus EAEC in the Asia Pacific', *Review of International Political Economy* 2, 3: 516–35.

Hirata, Keiko (2001) 'Reaction and action: analysing Japan's relations with the Socialist Republic of Vietnam', in S. Javed Maswood (ed.) *Japan and East Asian Regionalism*, London: Routledge, 90–117.

Hollis, Martin and Steve Smith (1990) *Explaining and Understanding International Relations*, Oxford: Clarendon Press.

Hook, Glenn (1996a) 'Japan and the construction of Asia Pacific', in Andrew Gamble and Anthony Payne (eds) *Regionalism and World Order*, London: Macmillan, 169–206.

—— (1996b) 'Japan and contested regionalism', in Ian G. Cook, Marcus A. Doel and Rel Li (eds) *Fragmented Asia: Regional Integration and National Disintegration in Pacific Asia*, Aldershot, Hants: Avebury, 12–28.

Hook, Glenn D., Julie Gilson, Christopher W. Hughes and Hugo Dobson (2001) *Japan's International Relations: Politics, Economics and Security*, London: Routledge.

—— (2002) 'Japan and the East Asian financial crisis: patterns, motivations and instrumentalisation of Japanese regional economic diplomacy', *European Journal of East Asian Studies* 1, 2: 177–97.

Hook, Glenn D. and Gavan McCormack (2001) *Japan's Contested Constitution: Document and Analysis*, London: Routledge.

Hughes, Christopher W. (2000) 'Japanese policy and the East Asian currency crisis: abject defeat or quiet victory?', *Review of International Political Economy* 7, 2: 219–53.

—— (2002) 'Japan's security policy and the war on terror: steady incrementalism or radical leap?', CSGR Working Paper 105/02, University of Warwick.

Hurrell, Andrew (1995) 'Regionalism in theoretical perspective', in Louise Fawcett and Andrew Hurrell (eds) *Regionalism in World Politics: Regional Organisation and International Order*, New York: Oxford University Press, 37–73.

Ikenberry, John G., David A. Lake, and Michael Mastanduno (1988) 'Introduction: approaches to explaining American foreign economic policy', *International Organization* 42, 1: 1–14.

Jayasuriya, Kanishka and Andrew Rosser (1999) 'Economic orthodoxy and the East Asian crisis', Working Paper 94, Asian Research Centre, Murdoch University, <wwwarc. murdoch.edu.au/wp/wp94.pdf> (accessed 1 March 2005).

Johnson, Chalmers (1982) *MITI and the Japanese Miracle*, Stanford, California: Stanford University Press.

—— (1992) 'Japan in search of a "normal" role', Policy Paper 3, Institute of Global Conflict and Cooperation, University of California.

—— (1993) 'History restated: Japanese-American relations at the end of the century', in Richard Higgott, Richard Leaver and John Ravenhill (eds) *Pacific Economic Relations in the 1990s: Cooperation or Conflict?*, St Leonard, NSW: Allen & Unwin, 39–61.

—— (1995) *Japan: Who Governs?: The Rise of the Developmental State*, New York: W. W. Norton & Company.

—— (1998) 'Economic crisis in East Asia: the clash of capitalisms', *Cambridge Journal of Economics* 22: 653–61.

—— (1999) 'The developmental state; odyssey of a concept', in Meredith Woo-Cumings, (ed.) *The Developmental State*, Ithaca, New York: Cornell University Press, 32–60.

Kahler, Miles (1990) 'The United States and the International Monetary Fund: declining influence or declining interest?', in Margaret P. Karns and Karen A. Mingst (eds) *The United States and Multilateral Institutions: Patterns of Changing Instrumentality and Influence*, Boston: Unwin Hyman, 91–114.

Katada, Saori N. (1998) 'Collective management of international financial crises: the Japanese government in the Pacific rim', paper presented at CIS seminar, University of California.

—— (2001) *Banking on Stability: Japan and the Cross-Pacific Dynamics of International Financial Crisis Management*, Ann Arbor: University of Michigan Press.

—— (2002) 'Japan and Asian monetary regionalism: cultivating a new regional leadership after the Asian financial crisis' *Geopolitics* 7, 1: 85–112.

—— (2004) 'Japan's counterweight strategy: U.S.–Japan cooperation and competition in international finance', in Ellis S. Krauss and T.J. Pempel (eds) *Beyond Bilateralism: U.S.-Japan Relations in the New Asia Pacific*, Stanford: Stanford University Press, 176–97.

Katzenstein, Peter J. (1978) 'Introduction: domestic and international forces and strategies of foreign economic policy', in Peter J. Katzenstein (ed.) *Between Power and Plenty:*

Foreign Economic Policies of Advanced Industrial States, Wisconsin: University of Wisconsin Press, 3–22.

—— (1997) 'Introduction: Asian regionalism in comparative perspective', in Peter J. Katzenstein and Takashi Shiraishi (eds) *Network Power: Japan and Asia*, Ithaca, New York: Cornell University Press, 1–44.

Katzenstein, Peter J. and Takashi Shiraishi (1997) 'Conclusion: regions in world politics: Japan and Asia – Germany in Europe', in Peter J. Katzenstein and Takashi Shiraishi (eds) *Network Power: Japan and Asia*, Ithaca, New York: Cornell University Press: 341–81.

Kimura, Takayuki (1997) 'Japan-US relations in the Asian-Pacific region', in Richard L. Grant (ed.) *The Process of Japanese Foreign Policy: Focus on Asia*, London: Royal Institute of International Affairs, 37–71.

Komiya, Ryutaro, Masahiro Okuno and Kotaro Suzumura (eds) (1988) *Industrial Policy of Japan*, San Diego: Academic Press Japan.

Korhonen, Pekka (1998) *Japan and Asia Pacific Integration: Pacific Romances 1968–1996*, London: Routledge.

Krasner, Stephen D. (1978) *Defending the National Interest: Raw Materials Investments and U.S. Foreign Policy*, Princeton: Princeton University Press.

Krauss, Ellis S. (2000) 'Japan, the US, and the emergence of multilateralism in Asia', *The Pacific Review* 13, 3: 473–94.

Krugman, Paul R. and Maurice Obstfeld (1997) *International Economics: Theory and Policy*, Reading, Massachusetts: Addison-Wesley.

Kwan, C.H. (1994) *Economic Interdependence in the Asia–Pacific Region: Towards a Yen Block*, London: Routledge.

Leong, Stephen (2000) 'The East Asian Economic Caucus (EAEC): "formalized" regionalism being denied', in Bjorn Hettne, Andras Inotai and Osvaldo Sunkel (eds) *National Perspectives on the New Regionalism in the South*, London: Macmillan, 57–107.

Levin, Norman D. (1993) 'The strategic dimensions of Japanese foreign policy', in Gerald L. Curtis (ed.) *Japan's Foreign Policy After the Cold War: Coping with Change*, Armonk, New York: M.E. Sharpe, 202–17.

Light, Margot (1994) 'Foreign policy analysis', in A.J.R. Groom and Margot Light (eds) *Contemporary International Relations: A Guide to Theory*, London: Pinter, 93–108.

Lincoln, Edward J. (1992) 'Japan in the 1990s – a new kind of world power', *The Brooking Review*, spring: 12–17.

Lindblom, Charles E. (1959) 'The science of "muddling through"', *Public Administration Review* 19, 2: 79–88.

Low, Linda (1991) 'The East Asian economic grouping', *The Pacific Review* 4, 4: 375–82.

MacIntyre, Andrew (1999) 'Political institution and the economic crisis in Thailand and Indonesia', in T.J. Pempel (ed.) *The Politics of the Asian Economic Crisis*, Ithaca, New York: Cornell University Press, 143–62.

Mansfield, Edward D. and Helen V. Milner (1997) 'The political economy of regionalism: an overview', in Edward D. Mansfield and Helen V. Milner (eds) *The Political Economy of Regionalism*, New York: Columbia University Press, 1–19.

Midford, Paul (2000) 'Japan's leadership role in East Asian security multilateralism: the Nakayama proposal and the logic of reassurance', *The Pacific Review* 13, 3: 367–97.

Milner, Helen V. (1992) 'International theories of cooperation among nations: strengths and weaknesses', *World Politics* 44: 466–96.

—— (1997) *Interests, institutions, and information: domestic politics and international relations*, Princeton: Princeton University Press.

Miyashita, Akitoshi and Yoichiro Sato (eds) *Japanese Foreign Policy in Asia and the Pacific: Domestic Interests, American Pressure, and Regional Integration*, New York: Palgrave, 2001.

Morrison, Charles E. (1988) 'Japan and the ASEAN countries: the evolution of Japan's regional role', in Takashi Inoguchi and Daniel I. Okimoto (eds) *The Political Economy of Japan: Volume 2. The Changing International Context*, Stanford: Stanford University Press, 414–45.

Muramatsu, Michio and Ellis S. Krauss (1987) 'The conservative policy line and the development of patterned pluralism', in Kozo Yamamura and Yasukichi Yasuda (eds) *The Political Economy of Japan: Volume 1 The Domestic Transformation*, Stanford: Stanford University Press, 516–54.

Nakanishi, Hiroshi (2001) 'Japan's diplomacy in the twentieth century', *Japan Review of International Affairs*, summer: 106–29.

Neary, Ian (2000) 'Japanese foreign policy and human rights', in Takashi Inoguchi and Purnendra Jain (eds) *Japanese Foreign Policy Today*, New York: Palgrave, 83–95.

Nef, J. (1994) 'The political economy of inter-American relations: a structural and historical overview', in Richard Stubbs and Geoffrey R.D. Underhill (eds) *Political Economy and the Changing Global Order*, London: Macmillan, 404–18.

Nesadurai, Helen E.S. (1996) 'APEC: a tool for US regional domination?', *The Pacific Review* 9, 1: 31–57.

—— (2000) 'In defence of national economic autonomy?: Malaysia's response to the financial crisis', *The Pacific Review* 13, 1: 73–113.

Nester, William (1990) 'The third world Japanese foreign policy', in Kathleen Newland (ed.) *The International Relations of Japan*, London: Macmillan, 71–99.

Nishimura, Yoshiaki (1998) 'Russian privatization: progress report no. 1', Kenichi Ohno and Izumi Ohno (eds) *Japanese Views on Economic Development: Diverse Paths to the Market*, London: Routledge, 241–64.

OECF (1991) 'Issues related to the World Bank's approach to structural adjustment', OECF Discussion Paper 1.

—— (1995) 'The World Bank's East Asian miracle report: its strengths and limitations', OECF Discussion Paper 7.

—— (1995) 'Transition strategies and economic performance', OECF Discussion Paper 8.

Ohno, Kenichi (1998) 'Overview: creating the market economy', in Kenichi Ohno and Izumi Ohno (eds) *Japanese Views on Economic Development: Diverse Paths to the Market*, London: Routledge, 1–50.

Orr, Robert M. (1990) *The Emergence of Japan's Aid Power*, New York: Columbia University Press.

Pempel, T.J. (1977) 'Japanese foreign economic policy: the domestic bases for international behavior', *International Organization* 31, 4: 723–74.

—— (1997) 'Transpacific torii: Japan and the emerging Asian regionalism', in Peter J. Katzenstein and Takashi Shiraishi (eds) *Network Power: Japan and Asia*, Ithaca New York: Cornell University Press, 47–82.

Peng Er, Lam (2001) 'Japan's diplomatic initiative in Southeast Asia', in S. Javed Maswood (ed.) *Japan and East Asian Regionalism*, London: Routledge, 118–31.

Pharr, Susan J. (1993) 'Japan's defensive foreign policy and the politics of burden sharing', in Gerald L. Curtis (ed.) *Japan's Foreign Policy After the Cold War: Coping with Change*, Armonk, New York: M.E. Sharpe, 235–62.

Phillips, Nicola and Richard Higgott (1999) 'Global governance and the public domain:

collective goods in a "Post-Washington Consensus" era', CSGR Working Paper, 47/99, University of Warwick.

Pyle, Kenneth B. (1988) 'Japan, the world, and the twenty-first century', in Takashi Inoguchi and Daniel I. Okimoto (eds) *The Political Economy of Japan: Volume 2. The Changing International Context*, Stanford: Stanford University Press, 446–86.

Ramseyer, J. Mark and Frances McCall Rosenbluth (1993) *Japan's Political Marketplace*, Cambridge, Massachusetts: Harvard University Press.

Rapkin, David P. (1994) 'Leadership and cooperative institutions in the Asia–Pacific', in Andrew Mack and John Ravenhill (eds) *Pacific Cooperation: Building Economic and Security Regimes in the Asia–Pacific Region*, St Leonard, NSW: Allen & Unwin, 98–129.

Reich, Simon (2000) 'Miraculous or mired? contrasting Japanese and American perspectives on Japan's economic problems', *The Pacific Review* 13, 1: 163–93.

Rhodes, Martin and Richard Higgott (2000) 'Introduction: Asian crises and the myth of capitalist "convergence"', *The Pacific Review* 13, 1: 1–19.

Rix, Alan (1988) 'Dynamism, foreign policy and trade policy', in J.A.A. Stockwin *et al. Dynamic and Immobilist Politics in Japan*, Honolulu: University of Hawaii Press, 297–324.

—— (1993a) 'Japan and region: leading from behind', in Richard Higgott, Richard Leaver and John Ravenhill (eds) *Pacific Economic Relations in the 1990s: Cooperation or Conflict?*, St Leonard, NSW: Allen & Unwin, 62–82.

—— (1993b) *Japan's Foreign Aid Challenge: Policy Reform and Aid Leadership*, London: Routledge.

Rosenau, James N. (1980) *The Scientific Study of Foreign Policy* (reviewed and enlarged edition), London: Frances Pinter.

Rowley, Anthony (1997) 'Asian fund special: the battle of Hong Kong', *Capital Trends* 2, 13, <www. gwjapan.com/ftp/pub/nrca/ctv2n13b.html> (accessed 30 January 2002).

Schoppa, Leonard J. (1997) *Bargaining with Japan: What American Pressures Can and Cannot Do*, New York: Columbia University Press.

Shiraishi, Takashi (1997) 'Japan and Southeast Asia', in Peter J. Katzenstein and Takashi Shiraishi (eds) *Network Power: Japan and Asia*, Ithaca, New York: Cornell University Press, 169–94.

Shiratori, Masaki (1998) 'Afterword to the Japanese translation of the World Bank report "the East Asian Miracle"', in Kenichi Ohno and Izumi Ohno (eds) *Japanese Views on Economic Development: Diverse Paths to the Market*, London: Routledge, 77–83.

Smith, Steve (1997) 'New approaches to international theory', in John Baylis and Steve Smith (eds) *The Globalization of World Politics: An Introduction to International Relations*, Oxford: Oxford University Press, 165–90.

Soderberg, Marie (1996) 'Japanese ODA: the business perspective', in Marie Soderberg (ed.) *The Business of Japanese Foreign Aid: Five Case Studies from Asia*, London: Routledge, 72–88.

Soesastro, Hadi (1994) 'Pacific economic cooperation: the history of an idea', in Ross Garnaut and Peter Drysdale (eds) *Asia Pacific Regionalism: Reading International Economic Relations*, Sydney: Harper Educational, 77–88.

Stiglitz, Joseph E. (1998) 'More instruments and broader goals: moving towards the post Washington Consensus', WIDER Annual Lecture, Helsinki.

Stockwin, J.A.A. (1988) 'Dynamic and immobilist aspects of Japanese politics', in J.A.A. Stockwin *et al. Dynamic and Immobilist Politics in Japan*, Honolulu: University of Hawaii Press, 1–21.

—— (1999) *Governing Japan: Divided Politics in a Major Economy*, Oxford: Blackwell.

Strange, Susan (1988) *States and Markets*, London: Pinter.

Stubbs, Richard (1994) 'The political economy of the Asia–Pacific region', in Richard Stubbs and Geoffrey R.D. Underhill (eds) *Political Economy and the Changing Global Order*, London: Macmillan, 366–77.

Subcommittee on Asian Financial and Capital Markets (1998) 'Lessons from the Asian currency crises – risks related to short-term capital movement and the "21st century-type" currency crisis', Japanese Ministry of Finance.

Tadokoro, Masayuki (2000) 'Asian monetary crisis and Japanese policy reactions', paper prepared for presentation for a conference, University of Amsterdam, 3–5 February.

Takeda, Yasuhiro (1997) 'Overcoming Japan-US discord in democracy promotion policies', <www.okazaki-inst.jp/alliance-pro-eng/takeda.e.html> (accessed 5 February 2002).

Tanaka, Akihiko (1999) 'Japan and regional integration in Asia–Pacific', paper presented at the annual convention of the International Studies Association, Washington, D.C.

Taplin, Ruth (1997) 'Japan's foreign economic policy towards Southeast Asia', in Richard L. Grant (ed.) *The Process of Japanese Foreign Policy: Focus on Asia*, London: Royal Institute of International Affairs, 72–106.

Terada, Takashi (1998) 'The origins of Japan's APEC policy: Foreign Minister Takeo Miki's Asia Pacific policy and current implications', *The Pacific Review* 11, 3: 337–63.

—— (2003) 'Constructing an "East Asian" concept and growing regional identity: from EAEC to ASEAN + 3', *The Pacific Review*, 16, 2: 251–77.

Underhill, Geoffrey R.D. (1994) 'Introduction: conceptualizing the changing global order', in Richard Stubbs and Geoffrey R.D. Underhill (eds) *Political Economy and the Changing Global Order*, London: Macmillan, 17–44.

Wade, Robert (1990) *Governing the Market: Economic Theory and the Role of Government in East Asian Industrialization*, Princeton: Princeton University Press.

Wade, Robert and Frank Veneroso (1998) 'Asian financial crisis: the undergoing risk of the IMF's Asia package', Working Paper 128, Russell Sage Foundation.

Waltz, Kenneth (1979) *Theory of International Politics*, Reading, Massachusetts: Addison-Wesley.

Wan, Ming (1995) 'Spending strategies in world politics: how Japan has used its economic power in the past decade', *International Studies Quarterly* 39: 85–108.

—— (1995/1996) 'Japan and the Asian Development Bank', *Pacific Affairs* 68, 4: 509–28.

Watanabe, Akio (2001) 'Japan's position on human rights in Asia', in S. Javed Maswood (ed.) *Japan and East Asian regionalism*, London: Routledge, 66–89.

Wei, Ruan (2002) 'Japan should work with, not against', Asahi Shinbun homepage, <www.asahi.com/english/asianet/column/eng_020322.html> (accessed 10 August 2002).

Weiss, Linda (1998) *The Myth of the Powerless State*, Ithaca, New York: Cornell University Press.

—— (2000) 'Developmental states in transition: adapting, dismantling, innovating, not normalizing', *The Pacific Review*, 13, 1: 21–55.

Williamson, John (1990) 'What Washington means by policy reform', in John Williamson (ed.) *Latin American Adjustment: How Much Has Happened?*, Washington, DC: Institute for International Economics.

Wolferen, Karel van (1986/1987) 'The Japan problem', *Foreign Affairs* 65, 1: 288–303.

—— (1989) *The Enigma of Japanese Power: People and Politics in a Stateless Nation*, London: Macmillan.

Woo-Cumings, Meredith (1999) 'Introduction: Chalmers Johnson and the politics of nationalism and development', in Meredith Woo-Cumings (ed.) *The Developmental State*, Ithaca, New York: Cornell University Press, 1–31.

Woods, Lawrence T. (1993) *Asia Pacific Diplomacy: Nongovernmental Organizations and International Relations*, Vancouver: UBC Press.

World Bank (1991) *World Development Report: The Challenge of Development*, New York: Oxford University Press.

—— (1993) *The East Asian Miracle: Economic Growth and Public Policy*, New York: Oxford University Press.

—— (1997) *World Development Report: The State in a Changing World*, New York: Oxford University Press.

—— (1998) *East Asia: The Road to Recovery*, Washington, DC: World Bank Publications.

—— (2001) *World Development Report: Attacking Poverty*, New York: Oxford University Press.

Wyatt-Walter, Andrew (1995) 'Regionalism, globalization, and world economic order', in Louise Fawcett and Andrew Hurrell (eds) *Regionalism in World Politics: Regional Organization and International Order*, New York: Oxford University Press, 74–121.

Yamakage, Susumu (1990) 'Will Japan seek regionalism?', in Michael S. Steinberg (ed.) *The Technical Challenges and Opportunities of a United Europe*, London: Pinter, 147–63.

—— (1997) 'Japan's national security and Asia–Pacific's regional institutions in the post-Cold War era', in Peter J. Katzenstein and Takashi Shiraishi (eds) *Network Power: Japan and Asia*, Ithaca, New York: Cornell University Press, 275–305.

—— (1999) 'Japan-ASEAN relations during and after the 1997–1998 crisis', paper presented at CSGR annual conference, University of Warwick.

Yasutomo, Dennis T. (1983) *Japan and the Asian Development Bank*, New York: Praeger.

—— (1986) *The Manner of Giving: Strategic Aid and Japanese Foreign Policy*, Lexington, Massachusetts: Lexington Books.

—— (1995) *The New Multilateralism in Japan's Foreign Policy*, London: Macmillan.

Young, Oran R. (1991) 'Political leadership and regime formation: on the development of institutions in international society', *International Organization* 45, 3: 281–308.

Zhao, Quansheng (1993) *Japanese Policy Making: The Politics behind Politics*, Westport, Connecticut: Praeger.

Publications in Japanese

Adachi, Nobiru and Hideaki Shiroyama (1999) 'Okurasho no seisaku keisei katei', in Hideaki Shiroyama, Hiroshi Suzuki and Sukehiro Hosono (eds) *Chuo Shocho no Seisaku Keisei Katei*, Tokyo: Chuo Daigaku Shuppanbu, 233–49.

Aramaki, Kenji (1999) *Ajia Tsukakiki to IMF*, Tokyo: Nihon Keizai Hyoronsha.

Doi, Toshinori (1999) 'Ajia tsukakiki to kongo no kadai', *Fainansu* 35, 7: 17–34.

Hanai, Hitoshi (1998) *Shin Gaiko Seisakuron*, Tokyo: Toyo Keizai.

Hosoya, Chihiro (1993) *Nihon Gaiko no Kiseki*, Tokyo: NHK Books.

Igarashi, Takeshi (1999) *Nichibei Kankei to Higashiajia*, Tokyo: Tokyo University Press.

Ikeda, Tadashi (1996) *Kanbojia Waheieno Michi*, Tokyo: Toshi Shuppan.

Imagawa, Yukio (2000) *Kambojia to Nihon*, Tokyo: Rengo Shuppan.

Inada, Juichi (1989) 'Taigai enejo', in Tadashi Aruga *et al. Koza Kokusai Seiji 4: Nihon no Gaiko*, Tokyo: Tokyo University Press, 183–209.

—— (1995) 'Nihon no enjo gaiko', in Atsushi Kusano and Tetsuya Umemoto (eds) *Gendai Nihon Gaiko no Bunseki*, Tokyo: Tokyo University Press, 151–78.

—— (1997) 'Washinton konsensasu vs nihongata apurochi', *Gaikou Jihou* 1341: 13–29.

—— (2001) 'Ajia keizai kiki no seijiteki sokumen', in Yasutami Shimomura and Juichi Inada (eds) *Ajia Kinyu Kiki no Seijikeizaigaku*, Tokyo: Nihon Kokusai Mondai Kenkyujo, 17–38.

Inoguchi, Takashi and Tomoaki Iwai (1987) *Zoku Giin no Kenkyu*, Tokyo: Nihon Keizai Shinbunsha.

Iokibe, Makoto (1989) 'Kokusai kankyo to nihon no sentaku', in Tadashi Aruga *et al*. *Koza Kokusai Seiji 4: Nihon no Gaiko*, Tokyo: Tokyo University Press, 19–52.

—— (1999) 'Reisengo no nihon gaiko', in Makoto Iokibe (ed.) *Sengo Nihon Gaikoshi*, Tokyo: Yuhikaku Aruma, 225–66.

Ishikawa, Shigeru (1994) 'Kozochosei', *Ajia Keizai* 35, 11: 2–32.

Ito, Takatoshi (1999) 'Ajia keizai kiki to wagakuni no yakuwari', *Gaiko Foramu*, February: 26–31.

—— (1999) 'Ajia tsuka kiki to amerika no taio', *Kokusai Mondai* 467: 21–33.

Iwata, Shuichiro (1997) 'Beikoku no gunji senryaku to nichibei anpo taisei', *Kokusai Seiji* 115: 110–25.

Japan Defence Agency (various years) *Boei Hakusho*, Tokyo: Okurasho Insatsukyoku.

JETRO (various years) Boeki Hakusho, Tokyo: JETRO.

—— (various years) Toshi Hakusho, Tokyo: JETRO.

Kikuchi, Tsutomu (1995) *APEC: Ajia Taiheiyo Shin Chitsujo no Mosaku*, Tokyo: Nihon Kokusai Mondai Kenkyujo.

Kimura, Shigeki (1998) 'Ajia tsukakiki- kokusaikyoku kara mita kono ichinen', *Fainansu* 34, 7: 14–20.

Kimura, Fukushige (2000) *Nihon Keizai Shinbun*, Keizai Kyoshitsu, 31 October.

Kishimoto, Shuhei (1999) 'Shin Miyazawa koso no shimei to ajia tsuka kikin', *Fainansu*, 35, 2: 31–48.

—— (2000) 'Ajia keizaisaisei misshon houkoku no igi to jinzaishien', Fainansu, 36, 3.

—— (2001) 'Ajia kinyu senryaku no tenkai', in Akira Suehiro and Susumu Yamakage (eds) *Ajia Seijikeizai ron*, Tokyo: NTT Shuppan, 259–88.

Kohara, Masahiro (2001) 'ASEAN + 3 no wakugumi – hirakareta chiikishugi no tameni nihon ga dekirukotowa', *Gaiko Foramu*, March: 77–81.

Kojima, Tomonori (1992) 'Nihon no higashi ajia seisaku no tenkai', *Kokusai Mondai* 384: 18–31.

Kono, Masaharu (1999) *Wahei Kosaku*, Tokyo: Iwanami.

Kono, Yohei (1995) 'Nihon gaiko no shinro', *Gaiko Foramu*, January.

Kubota, Isao (1993/4) 'Higashi ajia no kiseki', *Fainansu*, December/January.

Kuriyama, Takakazu (1991) 'Taikenteki nihon gaikoron', *Chuo Koron*, November: 108–23.

Kuroda, Haruhiko (1999) 'Atarashii kokusai kinyu shisutemu no kochiku ni mukete', *Yomiuri Shinbun*, 18 November.

Ministry of Economy, Trade and Industry (various years) *Tsusho Hakusho*, Tokyo: Okurasho Insatsukyoku.

Ministry of Foreign Affairs, (various years) *Gaiko Seisho*, Tokyo: Okurasho Insatsukyoku.

Mohri, Ryoichi (2001) *Gurobalizeshon to IMF/Sekai Ginko*, Tokyo: Otsuki Shoten.

Muroyama, Yoshimasa (1997) 'Reisengo no nichibei anpo taisei', *Kokusai Seiji* 115: 126–43.

Ogasawara, Takayuki (2000) 'Kanbojia wahei to nihon gaiko', in Hiroshi Kimura, Zui Zun

Guen and Motoo Furuta (eds) *Niho Betonamu Kankei wo Manabuhito no tameni*, Kyoto: Sekaishisosha.

Ohba, Mie (2001) 'Chiikishugi to nihon no sentaku', in Akira Suehiro and Susumu Yamakage (eds) *Ajia Seijikeizai ron*, Tokyo: NTT Shuppan, 259–88.

—— (2003) 'Tsuka kinyu kyoryoku ni miru nihon no higashiajia chiiki keisei senryaku', in Susumu Yamakage (ed.) Higashiajia Chiikishugi to Nihon Gaiko, Tokyo: Nihon Kokusai Mondai Kenkyujo, 153–92.

Ohno, Izumi (2000) Sekai *Ginko: Kaihatsu Enjo Senryaku no Henkaku*, Tokyo: NTT Shuppan.

Ohno, Kenichi (1998) 'Ajia kiki no keizaigaku', *Shukan Daiamondo*, 25 April: 60–1.

—— (2000) *Tojokoku no Gurobarizeshon*, Tokyo: Toyokeizai.

Ohno, Kenichi and Izumi Ohno (1993) *IMF to Sekaiginko*, Tokyo: Nihon Hyoronsha.

Oyane, Satoshi (2004) 'Higashi ajia FTA: nihon no seisaku tenkan to chiiki koso', *Kokusai Mondai* 528: 52–66.

Sakakibara, Eisuke (1998) *Kokusai Kinyu no* Genba, Tokyo: PHP Shinsho.

—— (2000) *Nihon to Sekai ga Furuetahi*, Tokyo: Chuokoronshinsha.

Sakamoto, Kazuya (1999) 'Dokuritsukoku no joken', in Makoto Iokibe (ed.) *Sengo Nihon Gaikoshi*, Tokyo: Yuhikaku Aruma, 66–104.

Shiratori, Masaki (1994) 'Sekai ginko repoto higashi ajia no kiseki wo do yomuka', *ESP*, February: 70–81.

Sudo, Sueo (1996) *Tonan Ajia Kokusai Kankei no Kozu*, Tokyo: Keisho Shobo.

—— (1997) 'Nihongaiko ni okeru ASEAN no ichi', *Kokusai Seiji* 116: 147–64.

Tadokoro, Masayuki (1999) 'Keizai taikoku no gaiko no genkei', in Makoto Iokibe (ed.) *Sengo Nihon Gaikoshi*, Tokyo: Yuhikaku Aruma, 105–42.

—— (2000) 'Ajia ni okeru chiiki tsuka kyoryoku no Kosatsu', *Leviathan* 26: 45–69.

Takeda, Yasuhiro (1995) 'Tonanajia gaiko no tenkai', in Atsushi Kusano and Tetsuya Umemoto (eds) *Gendai Nihon Gaiko no Bunseki*, Tokyo: Tokyo University Press, 63–88.

Tanaka, Akihiko (1994) 'Higashiajia no anzenhosho to nihon no seisaku', in Susumu Yamakage (ed.) *Shin Kokusai Chitsujo no Koso*, Tokyo: Nansosha, 120–43.

Urata, Shujiro (2004) 'Nihon no WTO/FTA senryaku', *Kokusai Mondai* 532: 18–31.

Watanabe, Akio (1992) *Ajia Taiheiyo no Kokusai Kankei to Nihon*, Tokyo: Tokyo University Press.

—— (2000) 'Atarashii higashiajia no keisei', *Chuokoron*, June: 66–83.

—— (2001) 'Nichibei domei 50 nen no kiseki to 21 seiki eno tenbo', *Kokusai Mondai* 490: 26–41.

Watanabe, Toshio (2000) 'En wa ikinokorukotoga dekiruka', *Shokun*, September: 46–55.

Watanabe, Yorizumi (2004) 'WTO shin raundo no kanosei to FTA no douko', *Kokusai Mondai* 532: 2–17.

Yamakage, Susumu (1985) 'Ajia taiheiyo to nihon', in Akio Watanabe (ed.) *Sengo Nihon no Taigaiseisaku*, Tokyo: Yuhikaku, 135–61.

—— (1997) 'Shoki ASEAN saiko', *Kokusai Seiji* 116: 17–31.

—— (2001) 'Nihon no tai ASEAN seisaku no henyo', *Kokusai Mondai* 490: 57–81.

Yamamoto, Eiji (1997) *Kokusai Tsuka Shisutemu*, Tokyo: Iwanami Shoten.

Index